HOT
BUTTONS

edited by
Donovan R. Walling

Phi Delta Kappa Educational Foundation
Bloomington, Indiana

Cover design by Victoria Voelker

Library of Congress Catalog Card Number 96-72039
ISBN 0-87367-495-2
Copyright ©1997
by the Phi Delta Kappa Educational Foundation
Bloomington, Indiana U.S.A.

TABLE OF CONTENTS

INTRODUCTION

Controversial issues — "hot button" issues — abound in education. No day goes by without a newspaper headline or a television commentator trumpeting an *issue* about which people are talking — and disagreeing. Often the issues themselves are neither new nor dramatic. But the controversies that arise from them are grist for the media mill.

However, such controversial issues, when they are addressed with thoughtfulness and civility, provide grist for another mill, the mill of education reform and improvement. If educators, parents, politicians, and policy makers are moved by such controversy to seriously study education issues and to arrive at reasoned and responsible positions, then the professional dialogue may be enlarged. Out of this larger dialogue, solutions may be found to problems, and proposals to improve education for children and adults may be weighed and actions taken.

This book, which we call simply *Hot Buttons*, is a collection of essays that deal thoughtfully with 10 current controversial issues: accountability, assessment reform, character education, charter schools, constructivist teaching, gay and lesbian issues, gender equity, inclusion of students with disabilities, school choice, and sexual harassment. Some of these are "hot button" issues because of their various interpretations. Character education, constructivist teaching, and assessment reform are examples. Others are controversial at least partly on political grounds, such as accountability, charter schools, inclusion, and school choice. And still others raise social, ethical, and moral controversies. These include gay and lesbian issues, gender equity, and sexual harassment.

One goal of developing this book of essays was to collect in one place examinations of 10 current, controversial issues that readers and classroom educators may find informative and thought-provoking for themselves or their students. Developers of professional inservice programs and teacher reading and study groups will find this collection useful as background reading. Likewise, professors and students in teacher education and school adminis- trator preparation courses will find that these essays provide a good starting point for understanding some of the currents of thought in contemporary education.

A second goal was to showcase 10 recent fastbacks from the Phi Delta Kappa fastback series. The fastback series was begun in 1972 as a publishing project of the Phi Delta Kappa Education- al Foundation. Each short monograph, or *fastback*, is intended to be a focused, authoritative treatment of a topic of current interest to educators and other readers. Often the fastbacks have been characterized as "sophisticated primers."

The inception of the fastback series was one early realization of the desires of George H. Reavis, who created the Phi Delta Kappa Educational Foundation in 1966. Reavis (1883-1970) entered the education profession after graduating from Warrensburg Missouri State Teachers College in 1906 and the University of Missouri in 1911. He went on to earn an M.A. and a Ph.D. at Columbia University. Reavis served as assistant superintendent of schools in Maryland and dean of the College of Arts and Sciences and the School of Education at the University of Pitts- burgh. In 1929 he was appointed director of instruction for the Ohio State Department of Education. But it was as assistant su- perintendent for curriculum and instruction in the Cincinnati pub- lic schools (1939-48) that he rose to national prominence.

Reavis' dream for the PDK Educational Foundation was to make it possible for seasoned educators to write and publish the wisdom they had acquired over a lifetime of professional activi- ty. He wanted educators and the general public to "better under- stand (1) the nature of the educative process and (2) the relation of education to human welfare." The fastback series broadened that vision by creating opportunities for educators at all levels to publish on a wide range of education topics using a format that is highly accessible and affordable.

Today, more than 400 titles have been published in this on- going fastback series, and more than 7.6 million copies have been disseminated, literally around the world.

The essays in *Hot Buttons* are condensed (in all cases, only slightly) from fastbacks published between 1993 and 1996. Information about the original fastback is printed on the first page of each essay. This information will enable readers who want to focus on a particular issue or a set of controversies to locate the original fastbacks. Also, all of the fastbacks included in this book are in print as this book goes to press and can be purchased individually or in multiple copies for use in classrooms and discussion groups. Multiple-copy price discounts are available. Purchase information can be obtained by calling Phi Delta Kappa International at 1-800-766-1156 or (812) 339-1156.

ACCOUNTABILITY

by Jack Frymier

Accountability in education is not a new idea. More than a hundred years ago the British Parliament approved a "Payment by Results" plan for schools in Victorian England; teachers were paid according to students' achievement. The law eventually was repealed because of negative reactions from all parties involved. About 25 years ago the term "accountability" began to show up in the education literature and as an agenda item on programs of organizations for policy makers and educators in the United States. Hundreds of references have appeared since the mid-1960s.

Despite this long history, "accountability" still means different things to different people, and there is little consensus about how to use the concept intelligently and creatively in schools. In spite of, or perhaps because of, varied and conflicting interpretations, "accountability" as an idea continues to attract attention and interest, both inside and outside the profession.

Some are attracted to the promises and possibilities inherent in the idea of accountability; others are reluctant to accept arbitrary definitions imposed on the term (and then imposed on the schools). Because those concerned with accountability in education come to the discussion from different backgrounds and with different motives, they imbue the term with different meanings; and so debate continues. And because accountability is an issue that subsumes other issues, it is difficult to sort out problems from possibilities.

The purpose of this essay is to explore various issues inherent in the concept and practice of "accountability," as that term is applied to public education. Some of these issues are legal, some

This essay is condensed from Jack Frymier, *Accountability in Education: Still an Evolving Concept*, Fastback 395 (Bloomington, Ind.: Phi Delta Kappa Educational Foundation, 1996).

political, some practical, some psychological, some economic, some historical; still others are a function of common sense. All are "educational" in that they relate to schools and schooling in America today.

Let me put forward a working definition: To be accountable means to be answerable, to be responsible. To be responsible means to be legally or ethically accountable for the care of another; capable of making moral and rational decisions on one's own and therefore answerable for one's behavior; capable of being trusted or depended on; reliable; required to render account.

Responsibility, of course, can be assigned, assumed, or exercised. Therein lies the rub.

Issues Related to Accountability

The issues listed here are problems — by definition, an issue is a problem — complicating what "accountability in education" means in theory as well as in practice. This list of issues is not meant to be exhaustive, and the discussion of each issue is not definitive. The intent is to describe and illustrate.

Each issue is explicated briefly to highlight the complexities and nuances associated with "accountability" in the hope that such explication may prove useful to those who work with education policies. Although they are listed and discussed separately, all of the issues are inextricably intertwined; they are neither discrete nor unique, as the logical separation might imply.

My purpose is to further understanding as a precondition for intelligent action. Following are the issues:

1. Accountability Requires Evaluation
To be accountable means to be responsible. To assess responsibility, one must judge performance against a criterion. To judge performance against a criterion means to evaluate. Therefore, accountability requires evaluation. Indeed, it cannot be accomplished without evaluation. Thus the questions develop: Whose performance? Whose criterion? Which criterion? Which evaluation procedures?

The recent history of accountability (perhaps the last 25 years) suggests that there are, as yet, no agreed-on criteria and no agreed-on procedures. That may change, of course; but the professional and general literature is replete with instances of accountability plans that were proposed, adopted, tried, and then discarded. Examples include performance contracting, teacher testing, merit pay, student achievement, financial disbursement, student dropouts, and educational "bankruptcy." Proposed modifications in the National Assessment of Educational Progress (NAEP) currently are being touted as new possibilities in the area of accountability, and many states are in various stages of devising or revising their own accountability programs. The only notion that has been consistent over time is that accountability requires evaluation. The purposes of that kind of evaluation have never been clarified or ratified to the satisfaction of thoughtful persons, either inside or outside the profession.

2. Improvement or Control?

Evaluation can be used for improvement or control. In theory, evaluation should help people or improve programs. In the relationship between ends and means, evaluation is a key to progress and improvement in any endeavor.

For example, quality control in business and industry is aimed at improving the quality of goods or services before those goods or services are made available to the public in order to minimize negative reaction by potential buyers. Post-production, having a place to register complaints following sales or service, encourages patrons to criticize products or services and allows management to monitor goods and services in ways that will lead to improvement.

Criticism and thoughtful review are essential to progress. Auditing, for example, is done to ensure integrity in the transactions of a business. Evaluation of construction by building inspectors aims to assure prospective buyers that the building is safe and to ensure that it has been constructed according to code. Concerns for improvement always involve evaluation of goods or services, whether it be inspection of meat at the slaughter house, regulation of banks, or monitoring of waste pollution. The purpose of such evaluations is to protect and reassure the general public, to ensure quality, and to promote confidence in the system.

The theory is sound: Evaluative information that is valid, reliable, and current will make any operation better. However, in some instances the emphasis seems to be on control for its own sake. Many workers, whether in education or some other occupation, chafe at evaluation that is perceived as restricting those who are responsible for action. Electric companies react negatively to restrictions placed on their coal-fired generators, even when evaluative data indicate that polluted air is harmful to the general health. Car manufacturers resist government requirements to put air bags in cars, even though research indicates that air bags save lives. Police review boards that cover up inappropriate behavior by police officers view criticism from outside as "unnecessary" when it conflicts with their own view of what happened from an "official" perspective. Evaluation sometimes implies that those who work to maintain an ongoing operation (such as a bank, school, or factory) cannot be trusted to do the job effectively unless they are "checked on" by another agency — an agency that is not in the same "chain of command."

"Don't trust the professionals" is the implicit message in many evaluation efforts. Sometimes such distrust is warranted. When those who are responsible for any operation have an opportunity to bend the rules and promote personal gain (for example, a bank officer who is in a position to defraud the bank, or a pharmaceutical company that misrepresents evaluative data to gain approval of its product with a resultant financial gain), then external evaluation is appropriate.

People may refuse to make needed changes because such changes will require more effort or a change of behavior. Or such changes may require them to report friends or associates who engage in inappropriate conduct, thereby making internal evaluation awkward and generally ineffective. "Whistle blowers" usually have difficulty, especially when their criticisms are relevant and valid. In circumstances such as these, external evaluation also seems to be appropriate.

In theory, evaluation leads to improvement. In practice, evaluation sometimes is seen as a mechanism for control. Control that improves quality is positive. Control that blunts enthusiasm, stifles initiative, or thwarts creativity is negative. And control that improves the quality of products or services but irritates and frustrates the people who produce the goods and services will evoke resistance or apathy or both. To argue that the end justifies the means guarantees that difficulties will arise. That seems to be the situation in education now.

3. Are Teachers Accountable for Students' Learning?

One of the statements frequently made about accountability goes something like this: "Teachers must be held accountable for students' learning." That is not the only way people talk about accountability in education, but this statement summarizes what many people mean when they refer to "accountability in education." But what does the statement imply?

For example, what does "learning" mean? Learning has always been defined in terms of behavioral change. "Students learn," we say, "when they think differently, feel differently, or act differently as a result of the experience that has been provided by the school."

If "learning" means "behavioral change," and if "teachers must be held accountable for students' learning," then teachers must be held accountable for what their students do — in the classroom, on achievement tests, on the playground, and in the halls. It means that teachers are responsible for their students' behavior.

Two problems emerge from the notion that teachers are responsible for their students' behavior. One problem is legal and the other is psychological.

First, the legal problem. If teachers are responsible for their students' behavior (in other words, their students' learning), then, by definition, students are *not* responsible for what they do. Such a notion is antithetical to the whole history of Western civilization, at least since the Greeks: Individuals are responsible for their own behavior.

Even parents are not responsible for their children's behavior. If a child burns down a house or assaults another person, for example, the child is accountable, not the parent. If parents can not control a child, that child may be removed from the home; but if a child does wrong, the child is punished by the state. In legal terms, the child is responsible for what he or she does, not the parent. Some communities (Los Angeles, for example) have recently adopted ordinances that hold parents responsible for their children's behavior in gang-related activities, but those laws have been vigorously contested in the courts.

To argue that teachers must be held accountable for students' learning is to argue that teachers are responsible for what their students do. Such an argument absolves students of responsibility for their own actions. That leads to the second problem, the psychological one.

Psychologists use the phrase "locus of control" to depict one aspect of learned behavior, and they describe that behavior as "internalized" or "externalized." Nobody is born with an internalized locus of control; nobody is born with an externalized locus of control. Locus of control is always learned — at home, on the playground, in the school, and from interactions with peers and others.

Those who acquire an *internalized locus of control* evidence what might be described as a "can do" attitude. They feel "on top" of things. They are in charge of their own life. They believe that they can make a difference, that what they do counts, and that they can influence events or circumstances. Such people are self-motivated and "self-controlled."

Those who acquire an *externalized locus of control*, on the other hand, feel that they are not in charge of their own life and that what they do does not count. They think that they cannot make a difference and cannot influence events. They think other people or external forces are moving them hither and yon; they lack control over their own lives. "They made me do it. It wasn't my idea. It's their fault." Such persons are fatalistic, in the main. They have learned to vest control of their life in things and other people external to themselves.

If teachers accept the notion that they are accountable for their students' learning, then teachers will be forced by circumstances and logic to do things that foster development of an externalized locus of control on the part of their students, rather than an internalized locus of control. Teachers will insist that students do as they are told rather than think for themselves. Students will not be encouraged, or even allowed, to think. If they think, they may think thoughts that teachers do not want them to think. Thus teachers will be driven to *control* students' behavior: what students think, what they say (in classroom discussions and on examinations), and what they do. Such teaching will lead to the development of dependence rather than independence, the exact opposite of what thoughtful educators and non-educators agree ought to be encouraged.

Policy makers in education sometimes argue that "teachers must be held accountable for students' learning." If one asks legislators or school board members, for example, "Do you think teachers should be held responsible for what their students do in school?" many will say, "Yes." However, I suspect that if one pressed that notion further by asking, "Do you think policy makers should be responsible for their constituents' behavior?" every policy maker would immediately respond with an emphatic "No!"

"Well," one might continue, "what should policy makers be responsible for?" Most would immediately respond with "I am responsible *to* my constituents *for* my own behavior. I am responsible for what I do."

And that is right. Each person is accountable for his or her own behavior, but not for what other people do. Thus teachers must be held accountable for what they do as teachers, but not for what their students do. Teachers are responsible for teaching — for doing anything and everything they can to help their students learn. But teachers must not be held accountable for students' learning. Students must be held responsible for their learning.

11

Of course, such responsibility cannot be simply assigned to them by teachers. Teachers are responsible to help students learn how to assume responsibility, how to find and use information, how to study, and how to develop interests, acquire skills, and achieve positive attitudes toward learning and life. But teachers must not assume responsibility for students' learning or for what their students do. Doing so would negate a fundamental purpose of schools and schooling.

4. Freedom, Authority, and Responsibility

If a school board says to a superintendent, "We are going to hold you responsible for thus and so," the superintendent will invariably respond: "Then I presume that I have the authority from you to get thus and so done." Authority and responsibility go hand in hand.

However, in practice authority means freedom to exercise options, to make decisions, to act. Those who exercise options must be held accountable for their actions, thus authority and freedom and responsibility are locked together in fundamental and irreducible ways.

5. Freedom, Equality, and Accountability

There are two ways to think about equality in relation to freedom and accountability. One involves varying definitions of equality that have developed over time. The other relates equality to freedom in terms of the interaction of the two basic dimensions of any social system.

Consider some of the different definitions that have evolved. Early in our nation's history, equality generally was interpreted to mean "equality before the law." Later, "equality of opportunity" was set as a standard for providing all persons, regardless of race or gender, equal opportunities to achieve. Still later, equality was redefined to mean "equal allocation of resources" according to some pre-determined guide. Finally, "equal achievement" of outcomes (or equity) was set as a goal. All of these definitions are related to accountability in education; but because different people use different definitions at different times, communication is difficult and agreement impossible.

The problem is compounded because of the way political scientists use the concepts of equality and freedom in their descriptions of political systems. Freedom and equality are the basic dimensions of any social system, and they interact in ways particular to the culture. Every society uses these theoretical constructs in its interpretation of the kind of life it wants its people to live and the kind of government it establishes and maintains.

Typically, freedom is defined as the opportunity of an individual to exercise personal choice, to make decisions, to act on one's own. But freedom is a dimension; it has two ends. One end is characterized by choice or option, and the other end is characterized by non-choice or restriction of choice. In the same way, equality is a dimension. One end can be characterized as equivalency or sameness, the other as diversity or difference.

We can think of these two dimensions interacting in various ways. Theoretically, we can construct a social system in which choice is either minimized or maximized (the freedom dimension), and either sameness or diversity is emphasized (the equality dimension). Different cultures position the leverage point at different places on each continuum.

If choice is maximized and diversity is valued, that creates one kind of social system, one that is growth-oriented. If choice is minimized or eliminated and sameness is valued, that creates a different kind of social system, one that is control-oriented. If choice is maximized and sameness emphasized, apathy results. And if choice is minimized but diversity is valued, frustration results.

6. Education as a Social System

Consider a different point of view. The Bible says that "the Lord is our judge, the Lord is our lawgiver, the Lord is our king." God is presumed to perform all of these roles without difficulty.

When the Founding Fathers conceived the government of the United States and developed the Constitution as the authority

13

base for that new government, they followed the differentiation described in the Bible, and they assigned these functions to different branches of government. They felt that consolidation of authority under one entity might make sense when that entity was an all-knowing God, but it did not make sense with fallible human beings; and so they separated the powers of lawgiver, judge, and king.

What we call "separation of powers" in government was a deliberate separation of authority according to function. Different people are expected (indeed, assigned) to perform the different functions. But consider the three functions in a generic way. The first and second are intellectual; the third is action-oriented.

Legislating is actually planning; it is conceptualizing or hypothesizing or thinking through before doing. Making laws or developing policies is predicated on the notion that "if we formulate the policy this way, then maybe such and such will happen." It is thinking that precedes action.

The judicial function is evaluative. Judicial activity involves reflection after action, the thoughtful, unhurried review of a particular policy or program that has been questioned. For example, is a policy appropriate and consistent with the basic goals stipulated in the Constitution? Was the implementation of policy consistent with the processes guaranteed as "rights" in the Constitution? Judges evaluate after planning has taken place or after plans have been implemented by executives, but the judicial function is intellectual in nature and evaluative in form.

By contrast, the executive function involves action. Executives take the laws or policies that have been developed and convert those "ideas" into things: organizational arrangements, programs, or practices. Executives translate hypotheses into reality, plans into action, ideas into products.

This system of government exudes integrity. Although people in the system make mistakes, most citizens have confidence in the system because of this separation of "powers" or functions. Thus the U.S. system of governance is complete in the systemic sense and aimed at truth in the functional sense.

This system is mirrored, for the most part, at the state level. Within the framework of many state governments, a state board of education constitutes the policymaking branch of the educational endeavor; the state department of education is the executive branch. But there is no separate entity — no state education accountability board — assigned the evaluative role. However, because evaluation is almost universally seen as important, separate evaluation units usually have been established within the state board of education or education department. Such a system is not theoretically consistent with our system of government.

Seeing a need for evaluation, education policy makers *assume* evaluative functions or executives *assume* evaluative functions. Boards of education evaluate policies they have adopted, or professional educators evaluate programs they have developed to implement those policies. Thus a hierarchy of authority is created in which evaluators are responsible to (and thus beholden to) policy makers or executives. The system is not "clean." As a consequence, policy makers and executives pay attention to evaluative feedback if they want to and don't pay attention if they don't want to.

If policy makers or executives in education assume evaluative functions, such action represents consolidation of authority rather than separation of authority. Asked to pass judgment on their own policies, policy makers often conclude that they have done a good job. Or, if asked to evaluate the programs that they were responsible for developing and implementing, educators often conclude that what they are doing is both appropriate and effective. As the system has no independent judiciary, problems emerge.

Consequently, as a social system, education lacks the internal mechanisms to improve itself. The strengths of our system of government are rooted in the fact that benefits come with evaluation criticism. But education was not built that way. Education does not have a separate unit charged with the responsibility for evaluation, a unit that "stands alone" and is not beholden either to the policy makers or to the executive branch of the system.

Many educators, of course, oppose establishing an evaluation agency. "It would give such a group too much power," critics say.

But the power of evaluation already exists in different, much less useful ways.

7. Goals of Education and Accountability

Four things seem important in thinking about the goals of education and accountability: 1) whether the goals are general or specific, 2) whether the goals are measurable or directional, 3) whether the goals have been both clarified and ratified, and 4) what should be the benchmark against which to measure goals. Each of these points merits further discussion.

Many people argue that goals must be specific, while others maintain that goals can be stated in general terms. History suggests that specific goals get dropped by the wayside over time, whereas general statements of purpose are more enduring. In the Constitution, for example, the Preamble sets forth the goals of the United States: to form a more perfect union, insure domestic tranquillity, provide for the common defense, promote the general welfare. Those general statements have never been modified, and they still provide direction and guidance to policy makers, executives, and judges.

Should goals be measurable or directional? Such a question presupposes philosophical agreement among all parties concerned. To date, we have had little agreement in education on how the question should be answered; but the issue must be resolved before adequate and appropriate accountability measures can be devised.

The goals of education set forth by President Bush and the nation's governors are inadequate because they are too limiting in terms of time (for example, to increase the graduation rate by the year 2000) and because they have not been submitted to the people for ratification. There is no general agreement that the goals are worthy of pursuit. Likewise, goals such as New Jersey's, which require the state to provide "a thorough and efficient" education, are too nebulous and learning-free to be helpful, either to policy makers or educators.

There has been much attention over the years to clarifying the goals in education, but clarification of a goal is only half of the

16

equation. The other half relates to whether the goal is seen as acceptable by those involved. Is it attractive? Is it significant? Has it been "ratified" in the sense that people agree that the goal is important enough that it must be achieved? Clarification and ratification are both essential elements in thinking about education goals.

The Preamble to the Constitution sets forth the goals to be achieved by the nation. Those goals are general, not specific. But the fact that they have been both *clarified* and *ratified* gives power to the system.

Finally, what is the benchmark against which all activities or programs are measured to determine whether the education enterprise is effective? This relates to the "ratification" idea outlined above. It may be that what is needed in education is a constitutional convention of sorts, in which goals can be clarified and then submitted to the populace in a referendum and ratified. If ratified, such goals could serve as an agreed-on benchmark against which to measure educational efforts. Without a benchmark that has the general support of the total population, different parties (such as elected school board members, appointed superintendents, teachers, parents) can invoke first one criterion and then another, with the result that the system is disrupted. A benchmark must be specified and ratified by the people at large and not subject to change, even by elected representatives, except through traditional amendment procedures.

8. Professionalism and Accountability

Research by sociologists over the years has documented and described the reality of professionalism. According to this research, individuals and groups that are truly professional are characterized in six ways:

Professionals perform essential services. Professionals help other people. But the help they provide is neither a nicety nor a luxury; it is absolutely essential. The clients served by the professional cannot get along without the help. If a person has a heart attack, for example, that person must have assistance. He or she cannot deal with such a problem alone. Professionals help other people in the sense that they provide essential service to their fellow human beings.

Professionals have a unique methodology. Every truly professional person or professional group is characterized by the fact that practitioners have an elaborate methodology that they use when they provide the essential services to help other people. This methodology can be taught and it must be learned. No person is born knowing how to perform bypass surgery, do a root canal, draw up a contract, or prepare a warranty deed. Those who have a doctorate in physiology, for example, are not allowed to perform surgery; they have not acquired the specific techniques and methodological skills that surgeons have learned, even though they know a lot about human physiology. Nor do we allow mathematicians to build bridges, rockets, or roads; those functions are reserved for engineers. Professionals learn certain methodological skills, and it is the responsibility of professional schools to help prospective professionals acquire those special methodologies, those professional tools.

Professional practice is based on research. Every truly professional person or professional group bases practice on research. Physicians generally do not belong to the Church of Christ Scientist, for example, because that church advocates a method of healing that is not empirically verifiable.

Professionals make judgments that affect the client. Professionals spend most of their time making judgments and decisions that affect other people, and seldom do those affected know whether the decisions are appropriate or sound. For example, if a physician diagnoses a patient as having diabetes and prescribes insulin therapy, the patient does not know whether the physician's diagnosis or treatment is correct or incorrect. The patient can check with another physician, but he or she still does not know. The same thing is true in other areas. If an attorney says that the title to a particular piece of property is clear, the client has to accept the attorney's word; the client does not know. Professionals regularly make decisions that affect those they serve, and those affected seldom know whether the decisions are right or wrong. In practical terms, this means that the opportunity for exploitation is inherent in any professional person's role.

Professional groups have a code of ethics. Because the opportunity for exploitation is inherent in every professional person's activities, those groups that are truly professional have developed and adopted a code of ethics to give direction and guidance to members of their group.

Professional groups use the code to discipline members. Those groups that are truly professional use the organization's statement of ethics and its governance structure as mechanisms to insist that every member of the group adhere to the ethical standards. Practitioners who do not abide by the code of ethics are drummed out of the corps. Truly professional organizations have elaborate procedures for evaluating the activities of members to assure the general public that the service provided is of the highest quality.

Using these six characteristics as criteria, we can ask ourselves these questions: Do educators provide an essential service? Is there a methodology that is unique and peculiar to education? Is there a solid research base on which to predicate practice? Do educators make decisions that affect other people, and is it true that those affected do not know whether those decisions are right or wrong? Is there a code of ethics? Do educators use the code as a basis for disciplining members of the group who deviate from what is judged to be appropriate behavior for professionals?

Professionalism might be an internal accountability mechanism in public education, but general evidence suggests that the profession has not fully matured in terms of the six criteria outlined above. Obviously educators provide an essential service; obviously they make decisions that affect those they serve. It is certainly true that those who are affected do not know whether the decisions are good or bad. And there is research, but it is not used consistently. There also is a code of ethics, but few people have even read it. There is little evidence of self-discipline of members by the professional organizations; for example, nobody gets ejected from the professional organizations on the basis of evaluative data. Accreditation of schools by organizations such as the North Central Association of Colleges and Schools is an example of self-regulation by educators; but only institutions are affected, not individuals.

These observations are not criticisms. It took physicians more than 4,000 years to achieve truly professional status; educators still have a long way to go. Even so, the concept of professionalism might be thought of as an accountability notion. Over time it could be nurtured as a way to achieve better schools and better schooling.

9. Motivation and Improvement

Everybody assumes that schools and schooling can be improved. The question is: What will it take to get the involved people to improve? Said another way: What kinds of incentives will it take to motivate teachers and administrators to change?

Whether talking about students, teachers, principals, superintendents, board members, or legislators, one could make the case that the general rule in education should be: "Do it right," because "If you don't do it right, then you have to do it over." An unwavering commitment to excellence is the only way to ensure quality experiences for students.

Concern with excellence ("doing it right") is the driving force behind the demand for accountability in schools. Competence can be required by the system, but excellence can be realized only if individuals within the system go above and beyond the minimum competence level. So the question remains: What will it take to get the people who make policies and the people who work in education to "do it right?"

Accepting the fact that everybody in the system will have to work harder and better if schools and schooling are to improve, the discussion here must focus on teachers. Much is known about what is required to help students work harder and better in schools (for example, superb quality curriculum materials, methods that ensure greater student involvement, feedback that fosters positive self-concept development, practices that enhance the development of an internalized locus of control). But what motivates teachers to improve their teaching is less well-understood. Consider a hypothetical illustration.

Suppose someone (teacher, principal, supervisor, superintendent, board member) comes forth with a new idea to improve education practice. The proposed change might involve new subject matter, a different way of organizing time and space within the school, a unique approach to instruction, or variations in the way students are evaluated. The new idea would constitute, in effect, a hypothesis for change. Implicit in the suggested change would be a rationale something like this:

Here is a new idea. Other people have tried it, and they say it works. Researchers have studied it, and they say that children learn more, faster, and better. We have examined the proposal, and we think it would be an improvement over what we are now doing. Will you give it a try?

For teachers, the question becomes: "What does this proposed change mean for me?" What do those who hold out the prospect of improvement in schools promise teachers, who will have to take the new idea and make it work? An analysis of the situation suggests that something like this occurs:

Take this new idea and give it everything you've got. Learn the new teaching techniques. Use the new materials. If you work hard to make this innovation fly, we can promise you that your students will learn more and you'll feel good about it.

We promise teachers an increase in personal satisfaction if they do a better job and help their students learn more. Is that an adequate and appropriate incentive to encourage teachers to change? Is that sufficient motivation to foster educational improvement?

Some will respond: "Good teachers will accept that challenge. Good teachers want their students to do better; good teachers will give the innovation a try."

Even if that is the case for some teachers, what about the others? Is it realistic to depend only on "good" teachers to make significant improvements in schooling? By definition, teachers who are not "good" probably need to change what they do even more than teachers who are already "good." Thus the question remains: Is promising teachers that they will feel good and that their students will learn more if they adopt the proposed change an adequate and appropriate incentive to encourage them to change?

Look at the question from a negative point of view. If we reverse the logic, the rationale for change goes something like this:

If you don't take this new idea and give it everything you've got — if you won't work hard to make this change successful — then your students won't learn more and you'll feel bad about it.

If this analysis is correct, it suggests that the system promises teachers an increase in satisfaction if they try to improve and personal disappointment if they do not try.

Many current assumptions about how to motivate teachers to change are rooted in the concept of altruism. There is neither recognition nor reward for teachers who do better, nor is there disapproval or punishment for those who do not improve. Complete failures are gotten rid of, generally; but mediocre and uninspired teaching is condoned. There are few extrinsic motivational factors to encourage teachers to change, no incentives to do better, no negative consequences for doing poorly. In fact, there are no external incentives or disincentives in the system at all. The system presumes that every teacher is driven by intrinsic, altruistic goals; that every teacher aspires to do better; and that every teacher loves teaching and children and wants to do an ever-better job, day after day. Those are wonderful notions, but they do not correspond to the reality of human ambitions.

A commitment to public service and altruism is a powerful and noble ideal, but it is an unrealistic construct on which to build continuous improvement and better schools. The idea that those who are most effective in what they do will be recognized and rewarded is a central notion in the American culture. Even preachers who do a better job get a bigger church and make more money — and altruism supposedly is their stock in trade.

Negotiated agreements between teachers and school boards during the past 25 years have produced conditions of work predicated on an assembly-line mentality: Everybody gets the same amount of everything as everybody else — resources, time, space, recognition, salary, and the like.

The single-salary schedule epitomizes the idea of sameness for everyone that characterizes the assembly line. Without being fully conscious of what was happening, teachers' organizations historically have opted for contracts that guarantee members of the teaching group will not have incentives to improve.

When the single-salary schedule was set forth 50 or so years ago, the idea of such a uniform schedule made a lot of sense. At that time, men were paid more than women, whites were paid more than blacks, and married men with children were paid more than single men. Now, conditions have changed. Furthermore, the historical evidence is clear: Those who advocate raising all teachers' salaries as a basic condition for improving teaching (and thereby students' learning) have had more than 50 years of experience from which to conclude that society will not pay all teachers a high salary, no matter how logical such an argument might be. And pressure from the general public for a differentiated salary schedule has been unrelenting in recent years, despite teachers' reluctance to embrace such an idea.

10. State Laws and the Laws of Learning

There are two kinds of laws, those made by people and natural laws. The "laws of the State of Nebraska" represent the first type. The "laws of gravity" represent the second type. People are expected to abide by state laws; they *must* abide by natural laws.

Consider an illustration: People who learn to fly are confronted by the rules and regulations of the Federal Aviation Agency and by the law of gravity. They may choose to abide by the FAA regulations or not, and they may get by unnoticed, be caught and fined, or lose their license. But they must adhere to the laws of gravity in order to fly without mishap; fliers ignore gravity on pain of death.

In education there also are laws made by people and natural laws: statutes by legislatures and laws of learning. Those who prepare statutes that affect education sometimes develop laws that are at odds with the laws of learning. When that happens, there may be no immediate or visible "crash." But there will be a consequence. For example, some legislatures have adopted laws over the years that were designed to "build floors" under educational endeavors, only to find that the floors became ceilings in the minds of those who tried to abide by the laws. In other words, the laws lowered expectations and thereby achievement, even though the intention was to raise expectations and achievement.

The point is that people-made laws and natural laws must match and mesh. Good intentions are not enough. School policies must be in harmony with the laws of learning.

11. Accountability and Levels of Operation

Schools and schooling in America were established and are maintained in hierarchical terms: federal level, state level, district level, building level, classroom level. One can make even further distinctions within each of these levels. The point is that levels are a part of the education reality.

Sometimes one level in education makes accountability demands on units that are two or more levels beneath it. If a building principal makes specific accountability demands on students, for example, what happens to the teachers who were "left out," so to speak? What happens if a superintendent of schools makes specific demands on teachers in a district and ignores the principals of buildings in which those teachers work? Does being bypassed affect the thoughts and actions of people at other levels?

If state legislatures develop accountability policies that affect the schools at the building level, and if those policies are imposed and enforced by state departments of education, in practical terms that means that local boards and superintendents are bypassed. The question then becomes: What responsibilities do districts have to see that individual buildings fulfill state responsibilities? At the least, some district-level administrators feel left out, and they may feel that there is little incentive or logical reason to be concerned about fulfilling the imposed decisions. Or district personnel may actively work to circumvent the intentions of state officials. Skipping levels of authority may seem reasonable from one point of view, but often it results in havoc.

12. Choice and Accountability

Many people are dissatisfied with the quality of schooling in America. Evidence suggests that most children receive a good education, but some do not. However, there is a general perception that education in America is not as effective or "good" as it ought to be, even though "ought to" is almost never defined in ways that help educators or others improve schools. America is driven by its ideals, and its failure to provide superb education for every youngster is interpreted by many to mean that schools and schooling in this country must be improved. "Choice" is an idea set forth in response to the perceived dissatisfaction of some people with the schools.

The United States was founded on the idea of being able to exercise personal choice. Restraint, denial of options, coercion, and compulsion are seen as un-American. Americans have always defined "democracy" as the opportunity of individuals to exercise personal options without restrictions by government. As a result, Americans have almost unlimited access to all kinds of things: information, entertainment, travel, and alcohol, drugs, and guns.

Coupled with the historical emphasis on the importance of "freedom of choice," as the phrase is often used, is the theoretical and ideological concomitant of "competition" in economic terms. Many people point to competition as the driving force in America's economic system. It would probably be more accurate to say that competition results from the fact that people are free to choose which products or services they want to buy, thereby encouraging those who provide goods and services to compete for the opportunity to make a sale.

Theoretically, those who provide goods and services in a competitive environment have different ways in which they can "close a deal." Some emphasize quality, others emphasize low price, and others emphasize style or form. Those who choose a product or service generally accept the fact that they get what they pay for. If they pay for quality, they may or may not get style. If they pay for style, they may or may not get low price or premium quality. If they want all three, they have to pay for all three. Because America is a large nation with diverse people, different enterprises thrive because they offer different things to different people.

Within this historical framework of freedom and the ideological commitment to free enterprise, the idea of "choice in education" has emerged. But "choice" is not a new idea; it is the "voucher system" with a new name. First proposed by the economist Milton Friedman, the voucher idea was set forth in opposition to Marx's statement in *The Communist Manifesto* that one of the characteristics of a communistic society would be "free education for all children in public schools." The fact that Marx supported the idea of public education was enough for Friedman to reject it, despite the fact that "free education for all children in public schools" existed in the United States long before 1847, when *The Communist Manifesto* was written. America's concern with anti-communism in mid-century led many to accept the voucher system idea without careful thought.

The argument for the use of vouchers is based on the notion that schools are part of the economic system of the nation. The school is like a factory, Friedman argues, and the child is a product of the school. If we want to produce a better product, then we must create an institution harnessed to the forces of free enterprise, namely "choice."

But the school is not a factory, and the child is not a product. The child is no more a product of the school than the patient is a product of the hospital or the prisoner is a product of the prison. Those who accept the analogy of the school as factory and the child as product do a disservice both to the student and to the profession.

If the school is not a factory, is it reasonable to say that the school is a service industry? The answer must be "no." Industry, by definition, means "the commercial production and sale of goods and services," and schools have never been commercial in that sense. No one would argue that the state of Indiana or the United

States government are "service industries," in the sense that United Airlines or McDonald's restaurants are service industries.

Schools do provide services. They provide care for the child. They help students learn. Obviously the child is affected by what happens in the school, but the child is not a product of the school. Nor is the school an economic institution in the sense that a bank or a factory or a grocery store is an economic institution. The school is not expected to show a profit, for example, as are commercial enterprises.

But if other agencies are allowed to compete with schools, some argue, the public schools will have to do better or go out of business. Thus, by competition, education will improve. Allowing parents choice in education will be the engine that drives school improvement and reform.

The assumption in that argument is that schools as institutions and those who work in schools will be motivated by profit considerations. Ironically, the idea is appropriate for individual professionals, but not for schools as institutions. Individuals who work in education can be motivated by the idea of profit and gain, but schools are now, and always have been, nonprofit institutions. It takes money to operate schools, of course; but the basic commitment at the institutional level has always been service, not profit. Even the great universities of America are nonprofit institutions.

What would it mean if the basic mission of such institutions as Harvard University, the University of Chicago, or the University of Minnesota were redefined in profit-making terms? What would it mean for the purpose of a university to be changed from "pursuit of truth" to "pursuit of the dollar"? Or, what would it mean if the boards of education of the Toledo Public Schools or the Chicago Public Schools, for example, were expected to show a profit every year? Is that what taxpayers want?

School boards and administrators could do many things to reduce expenditures: increase class size, reduce teachers' salaries, or curtail expenditures for instructional materials. By under-spending, any excess funds (in other words, savings) could be treated as profits. Boards of education could take these "profits" and invest them. There are many ways that schools could get money and spend money differently, if their basic purpose were redefined so they would be expected to be profit-making institutions. Not wasting funds is one thing, but showing a profit is a very different thing.

Some proposals to implement choice in education would make public funds available to private schools. Neither the federal government nor any state government will likely provide public funds to private institutions without controls, and so the strengths and advantages that private schools currently possess would be lost. They will become public or quasi-public, rather than private institutions. And they will not be free to reject or eject clientele or impose the kinds of demands that they are now free to impose on students without being subjected to the legal constraints now imposed on public schools.

Furthermore, the issue of "separation of church and state" will not simply go away. If public funds are made available to private (parochial or independent) schools, and if policies supporting such allocations are upheld by the courts, the understandable frustrations of people with public schools of today will meld with the natural inclinations of like for like, thereby splintering and crystallizing groups and subgroups along social, religious, economic, and racial lines. America will be Balkanized even more than it has been in recent years, and the process will freeze distinctions among groups by guaranteeing compartmentalization and separation with economic incentives on a massive scale.

But the issue is much larger than the schools. Public money for parochial schools will change America in ways that are both unanticipated and undesirable. History makes it clear that when government and religion join hands, either the government becomes strong and the church becomes weak, or vice versa. There is not a nation in the world in which the union of church and state has resulted in strong, effective government and strong, effective churches. Look at Iran: strong church, weak government. Look at England: strong government, weak church.

The only nations in which both government and church are strong are nations in which the wall of separation between the two institutions has not been breached. The book, *God Is Dead*, for example, was written by an Englishman. Such a proposition is almost unthinkable in the United States. But in England, with the government's long involvement — first with the Catholic Church and then with the Church of England — the church is a place where sightseers go, but from which local residents stay away in droves. Almost nobody goes to church in England. Churches there are local curiosities and historical artifacts, but seldom places of worship for more than a handful of local citizens. God is not dead. The church is dead. And the church is dead because religious leaders in days gone by sought to curry favor and join hands with those in political authority.

If we want to create such a system, under the law, then we ought to take those steps and adopt those policies with our eyes wide open and after extensive, probing debate. To adopt proposals that almost certainly will spell the dissolution of the public school, we must think and talk about such eventualities intensively, intelligently, and creatively. We dare not opt for "choice" because the word sounds good.

America might slip "sideways" into a dual system of schools under the rationale of saving money and improving education only to discover later, much later, that we lost both the idealism and the idea of the common school. In a nation that prides itself on prohibiting researchers from experimenting on participants without their full knowledge and informed consent, we must have complete disclosure when it comes to experimenting in this way with our public schools.

The concept of "choice" in its broadest sense is undeniably important. For example, helping children learn how to make intelligent choices may be the most important thing that schools can do for children. Do schools now help youngsters learn to choose wisely and well? Is allowing students and parents to choose their teachers unrealistic? Is expanding choice in terms of what is studied, how it is studied, or when it is studied possible without creating chaos and disruption in the school? Can schools teach children to make intelligent choices by denying them the opportunity to choose in school? These questions are worth exploring.

Compulsory education, compulsory attendance laws, compulsory course requirements, compulsory assignment to particular buildings or particular teachers — all are grating practices in public schools. Expanding options between schools and within schools are important ideas and ought to be instituted in more ways than we traditionally have done in public schools. But the wholesale embrace of school choice and vouchers should not be lightly undertaken.

Implications and Recommendations

Accountability means different things to different people, and those differences make communicating awkward and reaching agreement difficult. The relationships of freedom, authority, equality, responsibility, accountability, policymaking and implementation, and evaluation are complex. But those relationships must be explicated and comprehended if the possibility of improving schools through accountability is to be realized.

Accountability is an important idea in education. It can be a vehicle for self-renewal and improvement. But in most of its present forms, it is an instrument of control. New concepts of who is accountable to whom and for what are required. Restricting accountability practices to fiscal considerations or achievement testing is too limiting. Requiring one person or group to be accountable for another person's or group's actions is too demanding.

All children can learn. Schools exist to help people learn; and schools are a vital component of a democratic society designed to help people, especially young people, achieve goals that society stipulates should be achieved. But children are different from one another — indeed, each child is unique — and some differences make a difference in learning: age, ability, genetic makeup, home background, experience, interests, and needs. Public schools are responsible for helping every student learn, regardless of these differences. The diversity evident in any classroom requires education policies and practices that acknowledge the reality of individual differences and encourage and enable educators to respond to those differences effectively. Accountability policies and practices in education must include consideration of the differences that exist among students in schools.

Accountability requires evaluation. Evaluation can be used for improvement or control. Evaluation that fosters improvement is better than evaluation for control. Educators embrace the concepts and ideals of accountability that are improvement-oriented, rather than control-oriented. If educators have an opportunity to work with policy makers and others to specify education goals and then work to gain general acceptance of those goals, they will be enthusiastic about being evaluated.

Education lacks a "built in" component to evaluate the education enterprise. This void creates problems for policy makers and professionals in the schools, but "adding on" such a component without restructuring the total system probably would create more problems than it would solve. Policy makers are accountable to their constituents for clarifying goals, for enabling society to ratify those goals, and for relating the policies they adopt to the goals ratified in a reasonable, appropriate, and effective manner.

Similarly, parents are accountable to society for adequately preparing their children for school and for supporting the school's efforts to help their children learn. And administrators are accountable to policy makers for administering the policies that have been adopted, and to teachers for assisting them in becoming better teachers. Teachers are accountable to other teachers and to administrators for teaching — to help students achieve goals that society has agreed are important to be achieved — and to improve their teaching. They must acknowledge and respond appropriately and effectively to the individual diversity present in their classrooms; and they must provide safe, secure, and stimulating environments, appropriate and evocative curriculum materials, interesting and meaningful instructional procedures, and appropriate and helpful evaluation devices. Finally, students are accountable to their parents and teachers for their

31

own learning — in other words, for achieving the goals that policy makers have clarified and society has ratified. Accountability cannot be assigned by teachers. Responsibility must be assumed and exercised by students.

Two other issues bear mention: choice and national testing. Choice as an accountability concept is designed to encourage improvement in schools, and choice is important; but many of the current proposals for "choice" may change the fundamental nature of American society in undesirable ways.

Efforts probably will continue to implement a national testing program. Evaluating the complex processes and results in education is difficult. Valid and reliable instruments and procedures must be developed further than they have been developed thus far.

Bearing these issues in mind, I would put forward the following eight recommendations:

1. The goals of education should be clarified and then ratified. This process should be initiated by the legislature and completed by the people.
2. Policies, programs, and practices in schools should be evaluated in terms of the degree to which they contribute directly to the attainment of agreed-on (ratified) goals.
3. Educators should develop programs and practices to help students achieve the goals that have been clarified and ratified.
4. Policy makers should provide the resources and adopt the policies that will enable educators to provide programs and practices to help young people learn.
5. The legislature should establish accountability mechanisms, independent of both policy makers and professional educators, to determine the extent to which the goals of education have been achieved.
6. The accountability mechanisms established by the state should have authority to evaluate education policies, programs, and practices in terms of the extent to which the stipulated goals have been realized.

7. Professional organizations in education should assume responsibility for helping their members improve. If improvement efforts are unsuccessful, those organizations should recommend that ineffective people be removed from practice.
8. Public schools and universities should create collaborative working relationships that foster research and development activities that will improve both public schools and universities.

ASSESSMENT REFORM

by Herbert J. Walberg, Geneva D. Haertel, and Suzanne Gerlach-Downie

New forms of assessment result from education reforms, developments in psychology, and advances in testing technology. Much of the debate about assessment reform has relied on opinion, not fact. This essay analyzes contrasting opinions in the light of available evidence.

In this essay the term "traditional tests" refers to standardized, norm-referenced, multiple-choice achievement tests administered using a paper-pencil format under standardized conditions. These tests are used to measure individual student performance so that students' scores can be compared. During the past decade such traditional tests have been challenged.

The term "alternative assessments" means all assessments other than traditional tests. Alternative assessments include essays, portfolios, interviews, simulations, projects, and performances. Many alternative assessments, such as assigned written compositions and portfolios of artwork, have been used for decades; thus some of them are neither new nor untested.

The term "authentic assessments" refers to assessments, especially performance assessments, that purportedly measure valuable, real-world, complex tasks. Authentic assessments often are contrasted with traditional tests and promoted as being a significant improvement over the limitations of traditional tests. In this essay, the term "authentic assessments" is rarely used. The term "authentic" is a rhetorical device that suggests that traditional assessments are inauthentic or do not measure important knowledge

This essay is condensed from Herbert J. Walberg, Geneva D. Haertel, and Suzanne Gerlach-Downie, *Assessment Reform: Challenges and Opportunities*, Fastback 377 (Bloomington, Ind.: Phi Delta Kappa Educational Foundation, 1994).

or skills. The claims of the authentic assessment advocates have yet to be proved.

Influence of Education Reform

During the past decade, American public schools have been in the throes of reform. Apparent poor student performance on basic skills and knowledge tests, low levels of achievement for U.S. students compared to their international counterparts, and low rates of adult literacy have caused educators, as well as the general public, to call for reforms. The reform of student assessment is an essential component of the revitalization of American schools.

Accountability. The public values assessment data as a means to evaluate students, school systems, reform efforts, and the standing of U.S. students compared to students in other nations. Since accountability places responsibility for the success of the students on their teachers, it has become a central feature of education reform. Some reformers believe that the education system will improve only if teachers are held accountable for their students' test performance, because assessment data are the best evidence that schools are reforming. Adequate levels of achievement should be defined in terms of national standards, as well as comparative standards of progress among students. Thus some reformers argue that the quality of education will be improved only by establishing high standards of achievement and holding teachers responsible for ensuring that their students meet those standards.

Proliferation of Testing. Elementary and secondary students take an estimated 127 million separate standardized tests each year as a result of district and state mandates (National Commission on Testing and Public Policy 1990). During 1986-1987, approximately 105 million standardized tests were administered to 39.8 million public school students. Of these, more than 55 million were tests of achievement, competency, and basic skills administered to students in compensatory and special education programs. Some two million tests were used to screen prekindergarten and kindergarten students, and 41 million tests were administered in regular

36

classrooms in grades 1 to 12. The General Education Development testing program, the National Assessment of Educational Progress (NAEP), and admission requirements for a variety of colleges and secondary schools accounted for an additional six million to seven million tests (Neill and Medina 1989). The National Commission on Testing and Public Policy (1990) reported that test revenues doubled between 1960 and 1966, and increased fivefold between 1967 and 1980. The revenues increased from approximately $40 million in 1960 to $100 million in 1989.

High-Stakes Testing. Whenever important consequences are attached to test results, it is considered high-stakes testing. The Scholastic Aptitude Test (SAT) and the American College Testing program (ACT) have always been high-stakes tests for college-bound students, because receiving a poor score may result in the test taker being denied admission to the college of choice. School systems may suffer enrollment drops because of the importance given to test scores by some community members. Even the real estate market may be affected by the newspaper reports of local test scores and the ranking of schools and districts according to their test scores.

Media reporting of test scores has raised the stakes for schools and students. Teachers feel pressured to improve test scores and to cover tested material. Some districts use assessment scores to determine merit pay and dismissal decisions. Increasing the stakes of tests for teachers and administrators can exacerbate problems of overzealous test preparation and teaching to the test. Darling-Hammond (1991) listed the negative consequences of using test scores to make decisions about rewards or sanctions for schools and teachers, including:

> designating large numbers of low-scoring students for place-ment in special education so that their scores won't "count" in school reports, retaining students in grade so that their rel-ative standing will look better on grade-equivalent scores, excluding low-scoring students from admission to "open enrollment" schools, and encouraging low-scoring students to drop out. (p. 223)

In many states test scores have risen in the first few years following the introduction of a high-stakes testing program. Whether these increased scores reflect real improvement in student achievement or only gains specific to a particular test remains to be determined. Some studies show that dropout rates increase in schools with competency tests as a graduation requirement and test-based retention policies (Madaus 1991). Students usually are motivated to do well on tests if they see a relationship between their performance on these tests and their grades or college and job prospects.

Emphasis on tests can produce desirable effects on curriculum, teaching, and learning. High-stakes tests may serve to focus instruction and highlight students' and teachers' goals. Some researchers assert that a better match between what is taught and what is tested may revitalize an obsolete curriculum.

Influence of Psychology

Cognitive psychology challenges common views of learning, teaching, and assessment. The shift from behaviorism to cognitive psychology in the late 1950s initiated a new focus on how individuals learn, think, and acquire and apply knowledge. This new focus stimulated innovations in assessment practices.

Cognitive psychologists see learners as actively constructing knowledge structures that learners modify as their level of expertise rises. Behaviorists emphasize that higher-order understandings are the result of mastering discrete skills and prerequisite learnings. Thus behaviorists see teachers as knowledge transmitters who directly influence student learning, while cognitivists believe that teachers indirectly enhance student thought by asking questions, providing examples, giving instructions, and creating learning environments.

Behaviorists believe that complex processes, such as reading comprehension, can be broken down into a series of discrete skills. For behaviorists, tests are constructed by specifying behavioral outcomes that must be mastered for each instructional goal. In contrast, cognitivists believe that assessments should measure a wide range of thought, including knowledge, metacognitive processes, learning errors, and affective thought processes. Cognitivists measure knowledge by assessing the relationships among facts, principles, procedures, and beliefs. They measure metacognitive skills that an individual uses to appraise his or her own thinking, including the ability to plan, activate, monitor, and evaluate actions. Affective thoughts are measured through coping and self-regulatory skills.

Merlin Wittrock (1991) expresses the concerns of cognitive psychologists:

> Many standardized intelligence tests, achievement tests, and ability tests. . . were not designed to measure diagnostically useful cognitive and affective thought processes. . . . [T]hese tests do not measure student conceptions, learning strategies, or metacognition or affective thought processes relevant to instruction. (p 3)

Despite these claims from cognitive psychologists, many educators and other psychologists adhere to behaviorism or adopt an eclectic approach. Behaviorism is evident in mastery learning, computer-assisted instruction, and criterion-referenced testing. Cognitivists may strive to go beyond behaviorally developed tests, but they have yet to produce convincing, practical methods that can be used easily in classrooms.

Four broad understandings have emerged from cognitive psychology: 1) the description of subject matter in terms of declarative, procedural, and prior knowledge; 2) the characterization of increases in knowledge along a continuum from novice to expert performance; 3) the cataloguing of learning errors specific to subject areas; and 4) the identification of metacognitive processes and learning strategies that individuals use to manage their own learning.

1. Declarative, Procedural, and Prior Knowledge. Students organize knowledge into schemas that are unique to the subject matter. Declarative knowledge is a network of facts and ideas. A student's ability to retrieve information efficiently is directly related to the organization of his or her declarative knowledge. According to psychologists, achievement testing in a subject area should include both estimates of the amount of declarative knowledge a student possesses and how that knowledge is organized.

Traditional tests can provide a partial measurement of declarative knowledge. Items that require the student to recognize the correct answer can be used to assess the student's command of facts, principles, and vocabulary. Such tests may be less able to measure the way the student organizes information. Alternative item types, such as word associations or semantic maps, are more suited to measuring the organization of knowledge.

Procedural knowledge is knowledge of the processes and routines used in thinking. As knowledge becomes proceduralized, it becomes automatic and requires little attention by learners. The more quickly a student completes a task, the more proceduralized the knowledge and skills have become. There are no practical methods for teachers to test procedural knowledge, except through experienced observation.

Prior knowledge refers to the knowledge and skills that a student brings to the instructional setting. A student's idiosyncratic knowledge structures include not only the knowledge and skills they have acquired, but also their preconceptions, misconceptions, and beliefs. Information about a student's prior knowledge is useful when planning instruction.

The diagnosis of preconceptions, misconceptions, and beliefs can be accomplished through the use of constructed-response, alternative test items, as well as with multiple-choice items. Although facts and skills frequently are assessed, assessment of preconceptions, misconceptions, and beliefs is rarely used.

2. Novice and Expert Performance. Experts possess more complex knowledge structures than novices and efficiently organize their knowledge. They pay little attention to the surface characteristics of problems and carefully monitor their own problem solving. Experts generate rich problem representations as a guide for selecting solutions. Assessing expertise is easiest in subjects such as mathematics, in which the content is explicit and problem solving is well understood.

Several techniques used to document novice and expert differences include transcripts of students' solutions to problems, semantic or conceptual maps, and word associations. Semantic maps show relationships among the words and concepts that students use. Word associations involve generating word responses to a stimulus word. These assessment methods are less suitable for classroom use than for research because they require training the test administrators, administering individual assessments, transcribing transcripts, and detailed analyzing and scoring of responses.

Studies of expert performance can identify milestones that students need to master en route to expert performance. These milestones can serve as a blueprint for test specifications. Assessments of students' subject matter expertise should consider: 1) the level of detail used to represent a problem, 2) the characteristics of the problem, 3) the conceptual skills and principles used, 4) the degree of organization and flexibility in reasoning, and 5) the selection and execution of solution strategies.

3. Learning Errors. Individuals make a variety of errors when solving problems in specific subjects. Some psychologists believe that errors are rule-governed. Rule-governed errors are exemplified by the systematic mistakes of elementary-age students when applying subtraction algorithms or doing place-value arithmetic. Other types of learning errors include naive theories and misconceptions. Naive theories are common prescientific beliefs that individuals hold about natural phenomena. For example, in astronomy, some students believe the sun rotates around the earth. As individuals mature and increase their knowledge of these phenomena, they shift toward more scientific conceptions.

Researchers stress error identification because it can be helpful in diagnosing learning difficulties and in developing remediation. Learning errors are more easily identified in mathematics or the sciences. In less-defined subject areas, such as the arts, compiling an inventory of learning errors is difficult.

Learning errors cannot be diagnosed using traditional tests. Researchers have developed alternative methods, including individual clinical interviews, semantic maps, and verbal transcripts of explanations. These individually administered assessments require large expenditures of time and money; thus there has been some interest in developing group measures of learning errors.

4. Metacognitive Processes and Learning Strategies. Metacognitive processes involve the self-management of thinking. These processes include planning, activating, monitoring, and evaluating one's actions. Metacognitive skills can be specific to a subject area or they can be general. Knowing that a particular strategy will enhance performance and knowing how and under what conditions to apply the strategy are metacognitive skills. Many reading programs, for example, now are designed to teach metacognitive skills.

Weinstein and Meyer (1991) identified several types of learning strategies, such as rehearsal, elaboration, and organization. Rehearsal requires the simple repetition of items in order to secure them in memory. Elaboration involves the addition of symbolic content, such as mental imagery, to increase the meaningfulness of the information to be learned. Elaboration facilitates the integration of knowledge by increasing the relationships among information in a student's knowledge structure. Organization transforms information into a format that is easier to understand. The construction of a timeline is an example of organization.

Comprehension monitoring is another metacognitive skill, which involves establishing learning goals, assessing their accomplishment, and modifying ineffective strategies. For instance, students may ask themselves questions about information in order to discover knowledge gaps. Affective strategies allow students to persist longer at difficult learning tasks and feel more effective. For example, when students schedule study sessions before an examination as a way to relieve anxiety, they are using an affective strategy.

The assessment of metacognitive learning strategies cannot rely on traditional tests. In research studies, students' metacognitive learning is exposed through structured interviews, self-report measures, observations, and occasional paper-pencil tests. In performance assessments, students provide extended oral or written responses that may reveal the metacognitive learning being used. In performance assessments, teachers can examine an essay, a science experiment, or a detailed written justification of a mathematics solution to gather evidence of the metacognitive processes a student is applying.

Because learning and study strategies affect achievement, they must be assessed separately from achievement itself. Traditional tests fail to provide information on metacognition or study practices. The Learning and Study Strategies Inventory developed by Weinstein, Schulte, and Palmer (1987) attempts to remedy these deficiencies. It contains 10 subscales, including attitude, motivation, time management, anxiety, concentration, information processing, selecting main ideas, study aids, self-testing, and test strategies. This inventory can help teachers to design optimally effective teaching and learning strategies for all students.

Technological Developments

Technological developments have lightened the work of psychometrists and educators by making assessments easier to develop, administer, and score. Computers can make assessment more efficient as well as create new learning environments. However, for technology to fulfill its promise, critical economic and technological barriers must be surmounted.

Test Development and Scoring. As computer capacity and speed have increased, computers have become more widely used in all aspects of testing, including managing, storing, and updating item banks. Item banks make it possible to develop customized assessments. Test items can be stored electronically by instructional objective, technical characteristics, and other categories. CD-ROM technology is being developed to store longer items for which students must construct or produce a response. Computers also have been used to generate tests using laser printers, which allow complicated drawings to be included.

The technology of "mark-sense" (or scannable) answer sheets made large-scale assessment much more feasible and made the printing of thousands of answer booklets obsolete. Optical mark-reading equipment can score more than 6,000 answer sheets in an hour.

Currently, computers can score free-response items by comparing students' responses with keyword lists or previous answers that have been sorted into correct, partially correct, and incorrect categories. Computers also have been used to score students' writing. They can provide general essay evaluations and specific suggestions for word use and sentence construction. But one difficulty in the computer scoring of essays is that the written works cannot be easily converted into machine-readable form.

Computer software can select, order, and administer test items to individual students at their convenience. These administrations usually require microcomputers and may include the use of televisions, slides, or audio recordings. Computer-based administrations do not require students to record their answers on test booklets or answer sheets. Rather, students use a keyboard, mouse, or touch-sensitive screen. In the future, students should be able to write their answers on a computer screen.

Computerized testing affords greater standardization of conditions, because the computer can present identical screens to all students. Students can take computerized tests at their own convenience and pace in public libraries or at home, using modems with "dumb terminals" or inexpensive personal computers. Computer-based assessment makes it possible to administer individual mastery tests or criterion-referenced examinations to a classroom of students, each of whom is at a different level of competence. The computer selects the appropriate items and the point at which to discontinue testing for a given diagnosis, thus reducing the amount of time that the student or the teacher needs to devote to classroom testing.

Moreover, test security can be enhanced. Since passwords and encryptions are employed, no paper version of an assessment need exist. Test items can be sequenced randomly among computers to reduce the chance for students at adjacent computer stations to cheat. A final advantage is the wide range of stimuli that can be employed in the computerized presentation, including audio and video material. Videodiscs can store up to 54,000 still images or 30 minutes of full-motion, color, video images (Blando and Ryan 1992).

Adaptive Testing. In computerized adaptive testing, the computer uses a student's previous answers to select subsequent items that are most suitable in terms of optimal measurement, motivation, and time savings. Computerized adaptive testing can cut testing time in half, because fewer items are required for reliable assessment.

Adaptive testing can be used for diagnosis and instructional feedback; selection, placement, and certification; and accountability or system-monitoring. For example, the Portland Achievement Level Testing program is a combined norm- and criterion-referenced battery employing computerized adaptive testing. The testing program serves three purposes: 1) to test students when they enter the district in order to place them in appropriate instructional programs, 2) to provide continuous assessment of the students throughout the school year, and 3) to select students for placement in special programs at any point during their enrollment. In addition, a version of the computerized adaptive test has been used for such accountability functions as the evaluation of compensatory education programs (U.S. Congress, Office of Technology Assessment 1992).

Integrated Learning Systems. Four decades ago, Ralph Tyler pointed out that "Measurement [should be] conceived, not as a process quite apart from instruction, but rather as an integral part of it" (1951, p. 47). Integrated learning systems (ILS) are computer systems that permit an individual student's test results to guide instruction. Because computers can store large numbers of items and rapidly calculate estimates of a student's ability following the administration of each item, shorter tests that are individually suited to the student and provide nearly instantaneous feedback also may enhance motivation and utility.

ILS technology is guided by two aspects of curriculum. One is instructional experiences that move students through the domain of content to accomplish educational goals. The other is the set of course standards that serve as milestones of beginning, intermediate, or terminal accomplishments. ILS make use of instructional activities that move students along a path of expertise marked by testing milestones. Thus ILS are able to provide continuous analysis, diagnosis, and monitoring of student learning.

ILS items can be presented as part of the instructional process. The successive screens displayed on the computer provide presentations, checks for understanding, practice, coaching, and feedback. At the request of the student or teacher, a "mastery map" can be displayed on the monitor that shows what the student has accomplished and what standards are yet to be completed. The standards can reflect student, teacher, or district goals. ILS may include the following features: displays of student progress and options, directed practice on tasks, on-line prototype answers to assessments, cumulative archives of individual student data, computer-guided coaching, predictions of learning rates to guide review, and minute-by-minute analyses of classroom and group performance to aid in classroom, school, and district instructional management. Over the past 30 years, ILS developed by vendors such as WICAT, Computer Curriculum Corporation, and Jostens have been implemented in a variety of school districts.

Conventional computer-assisted instruction programs, an early application of ILS, have been studied carefully. Research syntheses show that their effects on specific, short-term learning outcomes are greater than those of conventional teaching (Niemiec and Walberg 1987). However, the data on more advanced ILS applications using general, long-term educational outcomes have been less convincing.

Intelligent Measurement. The use of knowledge bases and inferencing procedures permits computer systems to produce "intelligent measurement" (Bunderson, Inouye, and Olsen 1989). Intelligent measurement requires a knowledge base that contains expertise specific to a subject area. Three types of intelligent measurement are applicable to education. The first type provides prescriptive advice, or intelligent interpretations. An expert system can model the knowledge of a teacher who is familiar with the subject area, the instructional management system, and the curriculum. The expert system can model good pedagogy, match instruction with characteristics of learners, and generate trajectories of student progress.

A second educational application is automatic holistic scoring. Knowledge bases used in automatic holistic scoring represent mastery standards for the assessment tasks and the scoring knowledge of experts. In automatic holistic scoring, an expert system performs the complex scoring of assessments, replicating the judgments made by human scorers.

A third application of intelligent measurement is the automation of individual profile interpretations. The output of the computer includes: 1) questions for counselors to ask students in order to clarify the students' performance and 2) interpretative commentaries. The automation of individual profile interpretations reduces the need for each teacher to be an expert in interpreting assessment results.

Adequacy of Current Assessments

As assessment has increased in importance, the technical merit of individual assessments has become more critical. Technical merit may be evaluated using, for example, the *Standards for Educational and Psychological Tests* (1985) or the *ETS Standards for Quality and Fairness* (1987). Because there is no consensus about what constitutes appropriate technical standards for alternative assessments, determining their merit is more difficult than determining the merit of traditional assessments. For example, how does one determine the merit of a geometry assessment that promotes enthusiasm by allowing students to use their artistic talents in answering questions but that does not meet traditional technical standards of validity and reliability? Three areas of debate have emerged: purposes of assessment, standards of technical quality, and costs.

Purposes of Assessment. Assessments should fulfill at least one of three purposes: 1) the monitoring of individual student progress and the diagnosis of learning difficulties, 2) the placement and certification of individual students, and 3) the evaluation and comparison of groups to ensure the accountability of the education system (Resnick and Resnick 1989).

1. Monitoring and Diagnosis of Student Learning. Monitoring individual student progress and diagnosing learning difficulties aid teachers in classroom management. Monitoring student progress usually is accomplished with teacher-made tests that help teachers determine instruction. Some teachers criticize standardized achievement tests as lacking the capacity to provide diagnostic information for the enhancement of day-to-day instruction.

Traditional tests have been criticized for their dependence on recognition items, their limited coverage of domains of knowledge, and their alleged failure to elicit a range of higher-order thought processes. Traditional multiple-choice achievement tests, it is argued, place too much emphasis on facts and procedures for solving well-structured problems that are presented without context. In addition, these traditional tests are limited in their utility to identify the characteristics of a student's learning. Of course, traditional tests were never intended to do all these things. They were intended as complements to such teacher assessments as essays and laboratory assignments, which can accomplish these things.

Critics of multiple-choice items argue that such items are easier because they require only that the student recognize a correct answer. This is in contrast to fill-in-the-blank or essay items, which require a student to recall appropriate information and to generate a response. In addition, multiple-choice items sometimes can be answered correctly by guessing.

According to Ward, Rock, and La Hart (1990), traditional and alternative item formats can be arranged along a continuum based

48

on several dimensions: 1) selection/identification, 2) reordering/ rearrangement, 3) substitution/correction, 4) completion, 5) construction, and 6) presentation/performance. For example, multiple-choice items are considered the most constrained, because they do not require a student to generate a response. Rather, the student selects an answer from those presented. Proponents of alternative assessments assert that the items used in alternative assessments are less constrained and can be used to measure more realistic and complex problem-solving than can multiple-choice test items.

Proponents of performance-based alternative assessments emphasize the complexity and authenticity of less-constrained items. They argue that performance assessments derive their value from examining actual performances, rather than from examining indicators of potential performances, as occur with traditional tests.

Many researchers and educators are wary of claims that alternative assessments can replace multiple-choice tests for monitoring student learning. Many valued educational tasks require simple recognition, and some skills (including higher-order thinking) and subject areas can be competently assessed using a multiple-choice format.

Some advocates argue that alternative assessments provide a multidimensional view of a particular skill or content area. Yet breadth of coverage often is traded for depth of coverage. Performance assessments are based on one or a small number of tasks and thus may assess only a limited sample of what a student knows compared to the dozens of facts and ideas than can be assessed using multiple-choice items.

Researchers have examined the equivalence of multiple-choice and alternative assessments in various subject areas. In this research, the knowledge measured and the scores assigned using multiple-choice and alternative items — in particular, open-ended items — are very similar. If the knowledge and scores assigned are the same, then the capacity of these two types of assessments to diagnose learning difficulties is equivalent. Thus alternative assessments, which may be costly and may lack technical standards, have yet to demonstrate more value than teacher-made and traditional multiple-choice tests.

2. Certification and Placement of Students. A second purpose of testing is to make decisions about placement in instructional programs and certification of mastery of a content area. Tests used for this purpose do not inform the management of daily classroom activities but are used to make administrative decisions about a student's progress through the school system.

Tests used for making high-stakes decisions, including placement and certification, must meet high technical standards that warrant their use as the single piece of evidence for making decisions about a student's future. Of course, better decisions are made when multiple sources of evidence are used.

The use of traditional and alternative assessments for the placement and certification of a diverse student body has been challenged with evidence of racial, ethnic, and gender differences in performance on these tests. Some critics contend that traditional tests are inherently biased and produce an adverse impact on some groups of students, and thus should play a minor role, if any, in high-stakes decisions. But cautions regarding technical quality, equity, bias, and adverse impact pertain to all types of tests and assessments used for high-stakes decisions, including alternative assessments.

Some researchers indicate that some alternative forms of assessment, at least initially, widen the performance gap between males and females and between socioeconomic and ethnic groups. In contrast, others cite evidence that the written essay part of advanced placement exams in various subject areas produce smaller gender differences than do the multiple-choice parts of these exams. Less information is available about the reliability and validity of alternative forms of assessment. Again, there is the question of proof. Simply criticizing multiple-choice items or misuse of traditional tests hardly makes an affirmative case for alternative assessments.

3. Comparison of Groups for Accountability. The third purpose of assessment is the comparison of groups of students in order to

evaluate schools, programs, states, and nations, and thus to maintain accountability. Typically, multiple-choice tests have been used for this purpose. Recently, alternative assessments using constructed-response items have been considered for use in large-scale testing programs.

Improved accountability requires not only accurate comparisons among groups but also measures of student performance on content in which students have received instruction. School district goals, instructional materials, methods, curricula, and assessments often are poorly aligned or integrated. School districts develop local goals and curricula but depend on commercial textbooks and standardized tests for instruction and assessment. Because these commercial textbooks and tests are prepared for national use, they rarely reflect all the local educational priorities.

This mismatch may lead to inefficiencies and morale problems. Teachers may use instructional materials that fail to reflect district goals, even though they will be evaluated in part on their students' attainment of those goals. Students may be examined on knowledge and skills they have not studied, or they may study content that is not considered a priority in their community but on which they will be tested. These mismatches have been identified as a cause of poor educational productivity in the United States. Poor alignment of instruction, materials, and tests cannot be eliminated simply by using alternative assessments, though the local development of assessments can ensure more agreement among the elements of instruction and their assessment. However, local assessments cannot serve the purposes of comparing districts, states, or nations.

The National Assessment of Educational Progress (NAEP), a congressionally initiated survey of education achievement, is a testing program used for monitoring student performance at the national and state level. Since 1969, NAEP has collected assessment data in reading, mathematics, science, writing, history/geography, and other fields. NAEP draws on a representative sample of schools that participate in the assessments. In 1990, for the first time, NAEP conducted state-by-state comparisons as part of the mathematics assessment. Advocates of NAEP believe that these comparisons hold educators accountable for their students' performance over time and also for the level of performance their students display in comparison to similar students nationwide.

Recently, both major political parties advocated a national examination system to monitor the nation's schools. Referred to as America 2000 during the Bush Administration and Goals 2000 in the Clinton Administration, this examination system proposes "world-class standards" in English, mathematics, history, science, and geography (U.S. Department of Education 1991).

Standards of Technical Quality. Reliability and validity are two key psychometric concepts that are applied to the evaluation of tests and assessments.

Reliability is the consistency with which a test measures content. One type estimates the consistency of the test to measure the same individual's performance on several occasions (test-retest reliability). Other types of reliability establish the equivalence of several forms of a test (parallel and alternate-forms reliability). Still other types of reliability establish whether each item on a test measures the same content (split-half or alpha reliability). Finally, inter-rater reliability estimates the consistency with which raters assign scores to an individual's performance.

The reliability of traditional multiple-choice tests is well documented. In contrast, little information is available on the reliability of many alternative assessments. The reliability information that is available tends to focus on inter-rater reliability of performance-based alternative assessments. Preliminary evidence shows that expert raters often lack consensus on their assessments of written essays, laboratory exercises, and other alternative tasks.

Vermont initiated the first statewide assessment to measure student achievement using portfolios, one of the more popular forms of alternative assessment. This statewide assessment is one of the few alternative assessment projects being dispassionately evaluated by an external evaluator. A recent article describing the assessment (Viadero 1993) revealed the difficulty of establishing adequate reliability when using alternative test formats: "A 1992 report by the RAND Corporation . . . finds that the 'rater reliability' in scoring the portfolios . . . was very low" (p. 18). Because of low rater reliability, the results were not reported at the school or district level.

Validity refers to whether a test measures what it is claimed to measure. Recently, psychometricians Linn, Baker, and Dunbar (1991) developed an expanded definition of validity that applies to alternative and traditional assessments. In their view, the evaluation of validity for all forms of assessment should, at the minimum, include evidence regarding directness and transparency, consequences, fairness, transfer and generalizability, cognitive complexity, content quality, content coverage, and meaningfulness.

Directness refers to the extent to which the assessment task matches the instructional goals. An example of the direct assessment of writing is when students are asked to produce a writing sample. In contrast, an indirect assessment of writing skill requires students to answer multiple-choice questions about correct punctuation or stylistic considerations. *Transparency* refers to the clarity of the criteria used in judging performances. Assessments with high transparency have high acceptability and are viewed as legitimate measures. Directness and transparency can be viewed as components of *face validity.*

Fairness requires the identification of potential sources of bias, such as rater effects or insensitive or irrelevant materials. Bias sometimes can be detected using statistics that identify items on which groups of test takers perform differently. These differences may not reflect true differences in test takers' knowledge but, rather, differences in their cultural experiences. Adverse impact on identified groups of students must be considered when judging the fairness of an assessment. An assessment should not result in members of any racial, gender, or ethnic group being evaluated differentially, assuming all groups of students are equally qualified. In addition, some students may need to be taught how to take tests more effectively in order to ensure a fair evaluation of their knowledge.

Critics of traditional assessments question the degree to which successful performance on traditional assessments transfers to real-world activities. Performance assessments are believed to have increased transferability to non-academic tasks.

However, performance assessments present special problems in terms of their generalizability. Because developers of performance assessments create tasks that are held to be realistic, complex, and contextualized, the assessment tasks require more time than traditional tests. As a result, fewer tasks can be administered. Thus such assessments provide fewer incidences of student behavior and a limited sample of student knowledge and skills.

When an assessment requires the test taker to use several abilities, as opposed to a simple, less developmentally advanced way to solve problems, it is considered cognitively complex. Complexity should be determined by analyzing the types of skills and processes students use to answer questions. Students can correctly answer items using processes and strategies other than those expected by the test developers. Thus items that were designed to assess students' higher thought processes may be solved using less-advanced approaches, or vice versa.

Judging the quality of an assessment should include a review of its content. Adequate content coverage should express the breadth and depth of the subject. Subject matter experts should systematically determine whether the assessment adequately covers current ideas and material of long-standing importance. This type of review is particularly important in the case of performance assessments that sample only a limited aspect of a subject area.

Whether students and teachers perceive assessment problems as meaningful affects their motivation and performance. When assessments are meaningful to students, their content is relevant to the students' experiences. Advocates of performance assessment believe that assessment can be meaningful learning. By this criterion, however, life in classrooms can never be as "authentic" as that outside.

Costs of Assessments. Beyond consideration of the money spent on all types of assessments, educators increasingly are concerned about the time students spend preparing for and taking tests and the time teachers spend preparing, administering, and scoring tests.

Based on a national survey, researchers Dorre-Bremme and Herman (1986) concluded that only modest amounts of student time are devoted to testing. At the elementary level, total testing time, in all subjects, averaged 76 hours a year, or 8.6% of the total class time of students. Elementary students took a test in reading and a test in math about once every eight days. High school students spent about 12% of their time taking tests in English and mathematics classes. A typical 10th-grader spent nearly 26½ hours annually completing tests in English and 24 hours annually completing tests in mathematics. A high school student took an English test and a mathematics test every three or four days.

Dorre-Bremme and Herman also found that both high school and elementary students spent the largest percentage of their testing time on teacher-developed tests and the next-largest percentage on tests included with curriculum materials. In contrast, minimum competency testing, on average, consumed a very small percentage of testing time. State- and district-mandated tests took about 25% of high school students' total testing time.

According to Dorre-Bremme and Herman, for each hour a student spent taking a test, a teacher spent two to three hours preparing for the test, grading the test, and recording students' scores. Interviews with elementary teachers indicated that they spent about 12% to 15% of their work time, both in and out of school, on achievement testing in all subject areas. This averages to about 200 to 250 hours throughout a school year. Similar figures were not available for high school teachers, but the researchers claimed that high school teachers spent about two hours outside the class for every hour of student testing.

The amount of time teachers devote to alternative assessments also has been a subject of debate but has not been well researched. According to one report, teachers in Great Britain, who have relied heavily on alternative assessments in the past few years, are displeased with the time commitment that such tests require.

Although alternative assessments may require more teacher time for development of the assessments and the training in their use, such time can be viewed as a benefit rather than a cost. For example, teachers involved in developing and scoring the California Assessment Program report that these processes are the most effective staff development activity in which they have participated (Carlson 1991).

The three basic costs incurred when conducting traditional or alternative assessments are: 1) money costs, 2) non-money costs, and 3) estimated opportunity costs. Money costs are the dollars spent on development, administration, scoring, and reporting results. Although estimates vary on the exact money costs of traditional tests and performance assessments, experts estimate performance items to be much more expensive. According to the U.S. Congress, Office of Technology Assessment:

> The costs of performance assessment represent a substantial barrier to expanded use. Performance assessment is a labor-intensive and therefore costly alternative unless it is integrated in the instructional process. Essays and other performance tasks may cost less to develop than do multiple choice items, but are very costly to score. One estimate puts scoring a writing assessment as 5 to 10 times more expensive as scoring a multiple choice examination, while another estimate based on a review of several testing programs administered by ETS. . . suggests that the cost of assessment via one 20- to 40-minute essay is between 3 to 5 times higher than assessment by means of a test of 150 to 200 machine scored, multiple choice items. Among the factors that influence scoring costs are the length of time students are given to complete the essay, the number of readers scoring each essay, qualifications and location of readers (which affect how much they are paid, and travel and lodging costs for the scoring process), and the amount of pretesting conducted on each prompt or question. The higher these factors, the higher the ratio of essay to multiple choice costs. (1992, p. 243)

Non-money costs for traditional and alternative assessments include expenditures of employee time, materials, equipment, space, and energy. Other non-money costs may be stress and a decrease in morale for students, teachers, and administrators. The enthusiasm produced by some of the hands-on activities used in alternative assessments must be weighed against the expenditures of time required to administer and score performance assessments. Traditional tests often are met with less enthusiasm by teachers and students but require a more modest expenditure of time, materials, and space.

Opportunity costs require educators to consider what is displaced for students and teachers when a testing program is implemented. When resources of time, money, and energy are invested in an assessment program, they are unavailable for other uses . For example, the time spent by teachers on administering and scoring assessments should be weighed against the time that could have been used for lesson planning, tailoring instruction to individual students, or upgrading teachers' content knowledge and pedagogical skills.

A second example of opportunity costs is provided by comparing the costs and benefits of using different types of assessments. Some educators argue that alternative assessments provide better data for diagnosing and remediating learning difficulties than do traditional tests. However, the opportunity costs of improved diagnostic information may include a loss of instructional time for students or planning time for teachers, and a reduction in the budget due to the expense of the alternative assessment. Alternative assessments may require more resources on the part of the education system than their promised benefits warrant.

Conclusion

Assessment is integral to the educational process. It serves three fundamental purposes: the day-to-day management of instruction, the classification and placement of students, and the maintenance of accountability for educators and students. Because of these fundamental uses, assessment has become a primary tool for the reform of education. In the past decade, educators have argued over the purposes, format, technical adequacy, and costs of assessment. New assessments are emerging from these debates. Some employ new item formats; others make use of computer-based technologies.

Psychological research is another influence on assessment. Psychologists have argued for assessments that measure students' knowledge schemas, pathways to expertise, and metacognitive learning and study strategies. However, leading education researchers have cautioned against hasty applications of cognitive psychology. Richard Snow and David Lohman assert, "Cognitive psychology has no ready answers for the measurement problems of yesterday, today or tomorrow" (1989, p. 320).

Alternative assessments, particularly those that are referred to as "authentic" because of their reliance on complex, real-life tasks, are viewed by some as a remedy for the misuse of traditional testing. Alternative assessments are regarded as having high face validity and close curricular and test alignment. Other advocates of alternative assessments see these tests as the best way to measure subject-matter expertise. They believe that expertise is better demonstrated in assessments that require extended performances and go beyond recognition items. Despite the supposed benefits attached to alternative assessments, there is little evidence of their wide-scale feasibility, practicality, and utility.

When the purpose of assessment is monitoring the educational standing of school districts, then traditional tests may be the assessment method of choice. Standardization and norming are necessary when comparisons among groups of students are to be made. The larger the pools of students being compared, the more important it is that the assessment procedure be affordable, objective, standardized, and easy to administer and score. These criteria are not easily met by many alternative assessments. Multiple-choice tests can serve the purpose of accountability and, with enhancement, can measure higher thought processes. When selecting an assessment, educators must be attentive to the trade-offs in cognitive sensitivity, technical adequacy, costs, and ability to fulfill the assessment purposes.

Alternative assessments promise much, but they require sober evaluation. There is little information about the technical characteristics of many new forms of assessment. Evidence of difficulties in the use of performance assessment — one form of alternative assessment — has surfaced. For example, Alan Purves, director of the international writing assessment, recently expressed disenchantment over the inability to establish comparable ratings among judges (Rothman 1990). This problem plagues not only writing assessments, but performance assessments of other subjects as well.

Studies by psychologist Richard Shavelson (1991) also cast doubt on the viability of a performance assessment as a sole tool for assigning grades to students. Based on his project, which develops science and mathematics performance assessments, he reported that large differences in a student's scores can occur depending on which performance assessment task is administered. In other words, different performance assessments that attempt to measure the same content do not rank students in the same order.

Computer-based technology promises to make assessment efficient and has demonstrated some impressive results. Optical mark-reading equipment, mark-sense answer sheets, microcomputers, hypermedia, artificial intelligence, and other applications have advanced assessment practices. Technologists claim that computers will be able to score complex, constructed responses; maintain cumulative mastery maps of student progress; present multimedia simulations; videotape student performances for further analysis; and train teachers on the administration, scoring, and interpretation of assessment results. Many of these components have been demonstrated separately. What is lacking, as yet, are large-scale systems that integrate a substantial part of the K-12 curriculum and instructional programs.

In the past, several computer-based innovations have been heralded as cure-alls. Although the feasibility of such technologies was demonstrated in university laboratories and military and business environments, their effectiveness in school settings was less well documented. Presumably, with national, or at least widely shared, goals that value technology for education, new technologies may become feasible for the nation's schools. Nevertheless, it is unlikely that computer-based technologies will be a panacea to our assessment ills in the immediate future. As in the case of all forms of assessment, open-mindedness and healthy skepticism are in order.

References

Blando, J.A., and Ryan, P. "Student Assessment: The Role of New Technologies." Paper presented at the annual meeting of the American Educational Research Association, San Francisco, April 1992.

Bunderson, C.V.; Inouye, D.K.; and Olsen, J.B. "The Four Generations of Computerized Educational Measurement." In *Educational Measurement,* 3rd ed., edited by R.L. Linn. New York: Macmillan, 1989.

Carlson, D. "Changing the Face of Testing in California." *California Curriculum News Report* 16 (January-February 1991): 1, 10.

Committee to Develop Standards for Educational and Psychological Testing. *Standards for Educational and Psychological Tests.* Washington, D.C.: American Psychological Association, 1985.

Darling-Hammond, L. "The Implications of Testing Policy for Quality and Equality." *Phi Delta Kappan* 73 (November 1991): 220-25.

Dorre-Bremme, D.W., and Herman, J.L. *Assessing Student Achievement: A Profile of Classroom Practices.* CSE Monograph Series in Evaluation No. 11. Los Angeles: University of California, Center for the Study of Evaluation, 1986.

Educational Testing Service. *ETS Standards for Quality and Fairness.* Princeton, N.J., 1987.

Linn, R.; Baker, E.; and Dunbar, S. "Complex, Performance-Based Assessment: Expectations and Validation Criteria." *Educational Researcher* 20, no. 8 (1991): 15-21.

Madaus, G. "The Effects of Important Tests on Students: Implications for a National Examination System." *Phi Delta Kappan* 73 (November 1991): 226-31.

National Commission on Testing and Public Policy. *From Gatekeeper to Gateway: Transforming Testing in America.* Boston, 1990.

Neill, D.M., and Medina, N.J. "Standardized Testing: Harmful to Educational Health." *Phi Delta Kappan* 70 (May 1989): 688-97.

Niemiec, R.P., and Walberg, H.J. "Comparative Effects of Computer-Assisted Instruction: A Synthesis of Reviews." *Journal of Educational Computing Research* 3, no. 1 (1987): 19-37.

Resnick, L.B., and Resnick, D.F. "Tests as Standards of Achievement in School." In *Proceedings of the 1989 ETS Invitational Conference: The Uses of Standardized Tests in American Education.* Princeton, N.J.: Educational Testing Service, 1989.

Rothman, R. "New Tests Based on Performance Raise Questions." *Education Week*, 12 September 1990, pp. 1, 10, 12.

Shavelson, R.J. "Authentic Assessment: The Rhetoric and Reality." Paper presented at the annual meeting of the American Educational Research Association, Chicago, April 1991.

Shavelson, R.J., and Baxter, G.P. "What We've Learned About Assessing Hands-on Science." *Educational Leadership* 49, no. 8 (1992): 20-25.

Snow, R.E., and Lohman, D.F. "Implications of Cognitive Psychology for Educational Measurement." In *Educational Measurement*, 3rd ed., edited by R.L. Linn. New York: Macmillan, 1989.

Tyler, R.W. "The Functions of Measurement in Improving Instruction." In *Educational Measurement*, edited by E.F. Lindquist. Washington, D.C.: American Council on Education, 1951.

U.S. Congress, Office of Technology Assessment. *Testing in American Schools: Asking the Right Questions.* Report No. OTA-SET-519. Washington, D.C.: U.S. Government Printing Office, 1992.

U.S. Department of Education. *America 2000: An Education Strategy: Sourcebook.* Washington, D.C., 1991.

Viadero, D. "RAND Urges Overhaul in Vt.'s Pioneering Writing Test." *Education Week*, 10 November 1993, pp. 1, 18.

Ward, W.C.; Rock, P.A.; and La Hart, C.L. *Toward a Framework for Constructed-Response Items.* Report No. RR-90-7. Princeton, N.J.: Educational Testing Service, 1990.

Weinstein, C.E., and Meyer, D.K. *Implications of Cognitive Psychology for Testing: Contribution from Work in Learning Strategies.* Englewood Cliffs, N.J.: Prentice-Hall, 1991.

Weinstein, C.E.; Schulte, A.C.; and Palmer, D.R. *The Learning and Study Strategies Inventory (LASSI).* Clearwater, Fla.: H&H Publishing, 1987.

Wittrock, M.C. "Cognition and Testing." In *Testing and Cognition,* edited by M.C. Wittrock and E.L. Baker. Englewood Cliffs, N.J.: Prentice-Hall, 1991.

CHARACTER EDUCATION
by Kenneth Burrett and Timothy Rusnak

I n 1980 a group of international scholars met to examine issues
related to the acquisition of values and moral development in
cultures worldwide. Out of that meeting came the formation of
the Council for Research in Values and Philosophy. The council
established research teams to explore the value traditions of
Western, Latin, Asian, and African cultures. These teams set out
to learn how values are developed in individuals as well as transmitted across generations.

The council's efforts resulted in three scholarly volumes that
provide the foundations for what we call Integrated Character
Education, the topic of this essay. These works address the philosophical, psychological, and educational dimensions of how
values are acquired and transmitted. In the first volume, *Act and
Agent: Philosophical Foundations for Moral Education and Character Development* (Ellrod et al. 1986), a team of philosophers
explore the concept of personal growth within culture. The team
focuses on the integration of such previously separated dimensions as intellect and will, knowledge and affectivity. This perspective provides a framework for reflection on the dynamics of
personal growth with implications for education.

A second volume, *Psychological Foundations of Moral Education and Character Development* (Knowles and McLean 1986),
focuses on psychological research in moral development.
Included are considerations of affectivity, especially those emotions judged to be most closely associated with morality. It makes
the connection between emotions and cognition and focuses on
both behavior and self-regulatory systems as a basis for character

This essay is condensed from Kenneth Burrett and Timothy Rusnak, *Integrated Character Education*, Fastback 351 (Bloomington, Ind.: Phi Delta
Kappa Educational Foundation, 1993).

development. Further, it details the impact of environment on the individual, as well as a person's deliberate actions to influence that environment. The "acting person" is seen as the mechanism for achieving personal integration, which leads to character development. Personal growth is seen as a function of knowledge, emotion, and environment. It occurs in developmental stages, as follows:

1. Ages 1 to 7: development of a sense of hope (openness and trust), autonomy, and imagination.
2. Ages 7 to adolescence: development of competence (beyond simply skill and technique) in the expression of self and of harmony with one's physical and social environment.
3. Adolescence: development of consistency and of fidelity predicated on a combined sense of ability and commitment.
4. Adulthood: development of a sense of justice, also love, care, and wisdom.

The third volume, *Character Development in Schools and Beyond* (Lickona and Ryan 1992), examines how the philosophical and psychological theory of character development can guide what is done in schools. It submits that: 1) cultural values are not simply relative or arbitrary but are clearly and objectively imbedded in our common cultural heritage; 2) current approaches to moral education fail to consider the connection between knowledge, feeling, and action; and 3) education can support cultural transmission and character development.

The Center for Character Education, Civic Responsibility and Teaching, established in the School of Education at Duquesne University in 1987, was selected to translate the philosophical and psychological theory undergirding character development into school practice. The center's work is carried out through annual summer workshops for teachers and expanded graduate and undergraduate courses at the university.

Integrated Character Education is founded on solid and well-researched principles of psychology and philosophy. The implementation model that has been developed demonstrates how administrators, teachers, community leaders, and parents can work together to foster character development in our youth.

To understand Integrated Character Education, it is helpful to see it in the context of earlier efforts in character education in the history of our nation. This is the focus of the next section.

The Tradition of Character Education in America

Character education, whether defined as ethics, citizenship, values, or personal development, has long been part of American education. In Colonial times necessary skills and knowledge were taught in the context of social expectations. Curriculum materials underscored the importance of relating content to community expectations. The *Hornbook*, for example, contained the Lord's Prayer, which children were expected to memorize. Later, the *New England Primer* taught basic skills necessary for a "proper life and eternal salvation." The alphabet and reading skills were presented using ample references to social and religious maxims. Thereby, students were prepared to participate in the economic, social, and cultural life of the community. This approach continued throughout the American Colonial period and well into the 19th century.

The recurring reliance on schools for the socialization of children was again demonstrated when Europeans emigrated to America in great numbers in the 19th century. They brought with them their religious, language, political, and social traditions, which were different and thus suspect by those who were established and in control of both the politics and economy of the nation. Those in control looked to the schools to provide a curriculum that would shape the "character needs" of this new citizenry. For example, the *McGuffey Readers*, first published in 1836, systematized reading instruction. In the second-level edition, the preface notes: "Careful attention is paid to develop the character of each student through selected stories." Some of the stories were: "The Good Boy," "The Good Girl," and "My Country." The intent, as conveyed by the titles, was to prepare the new immigrant students to choose responsible action in their new roles as American citizens.

Using many of the ideas espoused by Horace Mann, Henry Barnard was a primary shaper of the schools of this era. Barnard advocated extensive training in civic values but perhaps is most noted for his advocacy of transmitting American values in schools through the common denominator of the English language and through the teaching of a common cultural perspective. At the same time, many religious groups (particularly the Catholic Church) established schools in their churches and communities. Curricula often emphasized preservation of cultural traditions, especially religion and language. A typical school day included instruction in catechism, the native language, and social customs.

The rise of American public schools, coupled with that of private/parochial schools, underscores the importance our ancestors placed on achieving socialization goals through the schools. Rapid changes in American society in the 19th century continued to influence the course of education. However, true to its Puritan roots, America's concern with cultural development and general societal goals strongly influenced the curriculum and school practices.

Education for Virtue. By the early part of this century, schools were beginning to develop curricula that emphasized commonly accepted virtues, such as self-control, reliability, and duty. A popular middle-grade reading series, for example, featured three selections at the beginning of the text, which were intended to set the tone for the ensuing school year. The selections were: "Achievement" by Thomas Carlyle, "If" by Rudyard Kipling, and "A Man's Task" by Robert Louis Stevenson. Students often were required to memorize these works. Often mottoes carved over the entrance of school buildings underscored this emphasis on the "virtuous" life.

The Progressive Education Movement advocated the concept of social reconstruction. Based on the notion that schools could reform society, progressivism gained momentum during the Great Depression. This child-centered movement advocated the needs of the child; thus personal growth was a prime concern. This approach called on schools to affect the social order by emphasizing democracy, citizenship, and ethical character.

After World War II, the concern for virtue was reflected in the "Dick and Jane" readers, which exemplified a particular way to act, talk, and dress. The newly emerging electronic media exalted the perfect family, the perfect occupation, and the perfect way of life. This idealistic approach assumed supportive parents, friendly neighborhoods, and active community organizations. The school strove to nurture conformity in children by insisting on clear sets of do's and don't's. Character development was associated with patriotism. Soon, however, international and domestic developments would disrupt this "perfect system."

Uncertain Times. The civil rights movement and the Vietnam War created deep social unrest, calling into question many traditional values. The schools, reflecting the tumultuous state of society, became more sensitive to the complexity of values in a pluralistic and changing society. Differing views emerged as to how we should be teaching values and ethics in our schools.

The values clarification approach employed intriguing group-process techniques, such as the "Magic Circle" and the "Fishbowl." Teachers encouraged children to express their values, feelings, and beliefs. This was to be carried out in a secure environment of sharing and caring, with the focus on personal concerns. The premise was that as students interacted, they could express their own values while respecting those of others. However, critics charged that this approach focused too much on individual rights and feelings, to the neglect of societal responsibilities and of transmitting cultural traditions across generations.

Another, more sophisticated approach, called Cognitive Moral Development, engaged children in examining a problem that presented a moral dilemma. Led by a specially trained teacher, group discussions of these moral dilemmas were intended to make students think more altruistically. The theory underlying this approach is that there is a developmental sequence or stages of moral growth in each student. The embodiment of this model is the "just community," a school environment where teachers and students share decision making. This approach assumes that moral development is a function of cognitive deliberation, and it focuses on growth through the resolution of moral dilemmas.

Looking to the 21st Century. Character or values education continues to be as much a concern today as in any other period in our history. For example, a major theme of the 1992 presidential campaign was "traditional family values." Professional organizations, such as the Association for Supervision and Curriculum Development, have stressed the ethical development of children. States have adopted curriculum guidelines that address the broad goals of character education. Many schools and districts are developing their own curricula in character education.

What Is Integrated Character Education?

The Integrated Character Education model holds great promise as a means of fostering character in our youth. It recognizes both the affective and cognitive factors involved in educating the whole child and ultimately the responsible adult. The basic question is how to transmit the values of our heritage from one generation to the next, while supporting the personal development of our youth. To answer this question requires us to consider the nature of character education, including its goals and program criteria.

The Nature of Character Education. The terms, *ethics, moral, values,* and *character,* although carrying slightly different connotations, derive from a common tradition. Ethics refers to the study of and teaching about right and wrong, especially as defined in the philosophical traditions of our culture. Moral refers to personal behavior and also covers a group of concerns dealing with duties and responsibilities involving choices among value-laden issues. Values are general ideals individuals hold that determine their choice of action. Character describes a person's organized set of beliefs and values that influence actions related to ethical decisions.

These definitions are reflected in the various approaches to character education. Ethics education implies helping students resolve choices relating to ethical decisions. Values education emphasizes identification of fundamental principles or ideals guiding human activity. Moral education is concerned with development of judgments about what is right and with caring deeply about doing right. Character education is concerned with transmitting those cultural traditions that contribute to personal maturation.

The controlling principle of Integrated Character Education is its emphasis on the affective dimension of learning and decision making. The cognitive processes involved in decision making are inextricably linked to affective factors. Self-identity, commitment, and willingness to act ethically lie on the affective side of character. These affective dimensions of character represent the bridge between knowing and acting. Willingness to act on convictions becomes the integrating component between knowledge and feeling and promotes the growth of character.

Character commonly is defined using such terms as integrity, honesty, courage, sincerity, and truthfulness. If these qualities are practiced consistently, they are referred to as virtues. The Integrated Character Education model agrees in general with these popular definitions but holds that character is acquired. And since character is acquired, it can be fostered through education in the home, school, and community. It is the responsibility of educators to provide those conditions that are conducive to helping students confront problems, propose solutions, and then take constructive action. The Integrated Character Education model is based on the premise that individuals may choose and are responsible for their choices. Acting on choices validates character growth.

Goals of Integrated Character Education. Integrated Character Education is concerned with preparing youth to address life's moral and ethical problems, with the ultimate goal of developing mature adults capable of responsible citizenship and moral action. This is achieved through fulfilling personal development goals and social goals. Personal development goals include physical and

OUACHITA TECHNICAL COLLEGE

psychological health, positive self-concept, interpersonal skills, and demonstrating such qualities as being responsible and caring. Social goals include upholding the social system, belief systems, and intellectual traditions and preserving the physical environment.

Criteria for Character Education Programs. The Integrated Character Education model views student learning as having both cognitive and affective dimensions. Therefore, character education programs must meet certain criteria if they are to address both these dimensions. These criteria are explained below.

1. Character develops through responsible action. If good actions contribute to character development, then the educational setting should provide more than cognitive involvement with moral and ethical issues. The curriculum must allow students to confront meaningful questions in the school and community, to propose imaginative solutions, and to become involved in activities and actions to implement those solutions wherever feasible.

2. Character develops through interaction. Students develop character through interaction with peers, teachers, and community members. While society shapes the individual, each individual has the capability of shaping society through moral action. The character education curriculum needs to focus on interactions with the moral and ethical dimensions of our social, cultural, and ecological environments.

3. Character integrates the whole personality. The Integrated Character Education model supports the student in developing a strong sense of identity, which is the mainspring of moral commitment and action. The school should provide ample activities and experiences designed to foster moral and ethical growth, involving both the cognitive and affective dimensions of self.

4. Character involves consistent patterns of action. Psychologists tell us that one indicator of character is consistency in behavior over time and in different settings. The character education curriculum should be designed to help students commit themselves to a set of positive values and to act on them consistently.

The foregoing criteria stress the development of the whole person and interaction with the total environment. It follows then that character education should be a function of the total school curriculum. It must be fused with the academic curriculum, the extracurricular programs, and the administrative and social system of the school. It also means involving the family and community in creating a supportive environment for character development. Above all, Integrated Character Education must allow for active student involvement, for opportunities for personal growth through integrating the affective and cognitive dimensions of self, and development of commitment to a set of values that lead to consistent behavior and actions.

Six Key Principles for Implementing Integrated Character Education

Using the theoretical foundations and the program criteria described above, educators involved in the Integrated Character Education approach have identified six key principles that serve to guide implementation of character education in the classroom:

1. Character education is part of every subject, not just another subject.
2. The school and community are vital partners in the character education of youth.
3. A positive classroom environment supports character education.
4. Empowered teachers are in the best position to carry out the goals of character education.
5. Character education is encouraged through administrative policy and practice.
6. Character education is action education.

These six principles, taken together, serve as the basis for implementing an effective character education program. Each is discussed more fully below.

Character education is part of every subject, not just another subject. Character education includes those parts of every subject that uphold our cultural traditions and help youth to develop as functional members of adult society. Character education is not an "add-on." It is part of the academic learning of each student.

While teachers typically have specific objectives for each lesson, they often overlook potential character education content in the lesson. For example, while reading a selection of literature, students not only learn about the plot, setting, and point of view but also might examine the value of justice as reflected by the decisions of a central character. Interpreting the character's motive, intention, or reaction to the human condition through discussion or role playing gives deeper meaning to the reading selection and encourages the development of empathy.

One reading teacher indexes the stories she assigns by themes, such as honesty, fairness, justice, or respect for others. In planning lessons, she incorporates these themes into her teaching objectives and uses such instructional approaches as cooperative learning, whole language, or conflict resolution to get her students to interact with the ideas inherent in the stories. Thus character education becomes part of reading instruction.

Character education need not be confined to only the obvious subjects, such as literature or social studies. In one school a math teacher uses math activities that also have a social issue imbedded in the activity. For example, in learning how to construct graphs, the teacher uses data on recycling. As the students learn to graph the data, they also are given time to reflect on and discuss their individual responsibility in preserving and protecting the environment. This integrated approach combines mathematical operations with an exploration of individual responsibility for a serious ecological problem.

By analyzing each subject in the standard curriculum, teachers can identify concepts or ideas that can be incorporated into character education strands. As these ideas are systematized, themes will emerge that can become the basis of Integrated Character Education. Following are some typical themes supporting character development that cut across school subjects.

Personal Development Themes

self-identity	courage
health	conscience
sexuality	competence
friendship	fidelity
compassion	caring
self-respect	love
respect for others	decision making

Social/Cultural Themes

parent relationships	democracy
sibling relationships	freedom
religious beliefs	racism
human values	pollution
civic responsibility	global warming
civil rights	deforestation

Themes are imbedded in curriculum content. Where possible, the themes selected should be those commonly found in several subject areas. For example, the theme of decision making cuts across several subject areas. In science, mathematics, and technical subjects, themes can be generated by showing how the subject relates to the human condition in modern society.

Teachers and curriculum developers can support character education through:

- reviewing instructional material for themes relating to personal development and referencing such materials to specific learning objectives;
- reviewing national, state, and local documents for statements of goals relating to personal and social/cultural development;
- constructing a chart of ideas or concepts in various subjects that are focused on character themes;
- selecting teaching methods and activities that involve students in the process of reflection about moral/ethical issues;

- teaching lessons that integrate character education with the content being taught;
- evaluating student learning for evidence of understanding of and personal growth in matters of character.

The school and community are vital partners in the character development of youth. In the not-too-distant past, people lived and worked together in close-knit communities. The grocer was your friend; the policeman lived across the street. And who could forget the milkman who knew everyone on the block? At the heart of this community structure was the family. Often grandparents lived with the families. Newlyweds moved in with parents until they could afford their own place. Aunts, uncles, and cousins lived nearby and were part of the extended family.

Strengthening community ties were a constellation of organizations, often church-related, that brought people together and emphasized common values. Likewise, a number of social organizations also contributed to community life, collecting money for the poor, distributing food for the less fortunate, and aiding the disabled. Involvement with such organizations was part of living in a community. Leaders of these organizations were held in respect.

Schools also were an important thread in this social fabric. They provided a common experience for children growing up together. Teachers lived in the neighborhood and often taught two generations of the same families. There was a sense of security in the community with teachers and family providing clear expectations for the young.

Times have changed. Today our young are more likely to move away from the community. In many communities, social organizations have ceased to exist because of lack of interest. We travel to visit family, travel to work alone, travel to recreation, travel to go shopping, travel to worship. And often our children have to travel outside the community to go to school.

Now the schools are expected to fill the social vacuum resulting from a transient society. These expectations range from providing health care, hot meals, and personal counseling to personal hygiene and character guidance. Previously these functions were the responsibility of the family or community organizations. Now they have been assumed by the school — often with little involvement of parents and the community.

While there is no going back to the old ways, there are ways to bring schools and the community closer together. A major premise of Integrated Character Education is that schools and communities must cooperate in developing expectations for children and youth. When schools and communities work together, it builds strong personal ties and helps all citizens to be aware of their rights and responsibilities.

An example of this kind of cooperation is found in a school district near Pittsburgh, Pennsylvania. Not long ago this area consisted of several small communities, each with its own school system. The communities ranged from ethnic, blue-collar neighborhoods to a new suburban development and also included the wealthiest community in the Pittsburgh metropolitan area.

Predictably, with school district consolidation, many of the older neighborhood schools were closed and new facilities built. Children who once walked to school now were bused out of their neighborhoods. Some parents were bitter as they saw "their school" being abandoned or converted to apartments, a warehouse, or a nursing home. It was a difficult time for everyone.

A few years later, a new administrative team in the consolidated district recognized the need to bring together the communities they were serving. The team met with leaders representing school, religious, and community organizations to map a common strategy. Their first action was to establish a Citizens Advisory Committee, whose purpose was to bring a voice and a sense of equity to all communities in the district. Later the committee was strengthened by adding teams of teachers representing each school building in the district.

This alliance of citizens, school administrators, and teachers has addressed several substantive issues, including discipline, long-range planning, and curriculum improvement. More recently, the Citizens Advisory Committee has supported the development of an ethics education component in the curriculum. Through the efforts of this committee, the communities served by this school district have come closer together. They have developed some common purposes, which are reflected in the district's mission statement. It reads:

> Our mission, supported by a commitment to excellence, is to educate citizens who can reach in for ethical behavior, reach up for quality, reach another for service, reach together for the good of the whole, reach each other for mutual respect, and reach out for lifelong learning. Such citizens can change a nation.

This mission statement guides district policy. It is displayed prominently near the entrance of every school building in the district for all to see and serves to remind students and parents of the schools' high purposes and of their role in achieving those purposes.

Another example of a healthy school-community partnership is found in a small elementary school in Pittsburgh. At this school, teachers, students, and parents work together in a series of evening and after-school activities. Sponsored by the PTA, these activities range from parent-teacher-student talent shows to such school-wide activities as picnics, skating parties, plays, and a carnival. Any monies collected from these activities are reinvested in school activities and occasionally used to buy equipment.

The organizational structure of this K-8 school also lends itself to building community ties. Students are grouped in multi-age clusters: grades K-2 for the primary division, grades 3-5 for the intermediate division, and grades 6-8 for the middle school. Because children have homeroom and most subjects with the same teacher for three years, the student-teacher-parent relationship is personal and family-like.

This private, nondenominational school draws students from as far as 20 miles away. It demonstrates how active participation by parents who share common beliefs can build a sense of community in a school, even when the students come from a large geographic area.

What schools can do to foster parent-community participation:

- establish PTA and other parent-interest groups as a means of promoting community and parent involvement in schools;
- maintain frequent communication with parents;
- invite parent volunteers to accompany field trips or to serve as teacher or library aides;
- promote community or chamber of commerce days in school;
- invite community groups that support worthy causes to speak to students;
- sponsor programs to help parents better understand their children and the curriculum;
- open the school to community organizations during after-school hours;
- arrange with a community group to award a "student of the month" certificate;
- make the school a "beehive" of activity in the community.

A positive classroom environment supports character education. Teachers must attend as much to the instructional process as they do to the content being taught. How children are taught should model the ways in which we want them to act and behave. For instance, teaching methods and activities can be designed to foster group-process skills, analysis of personal values, creativity, inductive reasoning, and development of empathy.

A review of the curriculum will indicate which teaching methods are appropriate to achieve Integrated Character Education goals. For example, the goal of working cooperatively with others might best be achieved by using cooperating learning methods. In cooperative learning, students are given a task; they then make a plan for carrying out the task and divide the task into jobs for which group members assume responsibility. They critique each other and offer help if needed and conclude with a group report or presentation. Such an approach provides for disciplined inquiry and reflection, offers practice in group skills and democratic processes, and encourages individual responsibility as well as respect for each other.

Classroom teachers can promote a positive classroom environment through:

- making a positive classroom environment an instructional priority;
- assigning small-group work to promote team building;
- using teaching methods that promote social learning skills, such as cooperative learning;
- interacting with students in ways that respect student input;
- using peer teaching activities.

Empowered teachers are in the best position to carry out the goals of character education. In schools where the textbook is the curriculum and the administration is obsessed with structure and adherence to rigid practices, teachers have little leeway for innovation and creativity. By contrast, empowering teachers means giving them the autonomy to control instruction and curriculum. With Integrated Character Education, teachers must be empowered to address the affective dimension of learning and to pass on our cultural values and heritage to the next generation.

An example of empowerment is a program developed by a fourth-grade teacher in a school in a small coal-mining town near Pittsburgh, Pennsylvania, which had rapidly been transformed into a suburban community. She called the program "Grandparents' Day." It involved inviting the grandparents of her students to school to share their life and work experiences, as well as other memorable moments in their lives. This simple event generated so much enthusiasm among the students and faculty that it was expanded into a schoolwide experience.

This program demonstrates what can happen when an empowered teacher uses older citizens in her community to pass on their rich heritage to the young. Some of the qualities exhibited by these older residents were self-sufficiency, loyalty, honesty, and a strong work ethic; and the teacher emphasized these qualities in discussions with the children.

Grandparents' Day brought many benefits to the school and community. First, it rekindled a sense of community among these older citizens, who were given the opportunity to contribute to the children's learning. Several agreed to serve as volunteers in the school. Second, it made the children aware of their heritage and of the common values that guided the lives of their grandparents. For weeks after the event, the children discussed with pride the stories their grandparents had told them. Third, it helped to instill pride in the school and community. (One follow-up activity was the school's sponsorship of Environmental Awareness Week.) Finally, it stimulated new ties to the community. Local service organizations became active in school programs.

Another example of teacher empowerment is in a Pittsburgh area district where faculty take responsibility for their own professional development. With the support of the administration, the teachers organized into grade-level teams. They meet weekly to discuss student progress and to arrange their teaching schedules. The teachers also are encouraged to work in professional organizations. On any given week, several teachers may be out of the building working on professional activities, with their classes covered by pre-arrangement with a member of their teaching team.

This system, which has been in place for more than 15 years, has empowered many teachers to take on leadership roles in local, state, and national organizations. Others have been guest lecturers in local universities and have carried out innovative programs with nearby schools. The teachers report that through empowerment they are better teachers, they have a more positive attitude about the teaching profession, and high morale pervades their school.

When teachers are empowered, they are able to integrate meaningful discussions of character and culture throughout the curriculum and to engage students in purposeful action.

To become empowered, teachers should:

- become involved in curriculum projects by serving on committees and forming special-interest groups;
- take leadership roles in their schools;
- become active in local, state, and national professional organizations;

- subscribe to and read professional journals;
- communicate often with parents to let them know what is going on in the classroom;
- publicize special school programs to let the community know what the school is doing for children;
- work with administrators, teachers, and parents on implementing character education in the school;
- develop a personal professional growth plan;
- become involved in community activities, attend school board meetings.

Character education is encouraged through administrative policy and practice. Just as teachers must serve as role models for character growth in their students, so must administrators institute policies and practices that support character growth. Some of the ways administrators can do this are: 1) incorporating the goals of Integrated Character Education into all written documents they prepare, thus legitimizing instructional practices used to foster character growth; 2) modeling desirable behavior to serve as an example for others; and 3) creating a total school climate that supports the goals of character education.

In one district, the administration decided to incorporate character education goals into its long-range planning process. This process involved a series of meetings with input from teachers, parents, students, community organizations, and community leaders. The outcomes of this process included a behavior code for administrators, a guide for instructional practices that involve students in decision making and project activities, a community-relations plan, and a plan for coordinating all student programs to be consistent with district goals.

One example of coordinating student programs to be consistent with district goals was making the in-school suspension program a part of the district's character education program. Students under in-school suspension participate in sessions conducted according to the principles of William Glasser's Reality Therapy. These sessions are designed to promote personal development and responsible behavior choices. Thus in-class suspension becomes a formal class in character education, which is directly related to district goals.

Administrative policy and practice is a vital component of Integrated Character Education and can be carried out in the following ways:

- include character education in district and school long-range planning;
- include the goals of Integrated Character Education in written documents disseminated by the district, such as curriculum strands, district goals, discipline policy and student behavior codes, and staff-development publications;
- practice administrative leadership styles that model desired behavior patterns;
- design communitywide programs to support character education.

Character education is action education. Integrated Character Education involves students in discussion and reflection that ultimately lead to worthy actions. Reflection followed by worthy actions enables students to mature into morally responsible individuals.

Student action may occur at any grade level and takes many forms. For example, a private high school requires all students to participate in a community service project. This service might be working with youngsters in child-care centers or volunteering in agencies that serve abused spouses and children. A public high school sociology course includes a requirement of collecting and distributing food and clothes to needy families. A middle school, after studying a unit on ecology, "adopted" a small park that borders the school. In an elementary school, children write letters to and visit the elderly residents at a nearby nursing home. The nursing home residents reciprocate by sharing their knowledge and life experiences with the children.

Integrated Character Education combines knowledge and affect with positive action. Teachers can promote growth in character through action by:

- sensitizing students to value issues through role play and creative drama;
- having students take the opposite point of view in discussions;
- promoting higher-order thinking about value issues through appropriate questioning techniques;
- arranging action-oriented projects that relate to curriculum themes;
- involving students in planning and organizing the projects;
- using parents and community members to assist in the project, thereby showing students how adults volunteer for altruistic purposes;
- highlighting examples of class and individual cooperation in serving the school and community;
- making student service projects visible in the school and community.

Conclusion

The Integrated Character Education model focuses on the whole person and pervades a person's total environment. It cannot be achieved with an occasional lesson on ethics or values. It requires a learning environment that takes into account the six principles discussed in the previous chapter.

The next millennium will bring many perplexing problems associated with changing family structures, an aging population, and protecting the environment, to name but a few. Addressing all of these problems is the challenge of character education. Therefore, Integrated Character Education must become an overriding goal of education.

References

Ellrod, Frederick E.; Mann, Jesse A.; McLean, George F.; and Schindler, David L. *Act and Agent: Philosophical Foundations for Moral Education and Character Development.* Lanham, Md.: University Press of America, 1986.

Knowles, Richard T., and McLean, George F. *Psychological Foundations of Moral Education and Character Development: An Integrated Theory of Moral Development*. Lanham, Md.: University Press of America, 1986.

Lickona, Thomas, and Ryan, Kevin, eds. *Character Development in Schools and Beyond*. Washington, D.C.: Council for Research in Values and Philosophy, 1992.

Showers, Bruce; Showers, Beverly; and Weil, Marsha. *Models of Teaching*. Needham Heights, Mass.: Allyn and Bacon, 1992.

Ryan, Kevin, and Wynne, Edward A. *Reclaiming Our Schools: A Handbook on Teaching Character, Academics and Discipline*. New York: Macmillan, 1993.

CHARTER SCHOOLS

by Lori A. Mulholland and Louann A. Bierlein

School reformers continue to argue that the traditional public school structure in the United States is outdated and that restructuring must occur. Central to this argument is the notion that those closest to students (school — not district — personnel) should be given more authority and held more accountable for student results. With greater independence from a central authority, many contend, school personnel will develop innovative learning environments that more closely match students' needs. The difficulty lies in deciding *how* to make schools more autonomous and accountable.

Charter schools may provide part of the answer. The creation of such schools offers a viable means to integrate various reform ideas and to develop highly autonomous and accountable learning environments. They also force educators to question the wisdom of many conventional management and instructional practices. The broad goal of the charter schools movement is not simply to develop a few new schools, but to create dynamics that will cause changes throughout the entire public education system.

In its purest form, a charter school is an autonomous educational entity operating under a charter, or contract, that has been negotiated between the organizers, who create and operate the school, and a sponsor, who oversees the provisions of the charter. Organizers may be teachers, parents, or others from the public or private sector; and sponsors may be local school boards, state education boards, or some other public authority. Provisions in each

This essay is condensed from Lori A. Mulholland and Louann A. Bierlein, *Understanding Charter Schools*, Fastback 383 (Bloomington, Ind.: Phi Delta Kappa Educational Foundation, 1995). That fastback draws on the work of the Morrison Institute for Public Policy and was prepared under an agreement with the Arizona Board of Regents for Arizona State University.

85

school's charter address such considerations as the school's instructional plan, specific educational results and how they will be measured, and management and financial plans.

A charter school may be formed using an existing school's complete personnel and facilities or a portion of such a school (as a school-within-a-school). Or a completely new entity with its own facilities may be developed as a charter school. Once granted approval, a charter school becomes legally independent, able to hire and dismiss staff, sue and be sued, award contracts for outside services, and control its own finances. Operational funding is based on student enrollment, just as it would be for a public school or district. Because charter schools agree to be held accountable for education results, they are freed from all or many district and state regulations that may be perceived as inhibiting innovation, such as excessive teacher certification requirements, collective bargaining agreements, Carnegie units, and other curriculum requirements.

When the term of a charter school's contract expires, it may be renewed, providing that the school has achieved specified student results, has not violated any laws or grossly mismanaged its affairs or budget, and continues to attract students, parents, and teachers. Failure in any of these areas puts the school out of business.

The Appeal of Charter Schools

There are several reasons why charter schools are getting attention around the country. In an ideal setting, charter schools:

Enhance educational choice options. Charter schools can improve educational choices for students, parents, and teachers. They offer teachers a chance to work in more innovative, autonomous schools that use new or alternative teaching methods, philosophical approaches, and assessments. They offer parents and students a variety of learning environments often not available in public schools.

Permit true decentralization. Charter schools decentralize education in a way that traditional site-based management may not. As autonomous legal entities, charter schools are free to make all their own administrative and instructional decisions, and they are held legally liable for them. This arrangement avoids the problems encountered by schools that are site-based managed, but for which the district remains legally liable. Fully autonomous charter schools also receive their funding directly from the state, just as if they were school districts. (However, not all states grant full financial or legal autonomy to their charter schools.)

Focus on results, not inputs. In return for stricter accountability, charter schools automatically are exempted from all state and local laws and regulations except those related to health and safety, nondiscrimination and civil rights, fiscal accountability, and those agreed to in their charters. Although some critics challenge that this level of freedom should be granted to all school districts, it is questionable whether many school board members or district office personnel would be willing to sign contracts agreeing to resign if certain results are not met. Charter schools involve volunteers willing to test this concept.

Remain public schools. Charter schools subscribe to the American democratic ideals of the common school: They are tuition-free, nonsectarian, non-selective in student admissions, and do not discriminate on the basis of race, religion, or disability. A few states (such as Arizona and Minnesota) do not prohibit private schools from becoming public charter schools; however, these private schools must follow the same rules as public schools that seek charter status and public funding. This provision is one reason that individuals who are against private school vouchers often support the charter school concept.

Offer new professional opportunities for teachers. Charter schools offer teachers a chance to become directly involved in all phases of school operations, from curriculum planning to management. They also open the door for teachers to become school "owners," rather than just employees. For example, teachers may establish a cooperative or partnership arrangement within a charter school and contract with a sponsor (or subcontract with a nonprofit charter school management team) to organize and operate the school.

Foster a more market-driven education system. Enrollment in charter schools is voluntary, so the schools must be designed to attract education consumers. This aspect introduces competition into the system. If a charter school fails to produce agreed-on results, the charter can be revoked. Before such action, however, a school could lose the support of parents who "vote with their feet" and withdraw their youngsters from the school. Early evidence supports the notion that this form of education choice will pressure the entire education system to improve.

Furthermore, charter schools have features that appeal to both conservatives and liberals. For example, conservatives tend to support charter schools because they include elements essential to their reform efforts: choice, decentralization, and enhanced accountability. Liberals value charter schools for bringing together education reforms without abandoning the public school system. Indeed, maintaining the ideals of the common school is seen as a key component of charter schools. Thus charter school legislation has transcended party lines. In Minnesota, for example, efforts to legislate charter schools were initiated by Democrats; in Massachusetts, charter schools were largely a Republican venture.

Charter School Approval Process

A number of steps are involved in the creation of a charter school. Generally, the process begins with one or two individuals (the organizers) who want to create a charter school. These organizers develop a plan that provides a comprehensive view of the proposed school. During this stage, the state or a private organization may provide technical assistance to help the organizers draft a workable proposal.

Once an initial proposal has been developed, the organizers present their ideas to a sponsor, a group or board that can legally enter into a contract with the organizers and hold them accountable for results. The sponsor may or may not approve the organizers' plan, and revisions may be necessary. Should a plan not be approved, the organizers may have access to an appeals procedure. Moreover, there may be another state-level group or board responsible for final approval of each charter school proposal.

Further examination of the roles of key players in the charter school process is instructive. Different states may refer to these participants by different names, and their responsibilities may vary.

Organizers. Organizers are responsible for creating the school's vision, negotiating and revising the charter, gathering necessary information, acquiring support and resources, and walking the school plan through the chartering process. They must develop the instructional and management plans for the proposed charter school. After approval, the organizers continue their involvement through the operation of the school.

Possible organizers named in legislation include teachers, parents, community members, colleges and universities, nonprofit social service agencies, cities, and corporations. In some states, legislation permits any individual or group to organize a charter school. A school district also may generate its own proposal.

Sponsors. Sponsors of a charter school are responsible for approving and overseeing the school. They must ensure that the charter school proposal is sound and will serve the needs of students. They hold the school accountable for the results stated in their charter. In some cases, the charter also may specify a higher degree of involvement for a sponsor. For example, a charter might include a contract between the school and the sponsor for such items as school lunches or payroll services.

Laws in various states designate a number of groups or officials that can legally act as a sponsor. Most often, local school boards are among the possible sponsors. Other entities that may serve as sponsors include county or regional boards of education, state boards of education, state superintendents or secretaries of education, and, in the case of Arizona, a state board for charter schools. Many state laws also establish an appeals process to assist organizers who feel that a given sponsor inappropriately denied their proposals. In these cases, the appellate body may be an alternate sponsor or a higher level of government that is authorized to hear appeals.

Final Authority. Some state laws require a second level of approval beyond that of the sponsor. The final authority in these cases usually is a state education board, an education department, or an executive officer. The intent of this final review may be to ensure quality and consistency among charter school contracts, or it may be simply to allow the state to keep track of the number of established schools.

Technical Assistance Providers. To date, only a few states have appropriated funds to assist organizers and sponsors in their planning and implementation efforts, despite general agreement that some types of technical assistance are important. To address the need, some state education departments have taken on the role of providing technical assistance, while in other states, private individuals and groups have done so.

Charter School Governing Bodies. In keeping with the spirit of decentralization, charter schools are administered by site-based school councils or boards. These groups are responsible for setting school budgets, contracting for services, hiring and dismissing staff, selecting curriculum, and carrying out all other administrative functions of the school. State laws sometimes prescribe the composition of the governing board. For example, some states require the participation of teachers, parents, and community members; others allow charter schools to create their own management configurations as appropriate. In either situation, the overriding goal is to create schools that are completely site-managed.

Charter schools in some states also are allowed to contract with an outside corporation to run the school. This has created an opportunity for education corporations, such as the Edison Project, to manage public schools on a charter basis.

A "Model" Charter School Structure

Although great variations exist across charter school laws, 10 elements deemed to be essential for a successful charter school "model" have been extracted from the work of Kolderie (1993) and others active in the charter school movement. The belief is that charter schools will have the best chance to create improved learning environments and positively affect the overall education system if these elements are in place:

1. A variety of public or private individuals or groups may organize, seek sponsorship, and operate a charter school.
2. At least one public authority besides the local school board (for example, the county board, the state board, or a university) may sponsor a charter school.
3. Charter schools are considered discrete legal entities.
4. Charter schools, as public entities, embrace the ideals of the common school. They are nonsectarian, tuition-free, nonselective in admissions, nondiscriminatory in practices, and accountable to a public body.
5. Each charter school is held accountable for its performance, both by parents and by its sponsoring public authority. Failure of a charter school to meet the provisions of its contract results in its closure.
6. In return for stricter accountability, charter schools are exempted from state and local laws and regulations except those related to health, safety, and nondiscrimination practices, and those agreed to within the charter provisions.
7. A charter school is a school of choice for students, parents, and teachers; no one is forced to be there.
8. Each charter school receives the full operating funds appropriate to its student enrollment — in other words, it is fiscally autonomous.
9. Within a charter school, teachers have the option to work as employees, owners, or subcontractors. If previously employed in a district, they retain certain "leave" protections, such as seniority or retirement benefits, should they choose to return to district employment within a designated time.
10. There are no restrictions on the number of schools that can be created.

Although the above elements describe what some believe to be an ideal situation, no state has yet enacted legislation that contains every element. The radical nature of the charter school concept has demanded many political compromises. Four areas have tended to raise the most political concerns: 1) sponsorship options (especially by bodies other than the local school board), 2) legal autonomy, 3) funding formulas, and 4) employment protections given to teachers.

Pioneering Charter School States

Ray Budde, an expert on school district organization, has been credited with introducing the charter school concept in the late 1980s. Budde's ideas were based on a review of explorer Henry Hudson's "charter" with the East India Company to find a new passage to the Orient (Stuart 1994; Mulholland and Amsler 1992). Albert Shanker, president of the American Federation of Teachers, furthered Budde's concept by proposing that groups of teachers be allowed to start their own schools under a charter process. Translation from Shanker's proposal to practice occurred first in Minnesota where, after a tough political struggle, the nation's earliest state charter school law was passed in 1991. California followed with its own charter school law the next year; and by the end of 1993, six more states — Colorado, Massachusetts, Michigan, Wisconsin, New Mexico, and Georgia — also passed charter school-type legislation (Bierlein and Mulholland 1994). By summer 1994, Arizona, Hawaii, and Kansas had joined the list, and legislation was being developed or considered in almost a dozen other states.

In some states with charter school laws, any school developed is granted a great deal of financial and legal autonomy and automatic freedom from state and local rules. These states are considered to have strong charter school laws and, perhaps as a result, have more charter school activity than other states. In other states, charter schools remain part of their school districts and often must seek waivers from rules on a case-by-case basis. Limited charter school activity is occurring within these states, though legislators in several of them are attempting to strengthen their charter school laws. Following are the states with charter school laws, listed by the degree of autonomy allowed by the law and the year in which the initial charter law was passed.

More Autonomous Charter Laws

Arizona (1994)	Massachusetts (1993)
California (1992)	Michigan (1993)
Colorado (1993)	Minnesota (1991)

Less Autonomous Charter-Like Laws

Georgia (1993)	New Mexico (1993)
Hawaii (1994)	Wisconsin (1993)
Kansas (1994)	

A brief review follows of the laws and activities (as of February 1995) within each of the six states with stronger charter school legislation and two of the states with less autonomous charter school legislation.

Arizona. Passed in June 1994, this state's charter law is considered one of the strongest to date. Organizers may be any individual, a public body, or private organization. The three potential sponsors for schools are: a school district governing board, the state board of education, or the newly created state board for charter schools. Local boards are allowed to charter an unlimited number of schools, with the level of autonomy for these schools to be determined by the charter. Each of the two state boards is allowed to charter up to 25 schools per year, with such schools being financially and legally autonomous. All charter schools are automatically exempt from most state rules. The law also establishes a charter school stimulus fund of one million dollars to assist charter schools with start-up costs.

To date, 19 schools have been approved — 11 by the state board, seven by the state charter board, and one by a local school board. Examples include I'Tom Escuela, a trilingual (Spanish, English, and Yaqui) community-based charter school, and the Arizona Career Academy, which focuses on providing a coordinated program of core academic instruction, counseling, technical training, and experiential learning for challenged youths.

California. In September 1992, California adopted the nation's second charter school law, in part as a defense against the passage of a private school voucher ballot measure. California's law allows up to 100 charter schools and permits any individual to initiate a charter school petition. Potential sponsors include the local school district or, if an appeal is sought, the applicable county board of education. Entire districts also may apply for charter status. By law, California charter schools are financially autonomous, though funds continue to flow through the district to the school, and charter schools often contract with their districts to provide some services . The extent of each school's legal autonomy is determined within its specific charter agreement. To date, about 77 charter schools have been established, with the majority of them beginning operations in 1994-95.

California charter school proposals encompass a wide variety of innovative strategies. For example, Bennett Valley Charter School employs a home-based independent learning approach. Options for Youth Charter School focuses on dropouts and those at risk of dropping out. And Bowling Green Elementary School practices W. Edwards Deming's Total Quality Management. Unlike their counterparts in Minnesota, however, many California charter schools are being converted from existing schools, rather than being created entirely new.

Colorado. Legislation passed in June 1993 permits up to 50 charter schools to be created prior to July 1997. Afterward, the ceiling is removed. Under the law, any individual or group can enter into a charter school agreement with a local school board if "adequate" support from parents, teachers, and pupils is obtained. A charter school remains under the legal authority of its school board but receives at least 80% of normal per-pupil funding from the district. Seventeen charter schools had been approved by February 1995, with 14 of those in operation. There also were seven applications pending and five potential appeals to the state board. The state board can require local boards to grant charters if no valid reasons for denial exist.

Massachusetts. As part of a broader reform package, Massachusetts passed legislation in 1993 permitting 25 public charter schools. Each may be organized by two or more certified teachers, 10 or more parents, or by any other individual or group that successfully enters into a charter agreement with the state secretary of education. The state automatically grants legal and financial autonomy to charter schools.

Although the new charter schools are not authorized to begin operations until September 1995, the initial application process yielded 64 proposals, of which 14 obtained approval. One of these proposals will be subcontracted with the Edison Project, a for-profit enterprise. Other approved proposals include a Boston University plan for a residential high school for homeless children and wards of the state and a proposal for Benjamin Franklin Classical, a school that will offer a rigorous classical education for K-8 students. Thirty-six new proposals have been submitted for the remaining 11 charters allowed by the legislation.

Michigan. This state's initial charter law was passed in December 1993 and declared unconstitutional less than one year later as the result of a lawsuit brought by, among others, the teachers union and several state board members. In its ruling, a county circuit court found that the law usurped the state board's power to supervise public education and that charter schools are legally not "public." State legislators moved quickly to pass new legislation, which became effective in April 1995. This legislation addresses the key issues in the lawsuit. However, at the time of this writing, an appeal to the circuit court decision is pending. The new legislation is written so that, if the circuit court's decision is overturned, the initial legislation (with minor modifications) will supersede the new law.

Key provisions of Michigan's new law include that organizers (any individual or entity) may choose from four potential sponsoring bodies: local governing boards of larger school districts, intermediate school district boards, community colleges, and state public universities. The charter schools become legally and financially autonomous and are exempted from most state rules. To date, eight schools, which had been approved under the initial law, received funding to operate as alternative public schools. These and other schools are preparing to be rechartered under the new law.

Minnesota. Building on existing public school choice programs, Minnesota initiated the first charter schools legislation in 1991. The law initially authorized creation of up to eight legally and financially autonomous schools (referred to as "outcome-based schools") to be organized by certified teachers and sponsored by local school districts. Minnesota's legislation was modified in 1993 and 1994 to allow up to 35 charter schools across the state. An appeals process to the state board of education also was added.

During the 1992-93 school year, two Minnesota charter schools were operating. The first is City Academy, which is located in a donated city recreation building in St. Paul and offers a year-round program for approximately 50 at-risk adolescents and young adults ages 13 to 21. The second is Bluffview Montessori, a private K-6 school that converted to charter status in March 1993. Five additional schools with diverse program offerings began operating under their charters in the 1993-94 school year. Among these are Metro Deaf, a school for deaf and hearing-impaired students that emphasizes deaf language, culture, and history; Skills for Tomorrow, a vocational/technical school developed with the support of the Teamsters Union and the Minnesota Business Partnership that emphasizes applied learning through internships; and New Heights Schools, Inc., a pre-K through grade 12 school that emphasizes the needs of at-risk students. Six additional schools opened during 1994-95, and three have been approved to open in fall 1995.

The following two states grant less autonomy to their charter schools and are illustrative of other states with "charter-like" laws.

Georgia. Legislation passed in 1993 allows an unlimited number of charter schools to be converted from existing public schools. Public school personnel may apply to the state board for charter status if they obtain prior approval from their local school board, two-thirds of the school's faculty and staff, and a majority of parents at a meeting called to initiate a charter school petition. Charter agreements must emphasize school improvement and student outcomes. The schools are not legally autonomous from their districts, and the amount of funding they receive is specified in the terms of the charter agreement. Three schools are expected to apply to their local school boards during spring 1995 and to begin operating in fall 1995.

New Mexico. Legislation passed in 1993 allows five existing public schools to be granted charter school status by the state board of education. These charter schools will continue to function under the legal authority of school districts, and certain administrative costs may be withheld by the districts. During 1993-94, initial planning grants of $5,000 were provided to 10 schools to promote the charter concept. Four schools began operating under charters in fall 1994, each receiving a $15,600 grant to support their first year of implementation.

Sample Charter School Programs

As the list of charter schools grows, so does the variety of programs. Many schools use innovative methods not commonly found in public schools. Some incorporate new formats, such as year-round school, extended-day schedules, and integrated subjects. Others subscribe to particular education philosophies, such as open education, home schooling, the Montessori method, or back-to-basics. Still others create programs that target a specific sub-population of students, such as those at risk of dropping out, those whose native language is not English, or those who are young or expectant mothers. Or they focus on a special subject theme, such as science, math, computer technology, or languages. Most schools combine several of these elements with differing emphases.

In some schools the instructional methods and student populations do not differ greatly from those in place prior to charter status. For these schools, the significant difference is that they become fully site-managed and will be held accountable to the outcomes specified in their charter. The brief descriptions that follow provide a sample of some charter schools.

City Academy, St. Paul, Minnesota. Located in a former city recreation building in downtown St. Paul, City Academy opened in September 1992. The school is both legally and fiscally autonomous from the district and serves teens and young adults between the ages of 15 and 21, most of whom were considered at high risk for failure. Many of City Academy's students have experienced such problems as academic failure, poverty, homelessness, chemical dependency, violent or delinquent behavior, parenthood, and physical or sexual abuse. One primary criterion for admission to this school is that the student currently not be enrolled in any other school. The program serves 50 students and has a long waiting list. However, there are no plans to expand much beyond the current enrollment, because the staff believes that small size is what makes the program effective.

City Academy's founding was helped by a grant from the local utility company. The sponsoring district provides food service and transportation.

Minnesota law requires that teachers make up the majority of City Academy's seven-member board of directors. A representative from the utility company also serves on the board, and two positions are set aside for a student and a parent. The staff at City Academy consists of six full-time teachers, three part-time teachers for Spanish, music, and language arts/writing, and one full-time support person. The school contracts with a former state fiscal agent for bookkeeping services. Additional support is provided by the utility company, which conducts workshops dealing with vocational assessment, career planning, developing leadership skills, and developing job skills.

The utility company also offers job opportunities and mentoring to students. Freed from Carnegie units, City Academy has the flexibility to let students spend time "in the field" each week, working with a variety of community organizations. There they

98

can study such subjects as art, acting, and conflict resolution or gain job experience in such occupations as construction, clerical work, recreation leadership, and child care.

One objective of City Academy is to enroll students in Minnesota's postsecondary education program, which allows students to receive both high school and college credits for taking tuition-free college-level courses. Student outcomes are evaluated by the examination of portfolios, writing and math assessments, student self-reports, and reports from employers, if applicable.

Metro Deaf School, St. Paul, Minnesota. Metro Deaf School is located in a commercial building in downtown St. Paul. In 1994-95, it served 26 deaf and hard-of-hearing students, ranging from kindergarten through eighth grade. The focus of its program is both bilingual and bicultural, with instruction in overall language proficiency and deaf culture. American Sign Language is the primary language of instruction.

The Metro Deaf School staff includes six full-time teachers, one full-time aide, and one part-time aide. The school also contracts with instructors to teach extra classes and with specialists (social workers, interpreters, bookkeepers, and others) to provide various types of assistance. The school does not contract with the sponsoring district for any services. As with all Minnesota charter schools, Metro Deaf is legally and financially autonomous from its sponsor.

Connect School, Pueblo, Colorado. Located in a rural district, Connect School opened its doors in September 1993. By 1994-95, the school served 90 middle-school-age students in nongraded classes. The school leases space in a commercial building that was remodeled using a donation by the building's developer. The curriculum draws heavily on the principles of Theodore Sizer's Coalition of Essential Schools. The core studies of reading, writing, and math are taught daily, while social studies and science are offered in workshop-style settings with extended blocks of nearly three hours per subject. Frequent field trips and projects augment the schedule.

Connect School also features an extended school day, small classes, and a schedule that keeps the same children in class together for three years. Technology and parent and community involvement are very important. In fact, the school name was chosen to reflect the connections between education, technology, and the community.

Although the Connect School remains under the district's legal authority, it operates independently. According to Colorado law, the school receives 80% of normal funding, with the remainder going to the sponsoring district to cover the costs of payroll services, accounting, warehousing, and the use of a district school bus.

The school governing board consists of an advisory group and a director. Serving on the board are two teachers, three parents, one community member, and one student. Members are elected in September and serve a two-year term. The staff consists of five full-time teachers; a variable number of part-time instructors to teach band, physical education, and special classes; and a janitor who cleans bathrooms and the kitchen. Otherwise, the school uses volunteers for its support services. Parent volunteers help with office work, offer seminars in their areas of expertise, and tutor students. Students also contribute to daily operations by answering phones in the morning and cleaning certain areas of the school. The money saved by the elimination of support staff has made it possible for the school to purchase computers and to maintain staff salaries.

Student outcomes will be measured through standardized tests, portfolios, and student exhibitions. The charter specifies that 90% of students will perform at or above grade level using the district standardized testing program.

Jingletown Charter Middle School, Oakland, California. Opened in September 1993, this school originally served 120 sixth- and seventh-grade students, expanding to serve eighth-grade students by September 1994. Bilingual education is emphasized, as many of the students speak English as a second language. Core subjects are taught in two-hour integrated subjects blocks, one block for math and science and another for language arts and social studies. Spanish, physical education, and a homeroom/advisory session also are part of the curriculum.

The school employs three full-time teachers, as well as five part-time teachers for special subjects. The school is governed by a principal and a board of directors composed mostly of parents. Staff, students, and community members also serve on the board. Students must wear school uniforms, and parents are required to volunteer four hours to the school each month.

Jingletown Middle School is legally and financially autonomous, which is not the case with many California charter schools. School staff have not found it necessary to contract with the sponsoring district for any services. The school property is located in a park that is leased at a nominal rate from the Catholic Diocese of Oakland. Leased portable classrooms are the facilities for the school. The school has received donations from both corporations and individuals.

Horizon Instructional Systems, Lincoln, California. Horizon Instructional Systems offers educational and resource services to students and parents involved in home schooling. Serving 30 students when it opened in August 1993, it has expanded to approximately 1,100 students in kindergarten through 12th grade. Two-thirds of the students are taught at home by their parents, while one-third (mostly high school students) are self-taught. The school has a staff of 55 part-time resource teachers, who meet with their students at least monthly to assess progress, evaluate work, make assignments, or provide other support.

School facilities consist of two portable classrooms, one located near each of two district schools. The portables are used for training parents to educate their children at home. They also house resource materials for distribution and serve as sites for special classes on such subjects as computers, sign language, and art. Parents help to develop extracurricular classes and sports teams.

Although the school is not legally autonomous, it functions independently from its sponsoring district. A member of the sponsoring district's governing board is the chair of the school's governing board and, therefore, is informed about issues relating to the school. The school also contracts with its sponsoring district to provide custodial, bookkeeping, and business management services.

The school is held to the same outcomes required of all schools in the sponsoring district, though the charter permits modifications to be made to fit the individual education plans of students. Student outcomes will be assessed by both the state assessment instrument and evaluation of individual work and portfolios. Observations of student improvement by resource teachers and parents also are considered by the school.

Creating and Operating a Charter School

Charter schools offer a radically different approach to providing and managing public education, but not necessarily a smooth road. Eric Premack and Linda Diamond (1993) write of their experience in assisting charter school participants in California:

> Educators have operated under a system of rules and regulations which have not rewarded deep change. . . . There is an absence of models of alternatives that deal with all facets of schools — instruction and curriculum, finances, governance, staffing, collective bargaining, maintenance, and so on. Further, they have been confronted by a barrage of misinformation from opponents of the charter concept. . . . Teachers and administrators need assistance to escape the box of familiar ways of doing things; they need examples; they need expertise; and they need support to envision a new system and invent practical solutions to implementing it. (p i)

Although these issues are of concern for any reform activity, several are particularly key to charter schools. This section will provide a glimpse of the challenges being faced by charter school organizers. Where possible, solutions to common charter school problems are provided.

Planning. Organizers must develop a clear vision of what their school will look like; and they must gather support from teachers, parents, and other community members. Some organizers have incorporated year-long planning periods to help them create a clear, well-developed school plan.

Planning must result in agreed-on school philosophy, educational objectives, teaching methods, appropriate use of technology, administrative structure, and the roles of students and parents. Furthermore, these ideas must be articulated in the charter school proposal, because potential sponsors will have many questions, and organizers who have not thought through their vision will not seem credible.

Planning also should set the stage for future involvement of key participants. A proposal is more likely to be approved if a broad-based group of teachers, parents, community members, and business partners are involved from the start.

Technical Assistance. One of the most challenging tasks for school organizers and staff is to acquire the skills needed to operate a charter school. This is especially true in states that allow charter schools a high degree of legal and financial autonomy. Many new activities require skills not typically expected of school principals and teachers. Among these are the acquisition of property, purchase of insurance, negotiation of contracts and leases, solicitation of grants and donations, administration of the budget, and assignment of responsibilities to the sponsor.

The best solution is proper training and outside technical support aimed specifically at charter schools. Unfortunately, few states currently allocate money to their departments of education for the purpose of providing technical assistance to charter schools. As a partial remedy, some education departments offer the services of their existing personnel in an attempt to meet the needs of charter schools. In some states, technical support is provided by private groups and charitable organizations.

As charter schools begin to share solutions and resources, organized charter school networks have begun to appear. Among these are the Minnesota Charter School Network, the California Network of Educational Charters (CANEC), and the Colorado League of Charter Schools. The growing charter movement also has prompted the recent creation of the National Association of Charter Schools.

School/Sponsor Relationships. Although the degree of autonomy for charter schools varies from state to state, it is usually advantageous for charter schools to maintain cooperative working relationships with their sponsors. One obvious reason is that the schools are accountable to their sponsors according to the provisions of their charters. Furthermore, situations may arise in which the school might contract with the sponsoring district for services such as transportation or insurance that, because of their relative size, would otherwise be cost-prohibitive.

Most charter school participants who were interviewed for this essay reported good working relationships with their sponsors. In the best circumstances, their districts viewed them as testing grounds for methods and practices too new or innovative to put in place at all schools. Indeed, some charter schools, such as the Connect Middle School in Colorado, have agreed to share with their sponsoring district the lessons they learn through their efforts. Some schools also have discovered the benefits of placing a district representative on their governing boards.

However, some charter schools have found that their sponsors are uncomfortable in their new roles. Staff from one autonomous charter school in California reported that their sponsor had not been eager to approve their charter in the first place but could find no legitimate reason for denial. Since granting approval, the sponsor has maintained only minimal involvement with the charter school.

School Funding. Charter school legislation usually stipulates that state and local education money for operations follows students to their charter schools. The schools also receive special education and other categorical funds for which their students are eligible. Some states allow sponsors to withhold a percentage of funds to cover any administrative costs or payment for other services rendered.

A few states provide funding for start-up costs or capital equipment. New Mexico, for example, provides $5,000 planning grants to those developing proposals, while Arizona contributes to school start-up by having set aside one million dollars in a charter school stimulus fund.

Lack of start-up and capital funding has forced schools to find ways to stretch their dollars. One solution is to replace paid support staff with volunteer help from parents and others. Another solution is to employ some part-time staff. Cross-utilized staffing arrangements that cast employees in several different roles also result in savings.

Many schools have received generous donations from corporations and private citizens. Jingletown Charter Middle School, for example, received donations of furniture, a copier, a telephone system, videocassette recorders, televisions, and computers and printers for every classroom, as well as a large corporate cash donation specifically designated for math and science materials and smaller cash donations from individuals.

Another high start-up cost is for leased space. Many schools have obtained the use of buildings at very low rates. In the case of Minnesota's City Academy, the mayor of St. Paul donated the use of an empty city recreation building. Other schools solve their facility problems by making use of portable units, finding reasonably priced accommodations in commercial buildings, or obtaining university space. Sometimes a school facility has been provided free of charge for a specified period of time; in other cases schools have been charged a low rate offered only to nonprofit organizations.

Organized Opposition. Charter school legislation in its final version often differs markedly from the original proposal. Changes, in large part, result from political pressures from groups that hold a stake in the status quo; compromises are made to reduce resistance from these opposing groups.

School board associations often oppose the creation of autonomous charter schools. Historically, school boards have been the sole providers of and primary decision-makers for public education in their communities. Under charter school legislation, local school boards and district offices may find their roles and responsibilities greatly altered.

However, some school boards see a brighter side to the charter school picture, especially as an alternative to private school vouchers. Randy Quinn (1993), executive director of the Colorado Association of School Boards, writes that charter schools represent "a dramatic, very fundamental difference, one that forces the school board to re-examine its role. Rather than serving as provider, the board has an opportunity to become the purchaser of education services on behalf of the citizens of the community served by the board" (p. 2). He further suggests that, in the future, boards may want to aggressively solicit charter proposals to create diversity within their district, which would allow students, parents, and teachers more choices among schools and thus mitigate many previously unresolvable conflicts.

Teachers unions, too, have resisted specific charter school provisions. Though the unions tend to support charter school legislation in theory, they have expressed concern about key provisions of legislation — especially versions that call for autonomous schools — because of the implications for teacher employment. The National Education Association notes, "*under the right conditions* charter schools could become change agents promoting new and creative ways of teaching and learning" (National Education Association 1993, p.1. Emphasis added). Two such conditions are that only certified teachers be used and that district collective bargaining agreements be maintained. Teachers unions also have expressed the concern that charter school provisions could become a "back door" for private school vouchers.

Autonomy and New Governance Structures. With the exception of a few states that allow charter school organizers and sponsors to agree on the level of autonomy for charter schools, state laws usually specify whether a charter school will be autonomous or remain a part of a school district. This is a defining feature of the legislation, because the difference between a school that has relative autonomy and one that enjoys true legal autonomy is significant. A charter school with partial autonomy may be able to operate with a degree of independence from its school district, but it still falls under the district's legal authority. A truly autonomous charter school, on the other hand, holds an iron-clad guarantee of its independence. Such a school is legally organized as a nonprofit, cooperative, or private corporation as specified by its state legislation.

A school's degree of autonomy affects many aspects of its operations. One of these is school governance. Charter schools with true autonomy have full decision-making power and full liability for their decisions. In charter schools with partial autonomy, school governance may be similar to that of a site-based decision-making council. The council can make decisions, but the district school board retains final authority. Awareness of these limitations reduces the potential for friction between charter schools and their sponsors.

Similarly, charter governing boards can differ markedly. For example, Minnesota's legislation requires that a majority of a school's board of directors be teachers. Other states are less structured but usually prescribe a diverse membership on the governing board. The boards that have emerged thus far include representatives from many groups: teachers and staff, parents and students, representatives of the sponsoring district, and business partners. Some boards set up subcommittees or advisory boards to represent special interest groups. These auxiliary groups maximize involvement of the school community and decrease the workload of the governing board members.

Employment-Related Issues. Among the most politically charged aspects of a charter school program are employment-related matters. Depending on applicable state laws and charter agreements, teachers may or may not be considered employees of a sponsoring district. Therefore, many questions arise. Who hires and dismisses school personnel? What collective bargaining rights do teachers hold? Will teachers and staff have job security or retirement benefits?

A charter school's degree of autonomy also affects employment issues. For charter schools that are only partially autonomous from their districts, employment provisions usually mirror those of the district. In legally autonomous charter schools, on the other hand, these employment questions must be decided by the school's governing body.

Some state laws separate charter school teachers from district agreements and, instead, allow teachers the choice of forming a collective bargaining unit completely within their individual school or of not entering into collective bargaining at all. Other state laws leave the collective bargaining decisions up to individual schools.

It is possible for teachers to become school "owners," rather than just employees. For example, teachers might establish a cooperative or partnership arrangement within a charter school and contract with a sponsor (or subcontract with a nonprofit charter school management team) to organize and run the school. Teachers with an entrepreneurial spirit are drawn to an opportunity such as this.

Assessment, Results, and Accountability. A basic tenet of the charter concept is accountability for results. A school's charter specifies the outcomes that students will attain and how attainment will be measured. In interviews, charter school participants reported using a variety of measures, including performance assessments, standardized achievement tests, portfolios, self-reports, and teacher observations.

Although a great deal of effort has gone into developing accurate student assessments, such as portfolios and performance-based assessments that might supplement traditional norm-referenced exams, for the most part such tools remain in the development stage; Charter schools are thus faced with the dilemma of using conventional measures that may not suit their situations or using innovative assessment techniques whose reliability is debatable. Furthermore, even much less sophisticated measures, such as dropout and attendance rates, can be subject to ambiguous definitions and recording errors, thus complicating the issue of accountability.

Equity and Opportunity. Policy makers and charter school organizers must ensure equitable access and opportunity to learn not only for students in charter schools, but also for those who remain in traditional schools. Highly specialized educational programs offered by some charter schools could result in selective, and potentially discriminatory, admission criteria. Thus charter school states have attempted to head off such possibilities by requiring schools to develop admission procedures that do not discriminate against pupils on the basis of ethnicity, national origin, gender, or disability. In addition, some states have required charter schools to address racial and ethnic balance issues and to comply with existing court-ordered or voluntary desegregation orders.

Nevertheless, schools chartered to address the needs of a specific group (at-risk youth or pregnant teens, for example) will, by necessity, segregate students. What, if anything, should be done? Some educators contend that attracting students away from regular schools into specialized charter schools will reduce diversity in the first school and create artificial homogeneity at the second. Others, however, point out that many students with special characteristics tend to be failures in "regular" schools. These students should be allowed to attend "segregated" schools that target their needs if they can be successful there.

The validity of such arguments remains to be seen. The primary goal of the charter school concept is to increase educational choices. The challenge for education leaders is to create a system of innovative schooling opportunities that ensures equity for all students.

The Effect of Charter Schools

Because the charter concept is new and few states have funded evaluation efforts, the effects that charter schools have created so far must be extracted from informal reports. These positive and negative reports, as well as observable trends, indicate the following:

School environments are being created in response to student and parent desires. In some cases, charter schools are being created where there existed long waiting lists to enroll in similar programs. The Community Involved Charter School in Colorado now serves more than 1,000 students who previously were waiting for slots in another program. In addition, numerous charter schools are using multi-age/multi-grade classes, reducing class and school size, and using a Montessori-style approach, back-to-basics program, or some specific curricular emphasis.

Numerous at-risk students are being served. Many charter schools have chosen to target students who are not succeeding in the traditional public school setting. One example is Minnesota's City Academy, which reports that within its first two years, 75% of its initial group of students (all former dropouts) had completed graduation requirements, and most planned to attend postsecondary education. There is a long waiting list for this school and others like it.

Unique community and business partnerships are being formed. For example, the Skills for Tomorrow Charter School, a vocational/technical school in Minnesota, is being run with support from the Teamsters Union and key business leaders. Several schools are being operated or co-operated by universities, such as the Pueblo School for the Arts and Science in Colorado and the Saginaw Chippewa Academy in Michigan. In Arizona, the town of Guadelupe is a partner in the I'Tom Escuela charter school, hoping to reverse a long history of poor academic performance among its children.

Larger percentages of existing funds are being focused on instruction. Through the use of volunteers and other cost-saving efforts, some schools actually are saving money on the business side and reinvesting in instruction. For example, the Vaughn Next Century Learning Center in Los Angeles realized a $1.2 million surplus in its first year of operation. This surplus was used to enhance technology and other instructional supports.

Ripple effects are becoming visible across the broader system. Charter schools are intended not only to serve the students within their walls but also to help initiate other changes. To some degree, this is beginning to occur, especially in states with strong charter laws. For example, a Montessori program now is being offered by one Minnesota district after parents sought to establish such a program under charter law. In response to Massachusetts' charter law, the Boston Public Schools and the teachers union initiated a process for creating their own charter-like schools. These types of activities could have occurred without charter school legislation, but the pressure to do so was not present.

Charter schools are not immune from problems. A few events underscore the fact that charter school laws have glitches to be worked out, and mismanagement can occur. In November 1994, the Ingham County Circuit Court declared Michigan's charter school law to be unconstitutional, in part because the law usurped the state board's power to oversee public education. The suit was partially prompted by the approval of the Noah Webster Academy, which was a network of home-schooling families. It was feared that this network would use public funds to support religious instruction. In December 1994, changes were made to the law; and previously approved charter schools, with the exception of Noah Webster, were funded.

Some charter schools have had difficulty managing administrative operations. One school in Colorado was alleged to have faulty hiring procedures and to be in violation of open meeting laws. Other schools struggle to secure buildings and capital equipment. These types of problems were magnified in the case of the Los Angeles-based Edutrain Charter School, which lost its charter in December 1994 because of financial mismanagement.

Conclusion

Charter schools are not for the faint of heart. Involvement in their creation, governance, and day-to-day operation requires a large investment of time and energy and a high tolerance for ambiguity. Charter schools are, bluntly, uncharted waters. So what can be learned from those already working in charter schools?

Interviews with charter school organizers and staff in several states reveal that school start-up is one of the most time-consuming tasks. Many start-up problems are similar to those that confront any new small-business owner. Organizers and staff must create a vision of the school they want and prepare to translate that vision

111

into reality. They must consider sources for start-up funding, develop community contacts and involvement, and locate a facility. They must constantly evaluate their process and outcomes, making ongoing adjustments as necessary.

Although the task of organizing a charter school may seem daunting, those who are involved see it as energizing, exciting, and inspiring. Charter schools peel away bureaucratic layers, and many people are more willing to support an education effort that is accessible to them. Charter schools are viewed as a grassroots reform strategy.

Charter school participants who were interviewed by the authors also made the following point clear: Those who believe in the charter school concept and can meet the challenging work load will reap rewards not possible in other schools. Just the tremendous emphasis on collaboration has been a welcome change to many. Nevertheless, many questions remain: Will charter schools become just another fad that fades into oblivion in a few years? Or will they successfully integrate a number of promising reforms? And if they do succeed, will they dramatically change learning environments for a great number of students and teachers, or will they affect only those within their halls?

It is too early to answer these questions; but many educators, policy makers, and community members from widely diverse philosophical backgrounds believe that charter schools represent a bold reform attempt with great promise.

References

Bierlein, L., and Mulholland, L. "The Promise of Charter Schools." *Educational Leadership* 52 (September 1994): 34-40.

Kolderie, T. "The States Begin to Withdraw the 'Exclusive'." *Changing Schools* 21 (November 1993): 1-8.

Mulholland, L., and Amsler, M. *The Search for Choice in Public Education: The Emergence of Charter Schools.* San Francisco: Far West Laboratory for Educational Research and Development, October 1992.

National Education Association. *Are Charter Schools Better?* Issue Brief. Washington, D.C., June 1993.

Premack, E., and Diamond, L. *Redesigning Education: Supporting the Charter Schools Movement.* Berkeley, Calif.: BW Associates, January 1993.

Quinn, R. "Charter Schools: Now What?" *CASB Agenda* (August 1993): 2.

Stuart, E. "Chartering a New Course." *State Government News* (April 1994): 8-11.

CONSTRUCTIVIST TEACHING

by John A. Zahorik

Deciding how to teach is a problem that all teachers face throughout their careers. Ideas about how to teach often come from formal research and theory, but they also come from informal sources, such as personal experimentation and reflection, observation of and dialogue with colleagues, and memories of one's own teachers.

In the 1970s and 1980s research in particular was a dominant source for ideas about how to teach. It produced direct instruction. This type of teaching, which teachers everywhere were urged to adopt, is based on studies by Stallings and Kaskowitz (1974), Good and Grouws (1979), and others, as well as on the research-based framework developed by Hunter (1982). It consists of several well-known elements: readiness, instruction, checking, practice, and review. The research found that learning, as evidenced by standardized achievement test score gains, occurred when teachers got students' attention at the beginning of the lesson; directly instructed them concerning the content or skills to be learned; checked to determine if the content or skills were acquired and, if not, retaught them; provided practice activities so that the learning became internalized; and provided periodic reviews.

Although direct instruction is a supportable way to teach and all teachers undoubtedly use direct instruction to some degree in their teaching, it has serious limitations. Direct instruction is effective when the goal of instruction is to have students acquire and reproduce factual knowledge and well-defined skills. It can

This essay is condensed from John A. Zahorik, *Constructivist Teaching*, Fastback 390 (Bloomington, Ind.: Phi Delta Kappa Educational Foundation, 1995).

be a successful method when teaching adding and subtracting, word syllabication, and map reading in elementary classrooms and in teaching basic knowledge and processes in any subject in middle and secondary classrooms. As long as reproduction is the objective, direct instruction is effective and efficient. When the goal of instruction is more than reproduction, when the goal is understanding, thinking, and creation, direct instruction is of limited value.

Having foundational knowledge and skills in the traditional disciplines of language, mathematics, science, social studies, and the arts is of critical importance for everyone; but it is sufficient neither for us as individuals nor for us as a society. To be able only to reproduce what has been presented to us is to ignore the enormous potential that humans have for being self-directed, creative, and productive. As more and more reproductive tasks are being done by computers and other machines, human minds must be put to the more important tasks of which they are capable. In addition to greater personal fulfillment, focusing on more than the reproduction of basic knowledge and skills has economic and social benefits for our society. To be competitive in foreign markets, reports such as *America 2000* remind us, we need a workforce that not only is proficient in basic skills but also can think, apply knowledge, and solve problems.

Constructivist teaching emphasizes thinking, understanding, and self-control over behavior but does not neglect basic skills and knowledge. This type of teaching, which has emerged in recent years, is called constructivist teaching because it is based on the notion that humans are constructors of their own knowledge, rather than reproducers of someone else's knowledge.

The purpose of this essay is to examine the theory and practice of constructivist teaching and to suggest how teachers can decide what form of constructivist teaching they might want to use. In the next section the theory undergirding constructivist teaching is explored. This is followed by a section that details the teaching elements and basic types of constructivist teaching and another section that focuses on beliefs and their importance in deciding about constructivist teaching. In the last sections, threats to implementation are explored and the future of constructivist teaching is discussed.

Constructivist Teaching Theory

The dominant learning theory since the turn of the century has been behaviorism. The various forms of behaviorism, such as operant conditioning, respondent conditioning, and modeling, all share the view that learning is a response by the learner to various stimuli present in the environment. In this stimulus-response view, usually represented as the S-R unit, the learner is a passive reactor who is shaped by associating behaviors with their consequences. The learner is more or less helpless. Whatever he or she learns and does is a function of his or her environment.

Psychologists who support the S-R notion have examined how S-R units are acquired, retained, linked, and transferred, usually in regard to simple tasks and often involving animals.

Although adequate for explaining the learning of many simple behaviors, behaviorist learning theory cannot explain the learning of more complex behavior very well, perhaps because behaviorists have ignored the mental processes that mediate the S-R unit. Between the stimulus and the response is a mind. Humans do not blindly react to stimuli. They are perceiving, thinking beings with insights, reasoning power, and the ability to make decisions. Humans can and do select the stimuli to which they respond and choose a response that makes sense to them. A unit that more adequately represents the learning process is the S-MIND-R unit.

The realization that something more was needed to explain the rational, logical, cognitive process that occurs between stimuli and responses gave birth to cognitive psychology, which in turn has in large measure provided the theoretical basis for constructivist teaching. Of the cognitive theorists, one major figure has been Piaget (1971). He suggested that cognitive functioning involves the complementary processes of assimilation and accommodation. Assimilation is a shaping process in which new experiences are received through existing knowledge structures, while accommodation is reshaping the existing knowledge structures to accept the new experience. The whole process, which is driven by a desire to achieve equilibrium or balance between personal constructions and new experiences, results in a cognitive structure that is more integrated or accepts more ideas and that is more differentiated or contains more substructures.

This conception of learning spawned many related conceptions, such as Rummelhart and Norman's (1978). They posited three kinds of cognitive processing: 1) accretion, or the encoding of new information in terms of the existing structure; 2) restructuring, or the process of creating new structures; and 3) tuning, or the gradual modification of existing structures as a result of using them. In addition to cognitive psychology, brain-function research and postpositivist philosophy serve to support constructivist teaching. A synthesis of work from these areas yields the framework of ideas, or the theory, for constructivist teaching. These ideas concern conceptions of knowledge and humans.

Knowledge

Knowledge is constructed by humans. Knowledge is not a set of facts, concepts, or laws waiting to be discovered. It is not something that exists independent of a knower. Humans create or construct knowledge as they attempt to bring meaning to their experience. Everything that we know, we have made. Although there may be a reality that our constructions represent, this correspondence is not knowable. All that humans can know is that their constructions are compatible with other constructions they have made or know.

Knowledge is conjectural and fallible. Since knowledge is a construction of humans and humans are constantly undergoing new experiences, knowledge can never be stable. The understandings that we invent are always tentative and incomplete. Even the understandings that we have that appear to be immutable are not. It was not very long ago that the periodic table contained 83 elements, the solar system had eight planets, the angles of a triangle

118

equaled 180°, and dinosaurs were cold-blooded animals. Although the understandings that we invent are imperfect, it does not mean that they are equally imperfect. While still being conjectural and fallible, some constructions fit better with other constructions.

Knowledge grows through exposure. Understanding becomes deeper and stronger if one tests it against new encounters. These encounters can be experiences that individuals have with objects and events. But because understandings can be encoded in language, they can be social encounters. Individuals can share their knowledge and get feedback from others. Through these pooled and critiqued understandings, knowledge grows. The disciplines of history, law, botany, mathematics, anthropology, and others are agreed-on social constructions. They have undergone and continually undergo the elimination, alteration, and strengthening of meanings through collegial sharing. Knowledge is, as Leinhardt (1992) suggests, both individual and community property.

Humans

Humans have a built-in aversion to disorder. Understanding, or making meaning, is an unavoidable consequence of being human and driven by the survival instinct. As humans, we constantly are monitoring our environment. Those occurrences that are novel are made to fit one's existing order, or one's existing meanings are reordered in an effort to understand and take action to avoid harm. Making sense of things means relating them to one's existing organization of ideas.

Humans have internal knowledge structures that guide perception, understanding, and action. All humans possess networks of meanings that are constantly being revised. These meanings, which are the result of past experiences, both physical and social, guide the perception of new experiences. That is, we see new things in relation to our present knowledge structures. The structures shape the perception, but the perception also feeds back and shapes the structure. It is the developing internal knowledge structure that then directs behavior.

119

To accept the notion that internal knowledge structures guide perception is to accept the belief that a person always has a knowledge structure that can bring meaning to a situation. If we were asked to explain the transfer function of Pascal programming, many of us would be convinced that we had no previous knowledge on which to draw; but in the hands of a skillful teacher, we would see that we had existing knowledge structures to bring to the task. They may be embryonic, incomplete, or even wrong; but they guide perception and initiate understanding. At birth or shortly thereafter, knowledge structures in some form are available for our use and refinement.

Human learning is a matter of strengthening internal knowledge structures. As one becomes engaged in experiences, his or her existing knowledge structures are activated. These existing structures, as a result of the new experience, can become more complex with more connections; they can become altered to accommodate a new understanding; or they can become obsolete because the new experience has caused the creation of a new knowledge structure. This sifting and winnowing of prior knowledge structures constitutes learning.

Constructivist Teaching Practice

Constructivist teaching is guided by the previous six theory statements. It can take many forms; but whatever its form, it must help learners construct their own knowledge. It must help learners focus on what they currently know, be receptive to new information, fit the new information into the current knowledge structure or revise the current knowledge structure, and become aware of what they know and know how to do.

The following elements constitute one conception of constructivist teaching. These elements are equally applicable to teaching declarative knowledge — such as substantive facts, concepts, and generalizations — and procedural knowledge — such as skills, processes, and techniques.

Five Basic Elements

Activating prior knowledge. Since what is learned is always learned in relation to what one already knows, to one's existing knowledge structure, it is important that this prior knowledge be identified. Students and teachers need to be aware of students' knowledge structures, because these structures accommodate the new experience and guide the perception of the new experience. When students are aware of their prior knowledge, they can appreciate their vantage point and more readily decide if the new content fits into an existing structure or if a new structure is required. When teachers are familiar with students' prior understandings, they can better plan and provide learning experiences that build on these existing understandings. Or, if the existing understandings are faulty, if they constitute misconceptions, then the teacher can engage students in activities to change these misconceptions before proceeding with the new content.

Prior knowledge can be activated in many ways. Simply asking students what they know about the topic to be studied can be effective. But sometimes a less direct technique is more productive in drawing out what they know. Other procedures that can reveal students' prior knowledge include brainstorming the elements of some phenomenon or the causes of some event (such as brainstorming the planets and other aspects of the solar system prior to studying the origin of the solar system), creating a timeline of events leading up to the topic of study (such as U.S. military conflicts prior to Vietnam), and predicting the consequences of a demonstration or experiment (such as hypothesizing the effects of various environmental conditions on plant growth in advance of a study of photosynthesis).

Also, if the knowledge to be acquired is procedural knowledge, the teacher can have the students attempt to perform the actual skill, process, or procedure prior to instruction. Trying to plot two variables on a graph or write a persuasive essay can provide helpful information for subsequent instruction.

Acquiring knowledge. Students must encounter knowledge in a way that helps them determine the extent to which it fits their existing knowledge structures. The teacher needs to focus on wholes and to assist students in acquiring them. If students are to develop understanding, they need to see the "big picture" and its related parts. Understanding does not result when content is experienced as isolated bits of information. It does not result when depth is sacrificed for breadth and the coverage of prescribed amounts of subject matter. Focusing on wholes means to identify a few major ideas and to make them the center of instruction.

In declarative knowledge, wholes are concepts or generalizations and their related, interconnected facts. An idea — for example, that in industrialized societies the functions that less developed societies carry out in families are performed by institutions — is a whole. Its related parts might consist of the functions of education, medical care, manufacturing, government, and transportation. Another example is the idea that plants and animals exist in a symbiotic relationship. The supporting facts for this whole would consist of animals' need for food, shelter, and protection and plants' need for fertilizer, dispersion of seeds, nurturing, and so on.

In procedural knowledge, wholes are the complete skill or process and the sequential steps that compose it. An example is learning to square dance. Rather than painstakingly learning each step, body position, rhythm, and dance configuration and then putting them together to experience the dance, the constructivist teacher would show students the dance as practiced by competent dancers. The teacher also might have students attempt to perform the dance in a rudimentary way. Only after some sense of the whole is acquired would the parts that need attention be treated.

Teachers can assist students to acquire wholes and to fit them into their existing structures, or to use them as a springboard to alter structures or create new structures, in two ways: 1) They can arrange experiences and environments so that students come to see wholes and their parts, to see relationships and connections, or 2) they can directly present wholes and parts through lectures, demonstrations, and dialogue.

The type of assistance that constructivist teachers provide has been termed "scaffolding" (Collins, Brown, and Neuman 1990;

Rosenshine and Meister 1992). The scaffolding metaphor points to the notion that a building is standing in some form, but it cannot stand alone. It needs support until it is strengthened by the addition of bricks, mortar, and steel. Some buildings, because they are defective, need to be razed before they can be rebuilt into a sturdy structure. Scaffolding with students can take many forms, but it always builds on students' prior knowledge. In learning both declarative and procedural knowledge, it can consist of explanations, examples, analogies, manipulatives, graphic organizers, models, and answering questions. As students begin to acquire knowledge, the scaffold is withdrawn gradually until the "building" is standing on its own. That is, the teacher's help is no longer needed after the students have reached a state of cognitive equilibrium.

An example of scaffolding with an analogy occurred in a chemistry class. The topic was the electronic structure of atoms, the understanding of which is a prerequisite to understanding other chemical behavior. The students were asked to think about each electron as having a house address. Since each electron has four quantum numbers and no two electrons can have the same set of quantum numbers, quantum numbers are analogous to house numbers and can be used to locate or identify. By considering quantum numbers as house numbers, students were better able to understand quantum theory without a rigorous mathematical treatment.

Modeling, as an example of scaffolding, was used by a reading teacher to teach summarizing. The teacher summarized a passage read by the class. After the teacher summarized the passage, she analyzed her summary, showing how she eliminated trivial and redundant material, used global terms to classify more specific elements, and selected or invented topic sentences for each paragraph. As students attempted to summarize other passages, the teacher modeled summarizing if they had difficulty.

Understanding knowledge. Once students have been exposed to new content or skills, the process of understanding begins. The student compares the new information to his or her existing structure to determine if it fits into the structure and strengthens it or if it clashes with the structure and the structure needs to be altered. Teachers can assist the development of understanding by providing experiences that cause students to explore thoroughly the new content and to share their interpretations of the new content as it relates to their knowledge structures. Marzano states that "the most effective learning occurs when we continually cycle through information, challenging it, refining it" (1992, p. 67).

To thoroughly explore the content means to examine it carefully from both the inside and the outside in an effort to come to know its fine points. An inside exploration includes summarizing the content, paraphrasing its main ideas, reordering its parts, explaining its meaning, and defining its terms. An outside exploration includes comparing and contrasting it with other content, studying examples of it, creating analogies for it, extending it into new areas, evaluating it in relation to established standards, and classifying it into existing categories.

An inside approach that was used in a fourth-grade science class consisted of building a semantic map of terms associated with tornadoes as a way of summarizing a lesson on tornadoes. Another example might be having students compose a letter to Nelson Mandela, listing major questions they would like to ask him about the future of South Africa. This would be a follow-up activity after reading about and discussing South Africa and its problems.

Examples of increasing understanding from the outside are having students classify artists by style or period following several class sessions on famous artists and having students compare du Maurier's novella, *The Birds*, which they had been studying, with the Hitchcock film of the same name.

Sharing emerging knowledge structures is essential for understanding. When knowledge structures are displayed, others can react to them. They can provide perceptions and insights that cause the student to rethink his or her knowledge structure. Furthermore, those who are providing the critique cannot help but reconsider their knowledge structures as they hear and react to the structures that are being presented.

There are many ways in which knowledge structures can be shared and critiqued in the classroom. Dialogue between the teacher and students or among students in small groups in which students take turns voicing their interpretations, explanations, solutions, perceptions, and ideas can be effective in revealing developing knowledge structures. Other ways in which reasoning is made public in the classroom include oral reports, debates, role playing, demonstrations, simulations, and displays. However, each of these activities must be accompanied by critique. It is the critique that causes students to rethink their positions and either modify or confirm them, and thereby strengthen them. Perkinson (1993) sees critical feedback as the most important aspect of teaching for understanding.

Following is an example of sharing ideas that took place through a simulation activity. In a unit on wildlife conservation, after the class had acquired knowledge about wildlife management and engaged in activities to deepen their understanding, the teacher involved the class in simulating the management of a moose population over a nine-year span. The factors that influence moose herd size, such as weather conditions, forms of habitat destruction, community education activities, and reproduction formulae, were written on cards. The students, assuming the roles of wildlife managers, rangers, and statisticians, selected cards and indicated the decisions they would make regarding the herd in relation to the information on the card. As the class discussed the responses to the cards, students' understandings were tested in the public arena of the classroom. Their understandings about the effects of human invasion on wildlife habitat, reproductive habits of animal populations, the delicate balance of natural communities, and other understandings emerged and were made clearer.

Using knowledge. Providing activities for students in which they use the knowledge that they possess, and about which they are beginning to develop understanding, extends and refines their understanding.

The most effective activities for knowledge use are problem-solving activities that are *authentic, interesting, holistic, long-term,* and *social*. Activities that require students to engage in solving problems result in making knowledge functional. Students must synthesize and operationalize their knowledge as they attempt to solve the problem. This process causes them to continue to examine and build their knowledge structures.

Authentic problems are those that are likely to occur in the real world, though they can be either academic or practical. They can be the type of problem that a historian or a scientist might face, or they can be the type that occurs in day-to-day living, such as planning a meal or developing a budget. *Interest* is critically important if students are to extend their understanding through activity, because if they are not interested in the activity, they will not participate to a sufficient extent. Activities that are interesting to students are those that involve contrast or emotional intensity, according to Sylvester and Cho (1992). An activity that provides contrast is one that contains some surprising, unexpected, or incongruous elements, while an activity that is emotionally intense is usually one that deals with life themes, such as love, violence, money, and death.

A *holistic* activity is one that is broad and multifaceted and has not been unduly simplified or shaped for pedagogical purposes. For students to test and strengthen their understanding, they need experiences that challenge their knowledge structures. *Long-term* means that the activity will occupy students for several periods or days. A short activity may not engage students long enough for them to rethink their knowledge structures. Finally, all other things being equal, a *social* activity is more useful than a solitary one. When students work in groups to solve a problem, they have the opportunity to constantly voice ideas and receive feedback on their adequacy.

Many activities can cause students to use knowledge, such as construction projects, research papers, proposals for action, data-gathering investigations, decision-making tasks, policy development, and many others. Whatever the form, an activity can be conceived, organized, and experienced as a *convergent* activity or a *divergent* activity.

A *convergent* activity is one that has one or more known outcomes. The teacher arranges and influences the activity so that the students arrive at the predetermined answer or product. Often these predetermined outcomes will be various collective constructions that scholars have developed and accepted over a long period of time; they will be the basic concepts and processes of the disciplines. Constructivism comes into play as the students use their knowledge structures to arrive at these outcomes and alter their knowledge structures to accommodate the collective constructions that emerge.

A *divergent* activity, in contrast, is one in which the substantive outcomes are unknown. The teacher encourages original, creative outcomes. The students may build on collective constructions, but they produce their own, unique conclusions.

An example of a convergent activity from a secondary school mathematics class involved determining odds. The students computed odds for a set of state lottery games that varied by task and pool numbers. An example of a divergent activity is a second-grade project in which students — with the help of their parents — constructed a square for a class quilt that depicted a family tradition. The quilt was part of a home and family unit. Another divergent example is a middle school history activity in which students created magazines as they might have been written in 1945. This was the final task of a unit about World War II. In the odds activity only one outcome was possible, but in the other two activities students could create their own quilt squares and magazines.

Reflecting on knowledge. Students acquire knowledge, they deepen their understanding of it, and they use it in problem-solving situations. But if knowledge is to be fully understood and widely applicable in and out of school, they need to decontextualize it. This requires reflection.

Reflection refers to understanding what one knows, or metacognition. It is one thing to use knowledge to solve a problem, but it is another to become aware of the strategy one employed that led to the solution. Being aware of one's own knowledge results in self-control and autonomous behavior. It permits students to set goals and make plans to achieve them.

Activities that cause students to reflect are those that require them to step outside themselves and look back at what they have done. Such monitoring and assessment can take place in many ways. Journal writing is an especially good technique for stimulating metacognition. It brings to the surface understandings that often are relegated to the background during the heat of problem solving. Teaching what one knows to others also is an effective means for causing reflection. It demands careful consideration of what one knows so that it can be presented in an efficient and effective way.

Another useful activity is simulation or role-playing. This activity requires students to examine their actual behavior as they engage in hypothetical, analogous situations. Any planning or proposal writing, such as planning a field trip or proposing a policy regarding school lunch, also causes reflection and self-regulation. Comparing one's processes and understandings with those of others also is a good way to stimulate reflection, according to Collins, Brown, and Neuman (1990).

In addition to these and other techniques in which students are actively involved in performing a task, reflection on one's own understanding and behavior can occur as one watches another engage in reflection. The modeling of reflection by the teacher or another student can cause students to do their own reflecting.

The five basic elements of constructivist teaching are not as discrete in practice as they have been presented here. In classrooms the elements are commingled in many ways. Some reflecting tasks may occur during the acquiring of knowledge; prior knowledge may be activated at many points in the lessons; more acquiring of knowledge may be provided following the use of knowledge; and so on. Nevertheless, the order in which the elements have been portrayed represents a general style or pattern of teaching that teachers can and do use.

Four Types of Constructivist Teaching

The four types of constructivist teaching that emerge from these five elements are application, discovery, extension, and invention. The dimensions on which these types vary are *goal* and *order*.

Goal refers to the outcome the teacher is trying to achieve. It can be either a convergent outcome or a divergent outcome. Convergence, as previously defined, refers to a focus on predetermined ends, while divergence refers to novel, original outcomes. *Order* refers to the kind of lesson organization the teacher is using. The lesson can be organized in a logical way, in which activities that develop basic learning precede activities that promote more advanced learning. Or the lesson can be organized in a psychological way, in which activities may contain both basic and advanced learning. A psychological structure permits students to acquire knowledge in a way and at a time that is meaningful for them.

An examination of the four types of constructivist teaching, along with an example of each type, follows.

Application. The sequence of elements in application is the one that already has been discussed. The teacher begins by activating prior knowledge, then having students acquire some content or skill. Next, the teacher moves to activities designed to increase understanding. Then the teacher has students engage in a use activity and, finally, employs procedures that cause students to reflect on what they have learned. The use activity in this type of teaching is a convergent one that causes students to directly apply what they have learned.

A second-grade language lesson exemplifies application. In this lesson the teacher sought to develop understanding of folktales. The lesson began with the teacher eliciting students' favorite characters from stories with which they were familiar and asking them to tell why the characters were their favorites.

Names that were mentioned included Charlotte, Pippy Longstocking, Lyle Crocodile, and Amelia Bedelia. Students said that these characters possessed such qualities as "funny," "smart," "like me," and "tough." Following this introduction, the teacher

129

announced that the story for the day was "Anansi the Spider," a folktale from Africa. Before reading the story, the teacher had the class examine the pictures in the book and tell what they thought the story would be about.

After the story had been read, the teacher asked students to summarize the story, to ask questions of each other to check their understanding of the story, and to make predictions about what might happen next if the story were to continue. As this dialogue, which focused mostly on the events of the story, drew to an end, the teacher then asked students to describe the kind of character that Anansi is and to speculate on why he is considered to be a folk character. They indicated that they saw him as tricky, clever, and smart but also lazy and vain. A folk character, they concluded after the teacher synthesized and rephrased the students' comments, was the central figure in a folktale, a story that has no known author but has been handed down from one generation to another by a particular group of people. The folk character often represents the kind of figure that the group of people see as a hero, but can also have qualities that they do not admire.

Next the teacher asked students to choose a partner and assigned them the task of writing another version of the folktale featuring Anansi without changing the basic facts of the story. She explained that because folktales are handed down over time, slightly different versions of the same story often exist.

In later sessions these stories were shared, and the teacher asked students to record in their journals a definition of the term *folktale* and to describe a family folktale that might have been told and retold in their family.

This lesson on folktales fits the constructivist teaching application model. It begins with the teacher eliciting students' prior experiences with favorite story characters that can later be tied to folktales. The reading of the story represents the acquiring phase, and the dialogue following the reading deepens comprehension during the understanding phase. The process used here — dialogue relating to summarizing, clarifying, and predicting — is similar to what Palincsar and Brown (1984) describe as reciprocal teaching. The writing of additional versions of the folktale is the use phase, and the journal entry serves as the reflection phase. Although the use activity requires some creativity on the part of students, it is mostly convergent because the teacher is seeking only slight variations in the original story.

Discovery. The beginning point for discovery teaching is a use activity. Students engage in an activity that has been planned so that student involvement leads to a predetermined end. As students engage in the activity, they either acquire and understand the intended content or skills incidentally, as a byproduct of the activity, or the teacher provides experiences during the activity that foster acquisition and understanding incrementally. After the activity, other tasks may be done that enlarge students' understanding. The sequence is then ended with attention to reflection on the new learning that emerged.

Constructivist discovery teaching is illustrated by a fourth-grade science lesson on electricity. The objective of the lesson was to have students understand that static electricity results from negatively charged particles attracting uncharged particles. The lesson began with the teacher dividing the class into five groups and distributing a balloon, a piece of wool cloth, and a piece of graph paper to each group. She announced that the groups were going to explore static electricity by rubbing the balloon with the wool cloth and trying to make the balloon stick to the wall. They were to vary the rubbing time, measure the balloon rubbing time and balloon adhesion time, and record their findings on the graph paper. As the groups began to work, she elicited students' experiences with static electricity.

Following their responses concerning "shocks" on cold days, clothes that cling when they first come out of the dryer, and lightning, and after much experimenting with the balloon and wool cloth, the teacher distributed pieces of cotton cloth and aluminum foil. She told the groups to continue their experimentation and to record the results. She also suggested that they try to make the balloon stick to a door, a window, and other surfaces.

After the groups had experimented for 20 minutes, she had the whole class share their findings. The students presented their data about static electricity production. The teacher then posed the question that several students had begun to ask: How does static electricity work? Responses included the ideas that rubbing warmed up the balloon, made the balloon shiny, cleaned off dust, and created friction. However, some students thought it had to do with positive and negative charges. The teacher built on this response and finally explained about atoms and electrons.

Next, the teacher had the class read a portion of the science textbook dealing with static electricity. A discussion followed in which misunderstandings were clarified and static electricity was compared to current electricity.

The last activity of the session was having students write in their science journals. They were to summarize their understanding of static electricity and propose a plan for the most efficient and effective way to pick up spilled pepper using a balloon.

This lesson is a good example of constructivist discovery teaching because the teacher began with a use activity and had one outcome in mind that she wanted students to acquire. The balloon-rubbing activities provided a hands-on experience that the teacher could use to introduce the explanation of static electricity. During the early phases of the group activity, she also activated prior knowledge; the later part of the lesson, when she presented the explanation of what students were observing, was the acquiring phase.

Reading and discussing the textbook clarified the concept of static electricity; that was the understanding phase of the lesson. The journal entry, the last activity of the session, was the reflective phase. Summarizing the major understandings and solving the pepper problem contributed to metacognition.

Extension. Extension teaching is similar to application teaching with one important difference. The use activity is divergent, rather than convergent. The teacher begins with acquiring and understanding tasks, but they are seen as being preparatory to the activity that follows, rather than as the center of the lesson. They provide the basic knowledge on which students can draw as they attempt to solve a problem that the teacher presents or that the students identify for themselves. The problem requires them to put the basic knowledge together in novel ways and to go beyond the acquired new information. After the divergent activity is finished, the teacher provides for reflection.

Constructivist extension teaching is exemplified in a middle school social studies lesson. In this lesson the teacher's objectives were to have the students learn the characteristics of a Third World country and to speculate on why Third World countries exist and how they can move out of Third World status. The lesson began with a review of the characteristics of developed countries. The teacher and students together identified the characteristics that the teacher wrote on the chalkboard:

1. Most people live in towns and cities.
2. Pay is high and hours of work are few.
3. Machines do most of the work.
4. Enough food exists for all.
5. Life expectancy is long.
6. Medical care is available to all.
7. Most adults can read and write.
8. People have money and time for leisure.
9. Houses have running water and electricity.

When the class was satisfied with the list, the teacher moved on to the Third World countries. First, he asked if anyone had seen a travel program on television about a country that might be a Third World or "underdeveloped" country. Responses included India, Zaire, Somalia, and Mexico. After students shared their knowledge of these countries, the teacher led a discussion in which he proposed and elicited characteristics of Third World countries. Seven characteristics emerged that also were listed on the chalkboard:

1. Natural resources are not fully used.
2. Much work is done by hand.

3. Most products must be imported.
4. Many people are farmers.
5. There is a great dependence on one crop.
6. Many people are illiterate.
7. The population is growing rapidly.

Next, the teacher distributed written descriptions of four fictitious countries for which various characteristics and statistics were identified. The students were to read the descriptions and decide if each country was more developed or underdeveloped. After sharing and justifying their responses, several students volunteered additional characteristics of Third World countries. Three new items were added to the list:

8. Urban centers are overcrowded.
9. Housing is substandard.
10. Education is available to only a few.

Following this activity, the teacher initiated a group activity. Each of five groups was to identify a Third World country of interest; obtain economic, political, geographic, historic, and other information about the country; and try to explain why the country had not become developed and what it might reasonably do to become a more developed country. These investigations, which took several days to complete, resulted in reports shared with the total class on India, Cuba, Zaire, Somalia, and China.

The last activity was a class discussion on what each group did as it attempted to complete its task. The discussion focused on organizing and identifying goals, locating resources, developing and supporting arguments, and other matters.

The various aspects of extension teaching are apparent in this lesson. The review of previously acquired information about developed and underdeveloped countries activated prior knowledge. The brainstorming and proposing of characteristics was the acquiring phase. The understanding phase was the activity in which the students compared and contrasted the characteristics of developed and underdeveloped countries as they categorized the four fictitious countries. The group activity was the use element; here the students were engaged in a divergent task that required them to draw on and creatively use their knowledge of Third World countries. Reflection occurred as the class shared how they proceeded to investigate their actual Third World countries.

Invention. Just as in discovery teaching, the lesson begins with a use activity in invention teaching. But here the activity requires divergent thinking. The students encounter and try to solve a problem that has many possible answers, rather than one or more absolute answers. In working on the problem, the students acquire and come to understand content and skills that are needed to reach and support a solution. If an impasse is reached, the teacher may provide experiences so that students can continue toward solution. In invention teaching, as in discovery teaching, the elements usually are not separate or, indeed, separable. Again, the final part of the sequence should promote reflection.

A secondary school geometry lesson illustrates constructivist invention teaching. The teacher's intention in this lesson was for students to manipulate squares and to develop mathematical rules based on their observations. The teacher divided the class into four groups and gave each grid-lined paper, scissors, and rulers. They were asked to cut out squares of various sizes and arrange them in various ways in order to produce rules or laws regarding squares. Near the end of the class period, the groups were to report to the whole class about the rules they had developed, including an informal proof for each rule.

Each group cut out square units and manipulated the squares as the teacher moved from group to group offering assistance and raising questions. One group cut out two 5 x 5 squares and then cut each large square into 25 smaller squares. Then they found that the smaller squares could be reconstituted into a 50-square unit. They discovered that the side of the new, large square had a length equal to 5 times the square root of 2. The rule they composed was that the sums of the areas of 2 squares is itself a square, and the side of the new, large square has a length equal to the length of the small square multiplied by the square root of 2.

Another group measured the sides and diagonals of squares and found that the ratio of the side of a square to the diagonal of a square is always 7:5. In dialogue with the teacher, the group came up with the rule that the diagonal of a square is the square root of 2 multiplied by the length of a side, because the square root of 2 is approximately 1.4, or the product of 7 divided by 5.

A third group focused on areas and observed that the sum of the areas of a 3 x 3 square and a 4 x 4 square equals the area of a 5 x 5 square. That is, 9 squares plus 16 squares equals 25 squares. In response to the teacher's encouragement, the group also came up with 5 x 5 plus 12 x 12 equals 13 x 13 and 6 x 6 plus 8 x 8 equals 10 x 10. This group was unable to develop a generalization (rule) about area before the allotted time expired.

The fourth group maneuvered squares around the table in various ways and observed that three squares could be put together in such a way that an empty triangle is formed in the middle. One of their configurations resulted in a right triangle being formed in the middle. The rule they composed was that every triple set of squares in which the two smaller squares have a total area equal to the area of the largest square always forms a right triangle. When the teacher got to the group and read their rule, he asked them if it could be restated in terms of the right triangle. Their restatement (after several discarded attempts) was that the sum of the squares of the measures of the two shorter sides of any right triangle equals the measure of the largest side. Although discovering the Pythagorean Theorem was not the teacher's purpose, he did introduce the terms *legs* and *hypotenuse* and told them what they had produced.

In the reporting session that followed the activity, the three groups that generated rules presented and illustrated them. The remaining group shared its observations. Because this fourth group had not come up with a rule, the teacher asked the total class to try to compose a rule to fit the observations and to share it during the next class period. Also during the reporting session, the teacher asked questions about how the students arrived at their laws. He asked how they resolved false attempts, how they tested the law on additional observations, how they went about actually stating the law, and similar questions.

Although the constructivist teaching elements are not as evident in this example as in some of the other types of constructivist teaching, they were present in this invention lesson. The group activity involving squares was the use phase, but the acquiring and understanding phases were embedded in it. The use activity qualifies as invention because the students were free to create and manipulate squares in any way they chose and to develop whatever rules seemed to emerge. The teacher did not have specific mathematical rules that he intended would emerge or that he steered the groups toward. The fact that one group discovered the Pythagorean Theorem was coincidental.

However, it is true that in mathematics the rules that the students could possibly develop have undoubtedly already been formulated (perhaps in slightly different terms), while in another content area such as social studies or literature there is more opportunity for novel and extensive divergence. The acquiring and understanding phases occurred as the teacher monitored the activity of the groups. Through statements, questions, suggested rearrangement of the squares, challenging drafts of the rules, scaffolding first rule attempts, and other ways, the teacher provided information and helped students to understand it. Some drawing on prior experience also was exhibited during the monitoring process.

The last activity of the class, the reports with accompanying dialogue, constituted the reflection phase and contributed to metacognition.

The four types of constructivist teaching are not always as simple and straightforward as these examples. The cycle of the five elements is not always completed in one or two class periods; several cycles of one or more types can occur in one lesson; and abortive and partial cycles can occur.

Furthermore, the four types of constructivist teaching are not four parallel, equally constructive types; they represent a range of constructivist teaching based on the ends one wishes to achieve and the means that one prefers to use. All teachers can and probably would use all four types as they teach their students, but some types may fit a particular teacher better than others. The next section explores how to decide which types are a better fit and therefore have a greater chance of being used effectively.

Constructing Constructivist Teaching

Deciding about constructivist teaching, or deciding about any instructional procedure, is a matter of examining possible instructional methods to determine which are consistent with one's beliefs. Research and theory are helpful in identifying ways to teach. But teachers need to decide for themselves which techniques they will and will not use. When reduced to their essential character, these decisions deal with beliefs about students, their human qualities and learning processes, and with beliefs about knowledge, its form and function.

If the beliefs about students and knowledge embedded in the technique or practice match the beliefs the teacher has about students and knowledge, the technique will be one that fits the teacher. In order to make decisions about constructivist teaching, two views of students and two views of knowledge are especially important.

One view of students is an active view. From this perspective, students are autonomous, can decide for themselves, wish to explore, and take responsibility for their behavior. They have the ability and desire to act on their own. They will enter into, plan, and pursue a task to a satisfactory conclusion.

A contrasting view of students is the reactive view. In this view, students seek direction, benefit from guidance, need to be stimulated, require organization, and want explicit limits. Rather than act on their own volition, they prefer to respond to an external structure. They benefit from logical sequence and from models and systematic coaching.

Of the two views of knowledge, one is the personal view. Significant knowledge from this perspective is the knowledge that students make for themselves. An understanding of major concepts and processes is important, of course; but this view of knowledge suggests that students' individual interpretations that result from creative and critical thinking are of greater importance. Here the goal of school is to have students reconceptualize existing structures and create new structures.

The other view of knowledge is the foundational view. Foundational knowledge consists of those powerful, collective constructions that have been developed over time through sharing, critiquing, and revising. This is the knowledge of experts in the various disciplines. The goal of schools, from this position, is to have students acquire this foundational knowledge and fit it into their existing knowledge structures or adjust their structures to accommodate it.

These views of students and knowledge represent reference points rather than dichotomous positions. Instead of believing one position to the exclusion of the other, most teachers probably support both positions on each variable to some extent, but they believe one more than the other. Beliefs are a matter of degree.

The direction toward which one leans in regard to the views of students and knowledge suggests which type of constructivist teaching may be appropriate for the particular teacher. Given the two belief variables and the two possible positions on each, four major belief patterns are possible: 1) reactive students and foundational knowledge, 2) active students and foundational knowledge, 3) reactive students and personal knowledge, and 4) active students and personal knowledge.

If one believes that students are mostly reactive and that foundational knowledge is more important than personal knowledge, the teacher may prefer application teaching. The logical order of starting with activating knowledge and progressing toward use and finally reflection says that students need organization, guidance, and models prior to using their knowledge. That the use is convergent suggests that important knowledge is the foundational, collectively constructed knowledge of experts.

If one believes the opposite, that students are generally active and that personal knowledge is more important than foundational knowledge, then the teacher probably will prefer invention teaching. Beginning teaching with a use activity that either includes the other elements or serves as an occasion for their later use is an indication that students are perceived as active individuals who can decide and act for themselves. The focus on divergent outcomes in the use activity shows that personal knowledge is valued.

Of the two remaining belief patterns, one is consistent with discovery teaching and the other is consistent with extension teaching. If a teacher believes in active students and foundational knowledge, he or she will likely be drawn to discovery teaching. In discovery teaching the lesson starts with a use activity, which reflects the view that students can make many decisions themselves, but the use activity is structured in such a way that students converge on predetermined ends.

If one believes in reactive students and personal knowledge, he or she will probably prefer extension teaching, which calls for a lesson in which preparatory information is acquired before students engage in a use activity, but the use activity is one that requires divergence through creative and critical thinking.

A case might be made for the proposition that, because of the beliefs about students and knowledge that underlie each type, invention teaching is the most constructivistic, application teaching is the least constructivistic, and discovery and extension teaching occupy middle positions with regard to constructivism. Certainly more constructivism may be occurring in invention teaching, where students develop personal knowledge on their own, or in extension teaching, where personal knowledge is the ultimate goal; but constructivism also is occurring to varying degrees in the other two types of teaching. If the focus of application teaching and discovery teaching were not an understanding of collective constructions complete with an emphasis on prior knowledge and reflection (and the metacognition it produces), then constructivism may not result — but that is not the case.

In deciding which form of constructivist teaching to use, beliefs are of major importance. But they are not the only basis for deciding. Because of one's beliefs, the teacher is likely to prefer, and therefore to use, those techniques that are consistent with the beliefs. However, classroom demands will require that a range of techniques be employed. Students' ability and experience, as well as the subject and particular content or skill to be taught, will influence the type of constructivist teaching that is most appropriate at any given moment.

Threats to Implementing Constructivist Teaching

Regardless of the types of constructivist teaching a teacher may choose, the classroom setting contains potential threats to implementation that must be reduced or eliminated if implementation is to occur. Three major threats or constraints are student expectations, content coverage, and evaluation.

Student Expectations. The student's role in constructivist teaching is to willingly engage in activities; share thoughts in dialogue, journals, and other ways; pursue topics in depth; critique other students' ideas; cooperate in group tasks; and create meaning. Hands-on activities, cooperative learning, journal writing, and other procedures that are compatible with constructivism exist in some form in many classrooms; but a full complement of constructivist teaching practices probably is missing in most classrooms. Students are accustomed to more teacher control and direction, an emphasis on correct answers, not expressing their thought processes, extensive practice of skills, and similar conventional classroom events.

An abrupt change in role from the traditional to the constructivist may be unrealistic. However, if the teacher incrementally substitutes constructivistic practices for traditional practices, then students may begin to assume this new role. Authentic tasks, valuing of students' ideas, building on their current level of understanding, and respecting their judgments can encourage students to join in the process of constructing knowledge. Together these acts create a classroom climate of trust in which students will risk thinking for themselves and revealing their thoughts to others.

141

Content Coverage. In constructivist teaching, as in more conventional teaching, the content and processes that experts in the various disciplines have constructed over time are of central importance. However, in constructivist teaching, it is the students' careful interpretation and deep understanding of the content and processes — in contrast to the ability to reproduce them — that is of concern. Constructing knowledge by fitting new content into existing structures or by adjusting existing structures usually can not be done quickly, nor can it be easily contained within arbitrary boundaries. Yet the content from curriculum guides and textbooks that teachers are expected to use consists of volumes of facts, concepts, and skills in separate subject areas. However, the expectation of content coverage in each of the subject areas need not preclude the use of constructivist teaching.

To achieve content coverage, the constructivist teacher needs to search his or her content area for the most powerful, generative ideas, as Bruner (1960) advised many years ago, and to make them the main objects of attention. These ideas undoubtedly will subsume a myriad of facts, which will result in a degree of content coverage. And because of their breadth, they flow into other content areas. The ideas cannot be construed nor presented as natural laws. Their tentative, socially constructed nature must be communicated. Textbooks and other learning materials in which the content is embedded must be viewed as "scaffolding on which readers can build their interpretation," according to von Glaserfeld (1992, p. 175).

Testing and Evaluation. Even as portfolio assessment is gaining a foothold in many classrooms, achievement tests still are prevalent. School districts typically use standardized achievement tests at various grade levels, and state departments of education often require tests of various kinds to be administered in reading and other areas. Generally, these tests require students to reproduce on machine-scored forms the facts and abilities they have acquired. Their emerging knowledge structures and metacognitive skills are neither examined nor evaluated.

If one engages in constructivist teaching and learning, if one emphasizes thinking and understanding, lower test scores on standardized achievement tests are not inevitable. On the contrary, it is reasonable to believe that if one has deep understanding of a concept or skill, he or she should score well on a test — even though the test emphasizes recall of facts or display of skill segments.

However, the question of actually evaluating constructivist thinking remains. Portfolio assessment, in which students and teachers can see and reflect on progress over time, is a step in the right direction if the focus is on interpretation and understanding. Problem-solving "tests," in which students are required to extend and reconceptualize their knowledge in new contexts, also are a possibility. Observing how students approach the problem can reveal the present state of their knowledge structures.

Other threats to implementation, such as class periods that are too short for extensive thought, supervision practices that reward more nonconstructivist teaching, school disciplinary practices that support a behaviorist ideology, and bulging class enrollments, all constrain constructivist teaching. But they do not prevent its use in some form for teachers who are persistent and creative.

Constructivist Teaching and the Future

Whether constructivist teaching is an education fad and soon will vanish or be relegated to a back bench except for a few tenacious zealots is unknown. It would seem that it might have a longer life than many education innovations, because it is not just a technique whose value is judged by its ability to produce an immediate result. Constructivist teaching — unlike direct instruction, for example — is based on theory. It emerges from a cohesive set of ideas about knowledge and learning that have their roots in philosophy and psychology. The theory may become clearer, new elements may be created, and additional types may be developed; but the power of the ideas suggests that this way of teaching will be long-lived.

143

The question of whether to use constructivist teaching is in some ways inconsequential. Constructivism on the part of students, if we believe constructivist theory, is unavoidable. It will happen no matter what teachers do instructionally. Any and all student experiences result in student construction of knowledge. The issue, then, is whether we should let students construct on their own in spite of their classroom experiences or whether we should do whatever is in our power to encourage and facilitate constructivism through experiences specifically designed to promote the making of knowledge by students.

References

Bruner, J. *The Process of Education*. New York: Vintage, 1960.

Collins, A.; Brown, J.; and Neuman, S. "Cognitive Apprenticeship: Teaching the Crafts of Reading, Writing, and Mathematics." In *Knowing, Learning, and Instruction: Essays in Honor of Robert Glaser*, edited by L. Resnick. Hillsdale, N.J.: Lawrence Erlbaum Associates, 1990.

Good, T., and Grouws, D. "Teaching and Mathematics Learning." *Educational Leadership* 37, no. 1 (1979): 39-45.

Hunter, M. *Mastery Teaching*. El Segundo, Calif.: TIP, 1982.

Leinhardt, G. "What Research on Learning Tells Us About Teaching." *Educational Leadership* 49, no. 7 (1992): 20-25.

Marzano, R. *A Different Kind of Classroom: Teaching with Dimensions of Learning*. Alexandria, Va.: Association for Supervision and Curriculum Development, 1992.

Palincsar, A., and Brown, A. "Reciprocal Teaching of Comprehension-Fostering and Monitoring Activities." *Cognition and Instruction* 1 (1984): 117-75.

Perkinson, H. *Teachers Without Goals, Students Without Purposes*. New York: McGraw-Hill, 1993.

Piaget, J. *Genetic Epistemology*. New York: W.W. Norton, 1971.

Rosenshine, B., and Meister, C. "The Use of Scaffolds for Teaching Higher-Level Cognitive Strategies." *Educational Leadership* 49, no. 7 (1992): 26-33.

Rummelhart, D., and Norman, D. "Accretion, Tuning, and Restructuring: Three Modes of Learning." In *Semantic Factors in Cognition*, edited by J. Cotton and R. Klatzky. Hillsdale, N.J.: Lawrence Erlbaum Associates, 1978.

Stallings, J., and Kaskowitz, D. *Follow-Through Classroom Observation Evaluations, 1971-73*. Menlo Park, Calif.: SRA International, 1974.

Sylvester, R., and Cho, J. "What Brain Research Says About Paying Attention." *Educational Leadership* 50, no. 4 (1992): 71-75.

von Glaserfeld, E. "Questions and Answers About Radical Constructivism." In *Scope, Sequence, and Coordination of Secondary School Science: Relevant Research*, edited by M. Pearsall. Washington, D.C.: National Science Teachers Association, 1992.

GAY AND LESBIAN ISSUES

by Donovan R. Walling

Many teens struggle with questions about their emerging sexual orientation, but they have little access to adequate counseling or other support services. The reluctance of educators to deal candidly with teenage sexual orientation issues, particularly if that orientation is homosexual, places a significant number of adolescents at risk, not only of school failure but of personal and social crises — even death.

Estimates vary for the number of teens who are gay or lesbian, ranging from 5% to 15% according to some experts. A number of teens acknowledge a homosexual orientation without engaging in sexual activity. Others are sexually active, a significant percentage with multiple partners. A recent study by the U.S. Centers for Disease Control (reported in *Education Week*, 15 April 1992) found that 19% of all high school students have had at least four sex partners.

Family crises, personal alienation, and social estrangement are factors that place homosexual students at risk in the school setting and beyond. Suicide and the incidence of HIV infection among gay and lesbian teens are at higher levels than for the general teen population. According to some studies, up to 30% of homosexual or bisexual teens have attempted suicide; and gay and lesbian teen suicides account for about 30% of all teen suicides. AIDS is now the number-two killer of young men in the United States. According to one study (Brownworth 1992), 51% of HIV transmission in adolescents aged 13 to 21 occurs among homosexual and bisexual males.

This essay is condensed from Donovan R. Walling, *Gay Teens at Risk*, Fastback 357 (Bloomington, Ind.: Phi Delta Kappa Educational Foundation, 1993).

If educators are aware of problems associated with emerging sexual orientation and the ramifications for potential high-risk student behaviors, they will be able to deal more effectively with those problems and thus diminish the risks to gay teens. The purpose of this essay is to provide an overview of the major issues associated with teen homosexuality and the at-risk characteristics exhibited by gay teens, and then to suggest practical educational responses that school leaders can implement.

Understanding Teen Homosexuality

A significant minority of teenagers spend their adolescence uncertain about their sexual orientation (Flax 1992). In an extensive study involving nearly 35,000 junior and senior high school students in Minnesota, University of Minnesota researchers found that nearly 11% of the respondents were unsure about their sexual orientation. The uncertainty declined with age, from about 26% of 12-year-olds to 5% of 18-year-olds. In this same study, about 1% said they were bisexual or predominantly homosexual. Older students were less likely than younger students to identify themselves as bisexual.

Older teens were more likely than younger teens to report that they were homosexual or to report same-sex attraction and behaviors. Nearly 3% of the 18-year-old males identified themselves as homosexual, and more than 6% reported being attracted to other males. However, only 27% of those who reported being attracted to other members of the same sex identified themselves as homosexual. These statistics are consistent with earlier studies by noted sex researcher Alfred Kinsey, who concluded that perhaps 4% of men are exclusively homosexual throughout their lives, while 10% are exclusively homosexual for at least three years.

Females in the Minnesota study were less likely to identify themselves as homosexual (less than 1%), though they were more likely to report being attracted to members of the same sex. This statistic also is consistent with Kinsey's estimate that the rate of female homosexuality is about half that of male homosexuality.

While survey research of this type is informative, the data might be better interpreted as an indication of the degree of sexual orientation confusion, rather than as precise statistics on the prevalence of teen homosexuality. The Minnesota researchers conclude that "ultimately, the findings illustrate the complexities and difficulties in assigning sexual-orientation labels to adolescents." One difficulty is that teens' definitions of sexual orientation probably do not match those of adults. Another may be respondents' reluctance to divulge a nonheterosexual orientation, despite guarantees of anonymity.

To put these statistics in perspective, take a typical high school graduating class of 500 students, half male and half female. If the Minnesota sampling is representative, about 25 students are probably unsure of their sexual orientation. Seven males are homosexual by their own definition; 16 report being attracted to other males. If this same senior class is representative of the national sample of students taking the Youth Risk Behavior Survey conducted by the U.S. Centers for Disease Control (reported in *Education Week*, 15 April 1992), then 28.6% of these students (143) have had four or more sex partners, with male students being more than twice as likely as females to report that level of sexual activity.

It seems clear that defining sexual orientation emerges in a highly individualistic manner. For some teens, the knowledge that they are homosexual or heterosexual comes early. Others may struggle with ambiguity about their sexual orientation throughout adolescence and into adulthood. As Krysiak (1987) points out: "Students sorting out their sexual orientation may be looking for a simple label, and that simplicity may be unhealthy to the adolescent who may not yet be really ready to make a commitment to a lifestyle."

The statistics reported above would indicate that a substantial group of students may need some form of supportive intervention, either because of external responses to their sexual uncertainty or because of their own social and sexual behaviors. And how their families and their schools respond to these students' struggles may be the determining factor that puts these teens at risk.

Response of Family and Peers. The continuing debate over nature versus nurture in the development of sexual orientation frequently intrudes into the dialogue about homosexuality, but it is largely a side issue when dealing with gay teens. What matters when an adolescent declares a same-sex orientation is the reaction of parents and peers to that declaration.

Typically, parents, on learning that their child is gay, react with shock, disbelief, sometimes even blaming themselves. In all too many cases, the emotional turmoil created by the disclosure leads parents to reject the child. Case histories of homosexual teens are often stories of throwaways, runaways, suicides, and attempted suicides. In other cases, parents eventually arrive at a level of acceptance and can help the child to deal positively with his or her emerging sexuality.

Disclosure of homosexual orientation by a teen also raises the issue of rejection by the peer group. As Robert Schaecher (1989), health coordinator for the Calhoun School in New York City, points out, "Homosexuality threatens straight adolescents by raising uncertainties they would rather not deal with so openly." In many instances, the gay teen is subjected to harassment from other teens, ranging from name-calling — "fag," "dyke," "queer" — to physical abuse. Violence directed at homosexuals is a major problem that has its roots in the school peer group. Schaecher questions: "Do educators label student putdowns of gays as unacceptable — or do we just keep silent?"

Some form of advocacy for gay teens who are struggling with emerging sexual orientation is important because, as Krysiak (1987) points out, "gay people are the only minorities that do not have a parent as a role model." Nor are they likely to have a supportive group of peers. The struggle that gay teens face is exacerbated by guilt and fear of disclosure to parents and friends. These factors lead many adolescent homosexuals to adopt dysfunctional behaviors that can put them at risk.

Response of Schools. "For most gay and lesbian students, schools are not welcoming places but scenes of hostility and intolerance, say experts in the problems of gay and lesbian youth" (Willis 1991). The school culture reflects the heterosexual majority. The curriculum, with the exception of token mention of homosexuality in a health education class, generally is silent on issues of sexual orientation. Moreover, it is oblivious to the concerns of gay students in family-living courses, where the subject matter may be alienating, or at least irrelevant, to gay students. As Robert Birle, a former teacher and co-chair of the National Education Association's Gay/Lesbian Caucus, comments: "You don't see the curriculum dealing with the diversity of sexual orientation" (Willis 1991).

Schools often refuse to deal with homosexual issues out of a fear of community reaction. Parents frequently protest that if schools teach about homosexuality, then they are encouraging or approving homosexuality. As a result, schools are reluctant to make information available to students about support services, either those that reasonably might be expected from the counseling department or from community agencies outside the school. Also, school administrators often discourage distribution of information from community support groups or even the publication of a gay teen hotline number in the school newspaper. Thus the response to a fear of community protest cuts off potential help for students who are struggling to understand their sexual orientation.

Alienation and Crises. Any number of studies have demonstrated that gay teens are frequently placed at risk by the circumstances in which they find themselves at school. According to James T. Sears (1991), a senior research associate at the South Carolina Educational Policy Center:

> Being sexually different in a society of sexual sameness exacts a heavy psychological toll. Struggling to cope with their sexual identity, gay and bisexual students are more likely than other youth to attempt suicide, to abuse drugs or alcohol, and to experience academic problems. Of course, gay and bisexual students do not always display these symptoms — in fact, they may excel in schoolwork, extracurricular

151

activities, or sports as a means of hiding their sexual feelings from themselves or others. When they hide their feelings, however, their emotional and sexual development languishes.

In a study by researchers from the University of Washington and the University of Minnesota, 41 of 137 gay or bisexual men interviewed said they had attempted suicide. About half reported multiple attempts (Remafedi et al. 1991). According to the researchers, those who attempted suicide also were more likely to report having been sexually abused, having abused drugs, or having been arrested for misconduct. In a related study by the U.S. Department of Health and Human Services in 1989, gay and lesbian teens were found to be three times as likely to attempt suicide as heterosexual teens. Moreover, gay teens accounted for 30% of all teen suicides. Often, the toll exacted on gay teens is linked to visibility. As Robert W. Deisher at the University of Washington explains: "The majority of kids who are gay as teenagers 'pass' and no one realizes it." The more obvious a student is — that is, the more effeminate appearing or acting — the more likely he will be teased or harassed (*Sheboygan Press*, 31 May 1991).

At-Risk Behaviors of Gay Teens

The profile of at-risk behaviors observed in gay teens is not unlike that of any at-risk group of students. What is different is their underlying causes, which may be difficult to address because of the closeted nature of homosexuality. It is the underlying causes, however, that need to be identified and addressed by educators, parents, and other resource persons — and by the youths themselves — if these at-risk behaviors are to be changed.

School Failure. Three key characteristics that are common in disaffected students in general are also common in gay teens, albeit with a different spin: 1) poor self-image/low self-esteem, 2) alienation from the peer group, and 3) hostility toward authority. Each of these is discussed below.

1. Poor self-image/low self-esteem. Heterosexual youths find positive role models everywhere who affirm their "normality."

Teens struggling with defining their sexual orientation or who have identified themselves as homosexual seldom find positive gay models. Thus they are acculturated through models that tend to deny their sexuality in negative ways. This denial often is internalized as guilt and self-contempt.

Low self-esteem both arises from and leads to feelings of rejection. Even when students have not confided their feelings of sexual confusion to anyone, the rejection of "significant others" is often projected; and that anticipation of rejection can affect personal relationships.

Poor self-image is often evidenced in students who are:

- achieving below expected levels — that is, doing poorly in spite of average or above-average ability;
- failing to see a relationship between effort and achievement;
- displaying immature behavior;
- giving up on difficult tasks instead of persevering;
- not participating in discussions because they feel as though their opinions are not worth sharing or will be rejected.

2. Alienation from the peer group. The barriers that exist between being heterosexual and homosexual often leave gay teens with no trusted friend in whom to confide. Moreover, students who appear to be different often are treated with suspicion, distrust, and open hostility by their peers. Alienated from peers with whom they normally should identify, teenagers coming to grips with their homosexual orientation often act out that social estrangement in the following ways:

- being tardy for class;
- cutting classes;
- not participating in class activities (not dressing for physical education classes, not giving oral presentations, or not participating in other activities that call attention to themselves);
- not participating in extracurricular activities;
- failing to establish goals for a career future.

3. Hostility toward authority. Often coupled with alienation is hostility manifested by the rejection of those who have rejected, or

may be expected to reject, the gay teen. In school this hostility can be acted out in a variety of ways:

- not relating to authority or being rebellious, resulting in recurring discipline problems;
- expressing negative attitudes;
- running away from home or being truant from school;
- abusing alcohol or drugs;
- fighting or verbally abusing other students;
- being sexually aggressive.

As we shall see, the characteristics of low self-esteem, alienation, and hostility that lead to school failure for many gay teens also put them at risk of personal endangerment.

Depression and Suicide. As Robert J. Bidwell (1988) points out: "growing up gay or lesbian is living daily with a terrible secret that no one must ever know." Only a minority of gay teens "come out," or openly admit their homosexuality. Some are exposed by their behavior. But most live hidden lives, fearing the rejection that is a real possibility if their true sexual orientation is discovered. Many gay teens, when they reveal their homosexuality, are thrown out of their homes by their parents or run away rather than endure the physical and emotional abuse of their parents. For a significant number of gay teens, the ultimate response to the depressive effects of denial and concealment or the pain of being "out" is suicide.

The National Teen Suicide Audit, conducted by the Gallup Organization (reported in *Education Week*, 10 April 1991), found that 6% of American teenagers have attempted suicide and that another 15% "have come close to trying." Nearly half of these teens (47%) cited problems at home as the contributing factor. Other factors they identified included depression (23%), problems with friends (22%), and low self-esteem (18%).

The figures for gay teens are higher. Findings in earlier studies (Roesler and Deisher 1972; Remafedi 1987) are echoed in those reported recently by researchers in Minnesota and Washington, who found that 30% of homosexual male teenagers had attempted suicide — with about half of those reporting multiple attempts.

The warning signs for gay teen suicide mirror those of suicide generally:

- a depressed mood that lasts longer than two weeks;
- sleeping much more than usual;
- eating much more or much less than usual;
- restlessness, inability to concentrate in class or tolerate inactivity;
- not enjoying activities that used to be important;
- spending much more time alone; lack of interest in friends;
- feelings of hopelessness;
- sudden change in behavior or reactions; for example, a quiet person becoming suddenly boisterous, an outgoing person becoming exceptionally quiet or withdrawn.

Gay Teens and AIDS. Bidwell (1988) notes that "Many of those rites of passage through which other teens pass are not open to the gay and lesbian adolescent." The normal processes of dating — exchanging glances, sending Valentines, telephoning for a date, going to a movie, walking home hand-in-hand — are denied to the homosexual teenager. And without this healthy pathway toward initial sexual exploration, gay teens often resort to what Bidwell terms the "baths, bars, or bushes." Anonymous sexual encounters do little to foster intimacy or raise self-esteem. Instead, they are likely to increase feelings of guilt and estrangement.

Moreover, anonymous sexual encounters in this era of AIDS are fraught with dangers that go well beyond the normal complement of potential sexually transmitted diseases, such as herpes and gonorrhea. According to a report by Karen Hein, founder and director of the Adolescent AIDS project at the Montefiore Medical Center in the Bronx, "New York accounts for 23% of all reported cases of AIDS among 13- to 21-year-olds in the U.S." (quoted by Brownworth 1992).

Other cities and states present similarly alarming statistics. For example, one in four persons with AIDS in Georgia is an adolescent; and between 30,000 and 40,000 teenagers and young adults in the state are estimated to be HIV-positive. In Los Angeles and Miami, about 20% of reported AIDS cases are among adolescents; in Newark, New Jersey, the figure is 35%.

The highest number of new AIDS cases, according to the Centers for Disease Control, is now among men and women between the ages of 20 and 29. Finding this trend "extremely alarming," former Surgeon General Antonia Novello states, "There is no question that those cases were contracted during adolescence" (quoted in Brownworth 1992).

A study, "AIDS Among Adolescents," reported in the *American Journal of Diseases of Children* (October 1990) provides the following statistics on HIV transmission routes in adolescents aged 13 to 21 in the United States:

Homosexual/bisexual males	51%
Transfusion recipients	22%
Male homosexual intravenous drug users	8%
Heterosexuals	8%
Intravenous drug users	6%
Other	5%

In Karen Hein's words: "We've got to look at some new strategies, not just keep hauling out the old ones like telling kids not to have sex. . . . The point is that wishful thinking, 'Just say no,' and simplistic thinking ought to be part of the past history of the AIDS epidemic. Now we have a growing epidemic on our hands, and we need very, very bold steps to address it" (quoted in Brownworth 1992).

The School's Response to Gay Teens at Risk

If educators are to address the rights and needs of *all* students effectively, including those students who are homosexual or who may be struggling to define their sexual orientation, then they first need to examine their own attitudes and the institutional attitudes prevalent in their schools with regard to gay students. Many of these attitudes are not expressed openly. Others are reflected in school policies, practices, and curricula. Once educators recognize that gay teens have specific social, psychological, and educational needs that may be different from their straight peers, then they need to consider the kinds of support services that schools can provide for these students.

Dealing with Attitudes and Policies. The attitudes gay teens observe among their peers, teachers, counselors, and administrators will determine whether the school can address their needs.

When examining a school's attitudes about gay teens, it is helpful to think of a continuum from *exclusive* to *inclusive.* At the exclusive extreme, the school is blatantly homophobic. Gay students are subjected to verbal harassment, name-calling, labeled as AIDS carriers, or deliberately shunned. In some cases, school authorities look the other way when gay teens are harassed or physically abused.

Midway along the continuum, harassment may not be tolerated; but there is institutional silence on homosexuality. And the curriculum is silent as well. Teachers conduct their lessons on the premise that all students are heterosexual.

As the continuum becomes more inclusive, there is a recognition that some students may be questioning their sexual orientation and that some can be, or are, homosexual. School policies do not tolerate harassment, and the curriculum might give token recognition to a different sexual orientation.

At the fully inclusive end on the attitudinal continuum, teachers do not assume uniform heterosexuality and use language that recognizes sexual diversity. The curriculum reflects this recognition and acknowledges the culture and history of homosexuals as a group in a way that validates students' identity. In an inclusive school, teachers and counselors make it easy for gay students to approach them for advice and support.

Following are five "attitude indicators" that let gay teens know that they can ask for help or talk about their feelings:

157

1. Teachers and counselors use language that indicates an awareness of sexual diversity; they do not assume that all teens are heterosexual.
2. Teachers speak out against harassment and indicate that humor at the expense of gays is offensive.
3. Teachers recognize and openly discuss the contributions of homosexuals; for example, an English class might read and discuss the works of gay and lesbian writers.
4. Teachers and counselors display books or posters that show they are open to discussing homosexuality.
5. Counselors invite students whom they believe to be wrestling with sexual orientation to discuss their feelings. (Gloria Krysiak shares this gay student's comment: "It has to be easier for you to ask than for me to just come out and tell you.")

Gay teens tend to be a very silent minority. Many have been taught by observation or through personal experience that rejection and pain can be expected from disclosure of their sexual orientation. In order to reach those gay teens who may be at risk, teachers and counselors will need to demonstrate their openness in everyday conversations and in the way they deal with selected curriculum content in their classrooms. Also, support for teachers and counselors who attempt to serve gay teens needs to be provided at the institutional level through policies and practices that include the following:

Development of non-discrimination policies. School employees need to be secure within the institution in order to work effectively with students, teachers, counselors, and administrators. Policies that affect the way school employees are treated get translated into how students are treated. Therefore, non-discrimination policies must begin with employment. Is it acceptable for a staff member to be gay or lesbian? If known homosexuals are routinely discriminated against in hiring, or if employees are fired or otherwise "counseled out" when their homosexual orientation is discovered, then the clear message to gay students is that they can never expect any meaningful support for their needs.

Development of inclusive curricula. Gay and lesbian issues are part of the human condition and need to be included in the curriculum through readings, discussions, or projects when appropriate to a specific course. And the language teachers use and the manner in which topics are addressed let students know whether it is permissible to deal with gay and lesbian issues candidly. Teachers should be free to — and encouraged to — include gay and lesbian issues in their lesson plans, in reading assignments, and in lists of potential topics for written assignments or class presentations. Individuals who are gay or lesbian, or parents of gay children, can be invited as guest speakers when appropriate.

The health curriculum is an area in which sensitivity to language is important. For example, when dealing with various prevention measures in an AIDS education unit, the phrase "abstinence until marriage" is not a context in which gay teens see themselves. A more appropriate phrase might be "restricting sex to a monogamous relationship," which better matches gay teens' circumstances and avoids imposing a heterosexual social context. Likewise, in "family living" contexts, the use of non-gender-specific language in discussions about relationships allows students for whom male-female pair configuration is an ill fit to enter the discussion.

Professional development. If teachers are to work effectively with at-risk gay teens, they must become informed about gay issues. Such professional development will include reading, interacting with informed professionals in the community, and becoming familiar with local resources, such as gay organizations, health care agencies, counseling services, and youth groups. Many of these local groups can provide films, books, pamphlets, and bibliographies, some of which can be used with students. It is also important that school officials endorse comprehensive professional development, because it conveys broad attitudinal support within the institution, as well as creates a cadre of professionals with specific skills and knowledge to assist at-risk gay teens.

Along with ongoing professional development, the schools should establish a professional library with resource information on gay and lesbian issues, the development of sexual orientation in adolescence, and other topics related to homosexuality.

Support Services for Gay Teens

When a school's attitudes and policies are responsive to the needs of gay teens, then educators can teach tolerance and acceptance. They can help gay teens understand themselves, as well as correct some of the stereotypes of homosexuality. They can debunk the myths that put gay teens at risk. Positive attitudes and policies within the institution also allow educators to create support services in the school for gay teens and to develop links with outside organizations, which can provide additional services for the diverse, individual needs of gay teens. Following is a description of some of the support services needed by gay teens.

The library. Accurate and up-to-date information is the foundation for helping students to help themselves. School libraries should abandon curricular silence about homosexuality and provide information that many teenagers need as they struggle to understand their sexual orientation. Libraries can provide basic support services by maintaining books, pamphlets, magazines, and audiovisual materials that discuss gay and lesbian issues. Both nonfiction and fiction works serve to validate that "being gay or lesbian is a natural variation of human sexual behavior; it may be deviant statistically, but not clinically" (Schaecher 1989).

Library resources serve gay teens directly, but they also can raise the level of awareness about gay and lesbian issues among students and staff generally. As knowledge about homosexuality increases in positive ways, incidents of homophobia and harassment of gay students tend to decrease.

Local gay/lesbian support groups or organizations often can provide bibliographies that librarians can use to familiarize themselves with available print materials, films, videos, and so on.

The counseling center. If counselors are viewed as knowledgeable about and supportive of gay and lesbian issues, then it is easier for students to approach them with questions about sexual orientation. Most adolescents are reluctant to discuss sexual matters with adults and feel awkward doing so. This reluctance is

160

intensified for the gay student who is worried about the reaction others may have to the disclosure of a homosexual orientation.

In particular, gay students may not be ready to face the reaction of parents and peers on disclosing their sexual orientation. So the first role of the counselor may be to help the student to prepare for the reaction prior to disclosure to parents, friends, and others whose acceptance may be problematic (Krysiak 1987).

Unfortunately, in some school districts, the policy requires counselors to inform parents when they discuss sexual matters with students. Students usually know whether they can confide in counselors; and so, when policy compromises counselor confidentiality, students in general — and gay students in particular — are reluctant to discuss sensitive issues with their counselors that they are not yet ready to discuss with their parents.

Under these circumstances, two courses of action are possible. First, counselors, teachers, and administrators can work to sensitize the school board to the constraints of existing policy and work to change the policy. Second, counselors and teachers can inform students about alternatives to in-school counseling, such as local youth group services and telephone hotlines.

Counselors are a key support service. They can help gay students understand themselves and develop appropriate coping skills. And they can channel gay students into self-protective strategies that help them eliminate inappropriate or dysfunctional behaviors that place them at risk.

A "Special Place." "I don't think I fit in anywhere. I don't know where the line is that I shouldn't cross. Maybe I'll always be alone." This comment from a student at New York's Harvey Milk School (quoted by Getlin 1990) is typical of many gay teens. In a very few communities across the nation, schools have established "special places" for gay adolescents. One of these is the Harvey Milk School in New York City. This school was established in 1985 by the Hetrick-Martin Institute for Lesbian and Gay Youth in cooperation with the New York City Board of Education. Named for the gay San Francisco supervisor who was assassin-

161

ated in 1978, the Harvey Milk School, located near Greenwich Village, is the nation's only public school for gay, lesbian, and transsexual adolescents. Students who attend the school find it to be a haven from their regular public school, where they were frequently harassed or ostracized by teachers as well as other students. Josh Getlin (1990), in a feature article about the school, writes about a 14-year-old lesbian who, prior to entering the Harvey Milk School, said she "felt safer hanging out on street corners than spending time in the schoolyard." The common feature of school-sponsored "special places" is that they are, fundamentally, dropout prevention alternatives.

While most school districts are unprepared philosophically or fiscally to provide an alternative school for gay adolescents, many might develop "special places" within schools, where gay and lesbian students can feel comfortable and learn to deal positively with their sexual orientation. A model for this type of program is Project 10, founded in 1984 by Virginia Uribe in Los Angeles.

Project 10 was organized as an in-school counseling program in response to the unmet needs of gay and lesbian students in the Los Angeles schools. The project is designed, according to its literature, "to keep students in school, off drugs, and sexually responsible." Project staff conduct workshops for administrators and other staff, provide direct student counseling, develop liaison relationships with community social and health organizations, and offer outreach services to parents.

Project 10 is not without critics, however. As any school that initiates an on-campus program for homosexual youth might anticipate, there are those in the community who see the project as a way of "legitimizing" homosexuality or "recruiting" teens into a homosexual lifestyle. Because of these criticisms, many school officials are more comfortable with referring students to community organizations, rather than establishing in-school programs.

Youth groups. Youth groups for gay teens exist in a number of larger communities. Usually sponsored by social service organizations, health agencies, hospitals, churches, or other institutions, most focus on some form of counseling or group discussion process dealing with self-esteem, personal values, responsible behavior, and related issues. And many attempt to structure a system of peer support.

A model for gay and lesbian youth groups is Indiana's IYG, with headquarters in Indianapolis. IYG, originally called the Indianapolis Youth Group prior to branching out to additional sites, is a social, support, and educational group for gay, lesbian, and bisexual youth under age 21. The organization has three primary goals: 1) to provide a safe, comfortable place for gay, lesbian, and bisexual youth to meet and socialize with others their own age; 2) to provide a support system for these youth; and 3) to educate them in ways to reduce high-risk behaviors, including behaviors associated with HIV/AIDS infection and with substance abuse.

Self-identified gay teens can participate in a variety of IYG activities:

- bi-weekly educational meetings;
- social events, such as dances and roller-skating parties, that provide a safe place for youth to socialize;
- a "toxic family" support group to help youth deal with mental and physical abuse from family and peers;
- retreats to develop self-esteem and leadership skills;
- peer-counseling training so that teens can be part of the support system for other youth;
- IYG Ambassadors, who present workshops and panel discussions on an outreach basis to gay, lesbian, and bisexual youth;
- IYG Interactive Theater, which presents skits to educate others about gay/lesbian/bisexual youth needs and to educate all youth about AIDS;
- a pen-pal network that matches youth under 21 with compatible pen pals from across the United States.

The founder of the IYG was Christopher Gonzalez, who was interviewed for this essay. Gonzalez served as IYG executive director until his death in 1994. According to Gonzalez, most of the teenagers involved in IYG programs come because of feelings of isolation and rejection. He pointed out that "Like members of other minority groups, gay, lesbian, and bisexual youth face discrimination, but generally more often and more severe. . . . Among other minority groups the family acts as a counterforce to the effects of discrimination; however, among gay, lesbian, and bisexual youth the non-accepting family can exacerbate the pressures rather than help to relieve them."

Gonzalez stressed that IYG group facilitators are not counselors, but youth in need can contact IYG for referral to crisis or ongoing counseling. IYG stresses a high level of professionalism in its interactions with adolescents. The organization does not encourage dating or sexual relations between members, and facilitators are not permitted to date youth group members. Personal information shared at IYG meetings is considered confidential.

IYG has received national recognition and is supported with funding from the Centers for Disease Control and the Indiana State Department of Health. During 1990-91, partial funding also was provided by the U.S. Conference of Mayors. The organization operates centers or chapters in nine other Indiana cities besides the headquarters in Indianapolis. The executive directors and other staff provide technical assistance to cities in several other states where there is interest in establishing similar gay/lesbian/bisexual support groups.

Hotlines. Contact with IYG usually begins with a call to the Gay/Lesbian/Bisexual Youth Hotline: 1-800-347-TEEN (1-800-347-8336), which operates Thursdays through Sundays from 7:00 p.m. until midnight EST. The IYG hotline, to date, is the only national, toll-free hotline for gay teens that is peer-facilitated. When a teenager calls, he or she talks to another teen who has participated in a 50-hour peer-facilitator training program.

Hotlines provide gay teens with a "risk-free" or anonymous way to get information that can, literally, save their lives. The Teens Teaching About AIDS hotline (1-800-234-TEEN —1-800-

234-8336 — Monday through Friday, 4:00 to 8:00 p.m. EST) also is peer-facilitated and can help any teenager learn more about HIV infection and prevention. Other hotlines respond to questions about AIDS for all ages (in English and in Spanish), runaways, and sexually transmitted diseases.

School leaders need to identify local hotlines that also may meet the needs of at-risk students. Gay teens, or any student for that matter, benefit when the school makes them aware of available resources. Many hotlines, like IYG's Gay/Lesbian/Bisexual Youth Hotline, can refer callers to direct assistance, such as youth groups, counselors, or health professionals who can help teenagers deal positively with questions and problems related to sexual orientation and other matters.

Conclusion

Fear of controversy, cultural taboos, and to some degree, an irrational fear of homosexuality have prevented many educators from dealing effectively with gay and lesbian young people. Fear leads to discrimination, and this discrimination has caused immeasurable losses to our nation's teenagers.

The climate in most schools is such that gay teens rarely are willing to expose themselves to the ridicule, harassment, and abuse that comes when they openly acknowledge their sexual orientation. Instead, they hide their sexuality in order to pass for "normal." Such concealment takes a terrible psychological and emotional toll. The result can be behavioral choices that place adolescents at risk of school failure, disease, and even death.

To counteract these conditions, educators will need to acknowledge that homosexuality is a variation in sexual orientation and that they have a professional responsibility to provide information, counseling, and other services to help gay teens understand their sexual orientation and to avoid high-risk behaviors. They will need to regard homophobic prejudice in the same light as other prejudices, such as racism or anti-Semitism. And they will need to take deliberate steps to eliminate the negative attitudes and actions of students and staff in their schools that place gay teens at risk.

References

Bidwell, Robert J. "The Gay and Lesbian Teen: A Case of Denied Adolescence." *Journal of Pediatric Health Care* 2 (1988): 3-8. (Reprinted in Project 10 Handbook.)

Brownworth, Victoria A. "America's Worst-Kept Secret." *The Advocate* (March 1992): 38-46.

Flax, Ellen. "Significant Numbers of Teenagers Unsure of Sexual Orientation, New Study Finds." *Education Week*, 15 April 1992, p. 4.

Getlin, Josh. "School Is a Special Place for Gay Students." *Milwaukee Journal*, 29 April 1990, p. G10.

Krysiak, Gloria J. "Needs of Gay Students for Acceptance and Support." *The School Counselor* 34 (March 1987): 304-307.

Lawton, Milton. "More Than a Third of Teens Surveyed Say They Have Contemplated Suicide." *Education Week*, 10 April 1991, p. 5.

"Nineteen Percent of High School Students Have Had at Least Four Sex Partners, Study Finds." *Education Week*, 15 April 1992, p. 4.

Remafedi, G.J. "Homosexual Youth: A Challenge to Contemporary Society." *Journal of the American Medical Association* 258 (1987): 222-25.

Remafedi, G.J., et al. "Risk Factors for Attempted Suicide in Gay and Bisexual Youth." *Pediatrics* 87 (June 1991): 869-75.

Roesler, T., and Deisher, R.W. "Youthful Male Homosexuality." *Journal of the American Medical Association* 219 (1972): 1018-23.

Schaecher, Robert. "Reducing Homophobia Among Educators and Students." *Independent School* 48 (Winter 1989): 29-35.

Sears, James T. "Helping Students Understand and Accept Sexual Diversity." *Educational Leadership* (September 1991): 54-56.

"Study: Thirty Percent of Gay, Bisexual Male Teens Tried Suicide." *Sheboygan Press*, 31 May 1991, p. 3.

Willis, Scott. "Teaching Gay Students." *ASCD Update* 33, no. 3 (March 1991).

GENDER EQUITY

by Eileen Veronica Hilke and
Carol Conway-Gerhardt

The issue of gender equity has been on the education fore-
front since the 1972 passage of Title IX legislation prohibiting sex discrimination in education programs that
receive federal funds. Since that time, several pieces of related
legislation have been passed; but gender inequity continues to
exist in schools. In fact, many articles, television broadcasts, and
radio discussions have alerted the public to the need for gender
equity in the school, workplace, and community.

Following are a few of the concerns that are addressed by advocates of gender equity:

- Girls start school academically ahead of boys but finish
  school academically behind boys.
- By high school, self-esteem in females falls dramatically.
- Males outperform females in the American College Testing
  Program (ACT) and on the Scholastic Aptitude Test (SAT).
- Math and science fields are dominated by males.

To counteract inequity, educators need a greater awareness of
gender issues and an understanding of strategies for change.
Through a cyclical model of awareness, analysis, action, and assessment, various individuals and responsible groups — such as
school boards, administrators, and teachers — can make a positive
difference for both sexes, but in particular for girls and women.
This essay provides practical suggestions for new and experienced
classroom teachers to develop gender equitable classrooms.
Parents, too, can learn various strategies to assist the process.

This essay is condensed from Eileen Veronica Hilke and Carol Conway-
Gerhardt, *Gender Equity in Education*, Fastback 372 (Bloomington, Ind.: Phi
Delta Kappa Educational Foundation, 1994).

Defining Gender Equity

The term *gender equity is* defined as follows:

Gender encompasses not only the concept of sex, but also the social and cultural meanings attributed to being female or male. Embedded in every social interaction is an underlying sexuality; thus the sex(es) of the persons engaged in the interaction, even though seeming to have no direct relation to what is going on, actually may be central to the interaction. According to researchers Biklen and Pollard, "Gender is the social construction of sex" (1993, p. 1).

Equity means "justice, impartiality, the giving or desiring to give each person his or her due," according to *Webster's Unabridged Dictionary.* Concern about gender equity arises from the differentiated expectations that people hold for females and males, based solely on sex difference. *Gender equity* and *sex equity* often are defined similarly.

For example, the Affirmative Action definition for *gender equity* is "the elimination of sex-role stereotyping and sex bias from the educational process, thus providing the opportunity and environment to validate and empower individuals as they make appropriate career and life choices."

Bitters and Foxwell (1990) define *sex equity* as "freedom from favoritism based on gender. Achieving sex equity enables both women and men of all races and ethnic backgrounds to develop skills needed in the home and in the paid labor force, and that suit the individual's 'informed interests' and abilities."

A typical school policy definition for *gender equity* is "equal education free of discrimination on the basis of sex. It means helping students free themselves from limiting, rigid, sex-role stereotypes and sex bias. It means students will understand, think about, and prepare for a future characterized by change, especially in male and female life roles, relationships, and careers" (Sheboygan Area School District 1991).

Several pieces of legislation have made gender equity a legal requirement. The basis of this legislation is Title IX of the Educational Amendments Act of 1972, which prohibits discrimination based on sex in education programs that receive federal funds. Regulations were issued in 1975 that cover many implementation issues, from admissions and employment in higher education to athletics, course offerings, counseling, and differentiated treatment of students in elementary and secondary schools (Rebell and Murdaugh 1992).

A comprehensive effort to infuse equity into education programs began in 1976 with the Vocational Education Act, which requires each state to hire an individual to oversee the implementation of gender equity initiatives in the vocational education system. The Career Education Incentive Act of 1977, which is no longer operational, had a goal to eliminate sex-role stereotyping and bias from career education materials. It was superseded in 1978 by Title IV, under which Sex Desegregation Technical Assistance Grants were provided to local education agencies to deal with sex desegregation. Over the next decade, the impact of this legislation waned. But in 1987 the Department of Education resumed providing grants to help schools and communities deal with race, sex, and national origin biases. These grants took their impetus from earlier legislation, the Civil Rights Act of 1964.

The Carl D. Perkins Vocational Education Act of 1984 emphasized making vocational education accessible to all students. Grants were developed for single parents, homemakers, and young women. Equity program grants were intended to encourage self-sufficiency and eliminate sex-role stereotyping and discrimination in vocational education (Bitters and Foxwell 1990, pp. 15-17).

How Gender Inequity Affects Females

It will be helpful to examine gender inequity in order to understand gender equity. In the late 1980s the American Association of University Women conducted a poll of 3,000 school children. The association's subsequent report, *Shortchanging Girls, Shortchanging America* (1990), declared that girls face a pervasive bias against them from preschool through high school in textbooks, teachers, and tests.

A further synthesis of 1,331 research studies about girls in schools, *How Schools Shortchange Girls* (1992), revealed that girls and boys are not treated equally in our public schools and that they do not receive the same quality, or even quantity, of education.

The key concerns that have surfaced in research by individuals and the AAUW and other organizations include: 1) low self-esteem, 2) low academic achievement, and 3) low aspirations or limited educational and career goals for a high percentage of females. Each of these concerns is discussed below.

Low Self-Esteem. Without a doubt, family and societal influences already have made impressions on children before they start school. However, formal schooling too often brings systematic, if unintentional, neglect of girls' needs in the form of diminished quality and quantity of classroom attention. The result is low self-esteem.

The 1990 AAUW study showed that, on a self-esteem comparison index, girls start somewhat lower in self-esteem than boys in elementary school and drop off dramatically by middle and high school. Sixty percent of elementary girls and 69% of elementary boys say they are "happy the way I am," a key indicator of self-esteem. By high school, girls' self-esteem falls to only 29%, while boys' self-esteem declines to 46% (AAUW 1990, p. 11).

Shortchanging Girls, Shortchanging America reported:

- Teachers initiate more communication with males than with females in the classroom, strengthening boys' sense of importance.
- Teachers ask boys more complex, abstract, and open-ended questions, providing better opportunities for active learning.
- In class projects and assignments, teachers are more likely to give detailed instructions to boys and more likely to take over and finish the task for girls, depriving them of active learning.
- Boys are praised more often than girls for the intellectual content and quality of their work, while girls are praised more often for neatness and form.
- When teachers criticize boys, they often tell them that their failings are due to lack of effort. Girls are not given this mes-

170

sage, suggesting that effort would not improve their results (pp. 19-20).

Boys appear to have greater confidence than girls in their own talents, a connecting point between feelings and actions. In fact, almost twice as many boys as girls refer to their talents as what they like most about themselves. Boys who believe they are good at sports are particularly confident; as adolescents, they rate themselves four times as highly as girls do (Schuster 1991, p. 23).

Girls often express overwhelming concern about their body image, or how they see themselves physically. The focus on physical appearance or body image seems to be a significant component of self-esteem, which peaks during adolescence. Girls are socialized at an early age to believe that they should be thin and attractive. In fact, girls are "well aware that they are often judged on the basis of looks, whereas boys are more likely to be judged by their accomplishments or physical ability." This unrealistic and, for many girls, unattainable image is reinforced continually. From magazines to television and music videos, the "ideal woman" typically is portrayed as "white, tall, most often blond, and above all thin" (Jaffee 1991, p. 71).

Self-esteem shapes a person's ambitions and actions. Thus low self-esteem diminishes a person's future. Interactions in the educational setting coupled with "bigger-than-life" expectations from society, especially as they are portrayed in the media, help to diminish girls' self-esteem.

Low Academic Achievement. Academic achievement is so important to success in life that many parents begin to stress achievement before their children ever enter school. Also, the first communication from the school to parents often conveys some assessment of achievement. Thus a key question in gender equity is to what extent actual gender differences and differentiated treatment of boys and girls affect academic achievement.

Myra Sadker (1991) summarized the situation by indicating that elementary school girls are equal to or ahead of boys in every academic area, even math and science; but as they progress through school, girls fall behind boys, especially in math and science. Middle school seems to be the point at which boys forge ahead and girls fall behind (p. 42).

Often, what occurs is differentiated treatment for boys and girls. For example, when boys and girls have similar math scores, boys are more likely to be assigned to the highest ability group than are girls (Scott and McCollum 1993). Similarly, during science projects, "girls spent 25% less time than boys manipulating the equipment and four times as much time watching and listening" (p. 179).

In general, females earn higher grades on essays and score higher on Advanced Placement (AP) essay examinations. However, males score higher on the AP multiple-choice questions and, as a result, earn overall higher AP test scores. Analysis of this information indicates that performance on the multiple-choice section of the AP test underpredicts college grades for females, while essay test results are equally predictive for both sexes (Linn 1991, pp. 14-16).

When colleges assess the likely success of applicants, they usually use standardized tests. Sadker says, "Currently, according to standardized tests, males score better than females in both math and verbal sections of the Preliminary Scholastic Aptitude Test (PSAT) and the Scholastic Aptitude Test (SAT) and in most of the achievement tests students need to take to get into highly selective colleges" (1991, p. 42). Based on the American College Test-English (ACT-E) and the Scholastic Aptitude Test-Verbal (SAT-V), research shows that there are gender differences associated with cognitive responses. Males better discriminate among responses on multiple-choice questions, while females are better at organizing diverse ideas and writing effectively.

Female college graduates who plan to attend graduate or professional school do not score as well as males on the math and verbal sections of the Graduate Record Exam, the MCAT (for entrance into medical school), or the GMAT (for entrance to business school). However, in subsequent coursework, females get better grades than males. Some theorists contend that this occurs because standardized tests are biased against women. Others point to research that shows females are more likely to get high grades not just because of achievement, but also because of passive accepting behavior (Sadker 1991, p. 42). Statistics show that females earn slightly higher grades in high school and college mathematics courses, including the most advanced courses. "Within groups having the same course experience, males earn higher [test] scores while females earn higher grades" (Linn 1991, pp. 22-23).

Recent research by A.M. Gallagher cites another factor, pointing to the males' confidence in their mathematical abilities and females' lack of confidence as a motive for females to conform more readily to course expectations and to follow class procedures (Linn 1991, p. 29).

Pollard, who focused on analyzing gender differences in academic achievement, considered biological, sociocultural, psychological, and experiential factors. Out of her work, she concluded that such research is hampered by three problems: 1) inconsistent data on sex differences and achievement, 2) limited discussion of gender and achievement beyond the white middle class, and 3) inadequate attention to the relationship between achievement in the school and the workplace (Pollard 1993, p. 94).

Pollard pointed out, for example, that grade point averages from a large sample of seventh- and eighth-graders show that gender-role identity influences achievement more than biological sex does. Additionally, Pollard observed that studies of middle-class, white females overlook racial, ethnic, and socioeconomic factors. Pollard also found "that women between the ages of 25 and 32, who earned bachelor's degrees, were more likely to be unemployed (but looking for work) than men; and when employed, were more likely to be in lower paying jobs than men. Furthermore, when women held jobs similar to those men held, they earned less" (p. 96).

Pollard's research on gender differences in academic achievement reveal that the relationships among influential factors are truly multifaceted and cannot be predicted on the basis of sex alone. Despite encouraging evidence of successful academic achievement among girls and women, gender equity has not yet been achieved. Many women, Pollard believes, still are discouraged from achieving in certain areas, and others do not push themselves in school because of continuing perceptions that academic achievement is not feminine (p. 97). Even when females do achieve in school, they receive fewer rewards in the workplace. Adelman (1991) suggests that this fact sends a message to women that their achievement does not matter and ultimately discourages them from striving to excel.

Controversy continues over whether teachers respond to behavior more than to the sex of the student. If boys are more assertive or disruptive and teachers respond to their behavior, then girls receive less teacher attention because they are less assertive or disruptive, not because they are female. Another consideration is that teachers may expect boys to achieve more or to be more disruptive and may respond to these anticipated behaviors. Whether teachers are responding to real or anticipated behaviors, the consequence is that simply providing equal access to the same courses will not result in equal treatment.

For some educators, the answer lies in creating outcome equity — that is, having girls be as assertive and performance-centered as boys are. Johnston Nicholson says that educators need to believe that "girls are ready for leadership, ready for new opportunities, ready to respond to high expectations. This implies that we should be designing programs and environments for girls that emphasize risk more than comfort" (Johnston Nicholson 1991, p. 89).

Low Aspirations/Limited Goals. Since low self-esteem hampers girls' aspirations and actions, girls often "dream less, risk less, and try less when the time comes to make crucial decisions about courses of study and choices of careers" (AAUW 1990, p. 10). In fact, the AAUW survey shows that as girls grow up, they lose confidence in their abilities, expect less from life, and lose interest in challenging classes and careers, especially in math and science (p. 23). Girls are less likely than boys to feel "pretty good at a lot of things." When polled, less than a third of the girls expressed this level of confidence, compared to almost half of the boys. A 10-

174

point gap in confidence between boys and girls in elementary school increases to 19 points by high school (p. 26).

Although the general pubic believes that peer group pressure dominates the actions, values, and goals of teenagers, the AAUW survey shows that adults, including teachers and parents, actually have a greater impact on adolescents, and especially on girls. Understanding this phenomenon means realizing that girls' feelings about their academic performance correlate strongly with their relationships with teachers, who are predominantly female. One conclusion is that adults, including teachers, demonstrate less faith in girls' abilities than they do in boys' abilities, causing girls to lose their sense of academic self-esteem as they grow.

Less than 50% of the girls in elementary school said they feel pride in their schoolwork, and that proportion dropped to only 12% in high school. By contrast, boys tend to perceive adults as believing that they can accomplish things; thus boys usually have higher self-esteem as they go through adolescence (AAUW 1990, pp. 29-30).

One key concern is that girls often lose out on their potential futures in math and science. The AAUW survey found a crucial — and circular — relationship among self-esteem levels, interest in mathematics and science, and career aspirations:

- Girls and boys who like mathematics and science have higher levels of self-esteem; and girls and boys with higher levels of self-esteem like math and science.
- Girls and boys who like math and science are more likely to aspire to careers in occupations where these subjects are essential.
- Girls and boys who like math and science are more likely to aspire to careers as professionals. Indeed, this relationship is stronger for girls than for boys.
- Girls who like math are more confident about their appearance and worry less about others liking them.
- Girls and boys who like math and science hold onto their career dreams more stubbornly. They are less likely to

175

believe that they will be something different from what they want to be (p. 31).

Most girls and boys start out liking math and science and having confidence in their abilities, especially in the early grades. However, by high school the percentage of girls who like math drops 20 points from 81% to 61%, while the percentage of boys who like math drops 12 points from 84% to 72% percent (AAUW 1990, p. 32). In addition, girls perceive their difficulties with math as "personal failures," as "not being smart enough." Girls have internalized society's lesson that "girls aren't good at math and science" (p. 12). The boys perceive their problems with math as math itself being either "unimportant" or "not useful" (p. 32).

Science statistics are similar. The percentage of girls who like science drops from 75% in elementary school to 63% in high school. The percentage of boys who like science starts at 82% in elementary school and drops to 72% in high school. Those girls who dislike science in high school usually say science is "uninteresting," while boys who dislike it say science is "unimportant" (Schuster 1991, p. 35).

Career aspirations, as well as educational goals, tend to reflect students' perceptions, both in terms of liking subjects and believing they can be successful in those subjects or in careers based on those subjects. The challenge for teachers and parents is to help all students — and, in particular, girls — to identify and maintain high aspirations.

A Model for Eliminating Gender Inequity

Developing gender equity can be accomplished by using a cyclical model that incorporates four stages: awareness, analysis, action, and assessment.

The first task is to create *awareness* of the inequities that exist for students, particularly females, in the school setting. A committee should be developed and charged with devising a plan to promote gender equity. That plan should be shared with and approved by the school board. As part of the plan, staff, students, families, and community members should learn about ways that students are treated differently in their homes, schools, and communities based on their gender. Discussion should include potential negative consequences of gender inequity and ways to make positive changes.

Analysis centers on the stakeholders taking a serious look at their situation — classroom, home, worksite — and determining how and where gender inequity exists. Being aware of the problem allows each individual to isolate his or her verbal and nonverbal communications and to establish possible ways to work toward greater equity. Such analyses can be aided by gender equity checklists, videotaping for self-analysis, and peer interaction.

Taking *action* is the next step. In the classroom, this can mean simply waiting for all students — especially less demonstrative girls — to respond to a question, instead of accepting a blurted-out answer of a more aggressive student. It can mean taking positive steps toward creating a total school environment that respects all people and tolerates no putdowns.

Assessing the effects of strategies to promote gender equity will determine the next round of the cycle. *Assessment* can be accomplished through self-study and discussion, identifying specific classroom strategies and recording the results of their use, and peer coaching. The results of such assessment will direct the next awareness activity and analysis of additional needs.

Implementing the Model

In order to implement this model in schools, the school board, administrators, and teachers will play distinct roles. The following sections discuss these roles.

School Board Initiatives. Since the school board develops policies and allocates funds, it should play an integral role in developing, promoting, and implementing a gender equity plan. One way to develop awareness at the school board level is to invite a gender equity consultant to present an instructional session for board members. Such an activity may be as short as a half-hour or as extensive as a one- or two-day workshop. The awareness activity should include providing board members with information about current state and federal equity laws. This information will assist the board in understanding its legal responsibilities. In addition, a videotape of classroom situations might be useful to help board members identify specific examples of inequity. Commercially prepared videos on gender equity are available.

The board should participate in developing a gender equity team or committee, whose membership is a balanced representation of males and females from various racial and ethnic backgrounds. The team should be composed of 10 to 12 individuals drawn from the staff and the community. The purpose of this group is to analyze district policies and procedures, to broadly plan a gender equity program, and to assist in implementing the plan and then evaluating its success. The board also will need to budget for staff development, including the purchase of resource materials.

Principal Initiatives. The broad goals of the gender equity plan should allow individual administrators to develop equity objectives that are tailored specifically to their schools. Principals can make a positive impact in several areas:

1. School environment. Principals can sensitize staff and students to the importance of gender-fair posters, bulletin boards, and other visual materials that avoid sex stereotypes. Announcements over the school public address system and material in school publications should be gender-fair.

2. Staffing. Principals can take care to hire staff with males and females in all roles — teaching, clerical, food service, custodial. Employees should model gender equity awareness. Avoiding stereotyping is important, too. For example, there should be male primary teachers as well as female, and female high school science teachers as well as male.

3. Co-curricular activities. Principals should ensure that a balanced program of sports activities, equitably funded, is provided for boys and girls, and that coeducational sports also are available.

4. Parent involvement. Principals should actively involve staff and parents in the equity plan so that they feel a strong sense of ownership. The administrator can identify what already has been done and build on the efforts of the past. In addition, he or she can help to revise school policies and procedures as needed.

5. Staff development. Inservice programs can be arranged for teachers, counselors, and other professional staff with a focus on awareness and implementation of equity activities that can be used with students. Principals should ensure that support staff are aware of gender equity issues and that they have strategies for equitable treatment of students and others in the school environment. Students also should be informed about gender issues and equity policies.

Inservice programs for counselors should help them challenge stereotypes and learn how to counsel women about nontraditional roles. Student internships or job shadowing can help show women in successful, nonstereotypical careers. Females should be encouraged to take courses in technology and advanced math and science, so that their future career options are not limited.

Teacher Initiatives. Teachers are the key to effective change. They should be supported by the principal. A top-down administrative mandate to be more sensitive to the role of females will not be as effective as teachers collaborating to institute change. Empowering teachers to develop activities that change expectations for both male and female students is the most effective way to see a change in the classroom environment.

In terms of curriculum, the materials selected for classroom use and the way information is presented are important to gender equity. A review of the existing curriculum is a first step. Lessons and instructional materials should be evaluated for gender bias. Gender-neutral language is important; for example, "worker" instead of "workman."

Textbooks should portray both men and women in a positive manner. Female as well as male role models need to be represented in all resource materials. Teachers may need to check copyright dates and be aware that older materials sometimes contain gender stereotypes. Such materials can be used, but teachers also may want to use such texts as learning experiences to heighten students' awareness of gender issues.

Likewise, as teachers cooperate across departments, courses should be structured to encourage both sexes to take all classes. Boys should not be made to feel uncomfortable taking family and consumer education classes; girls should feel comfortable in technology education. Schedules should facilitate gender equity, and classes should not be scheduled so as to force students to choose between fields.

In terms of instruction, students should not be divided by sex. Boys and girls should work together as lab partners and reading partners. Segregation leads to unhealthy competition. Teachers should praise students who work together cooperatively and share leadership roles.

Techniques that foster achievement and equity include: 1) coaching — assisting the learner through modeling and dialogue that develop problem-solving skills; 2) collaborative learning — fostering an environment where cooperative instead of competitive learning occurs; 3) interdisciplinary teaching — dealing with real-world problems from different subject areas; and 4) hands-on projects — allowing students to demonstrate knowledge (Vandell and Fishbein 1990, p. 4).

Technology instruction is particularly important for female students. According to Burstyn, "Our society rewards those who develop skills related to technology. So long as women are not expected to work at or accept jobs involving the use of sophisticated technology, they will be denied access to the economic and social power the jobs provide" (1993, p. 114). Some of this instruction can be done through teacher modeling, such as when a teacher uses interactive technological systems.

Many classroom activities can promote gender equity. Following are sample activities that can be adapted for a particular grade or subject.

1. Ask students to select a book and to review the text and illustrations for the roles that females and males portray. Discuss the differences between historical fiction and contemporary works. Look at the copyright date and discuss how attitudes toward gender roles have changed over time. Identify stereotypes.

2. Ask students to research three careers of interest to them. Have them determine the type of education required and write a list of personal expectations for a future job.

3. Invite a guest speaker to talk about advantages and disadvantages of a particular career. The teacher might avoid stereotyping, for example, by inviting a male nurse instead of a female nurse.

4. Ask students to watch three prime-time television shows and determine the level of respect, intelligence, and responsibility assigned to each character. If gender inequity is observed, ask students how the script might be rewritten to make the show more equitable.

5. Help students to brainstorm examples of gender stereotyping. List the ideas on the chalkboard to enhance awareness of bias.

6. Ask students to rewrite a traditional fairy tale, assigning positive traits to both male and female characters.

7. Help students design and administer a survey that asks younger children about their favorite toys and why they enjoy playing with them. Analyze the similarities and differences between boys and girls.

8. Invite students to analyze magazine ads. How are sex stereotypes used to sell merchandise?

9. Review historical fiction to analyze female roles. For younger children, read passages from such books as *Caddie Woodlawn* by Carol Ryrie Brink, *Little Women* by Louisa May Alcott, or *Little House on the Prairie* by Laura Ingalls Wilder. List the jobs that female characters perform. Compare the work and social expectations of the historical time period with today's expectations.

10. Ask students to choose a famous person they admire. List positive and negative characteristics of this person. Explain his or her job, relationships to others, and positive things done for society. Has gender either helped or hindered success?

In terms of self-assessment, teachers can check on their own biases by asking a colleague or the school media specialist to video-tape a segment of their teaching day. Then, in the privacy of their home or classroom, teachers can analyze their teaching behaviors. This self-check activity will enhance teachers' awareness of how they present information and interact with students. If teachers feel comfortable sharing the tape, a colleague can view the video and offer suggestions to overcome stereotyping.

Following is a self-check that will help teachers become more aware of their own biases.

- Do I treat boys and girls fairly in my classroom?
- Do I use gender-neutral or nonsexist language (for example, police officer instead of policeman)?
- Do I avoid stereotyping expressions (for example, "woman driver" meaning poor driver)?
- Do I help my students to recognize stereotyping and bias?
- Do I confront examples of stereotyping and bias when they occur?
- Is my classroom arranged for positive interaction between males and females?
- Do I call on boys and girls equally?
- Do I encourage both boys and girls to take on leadership roles?
- Do I have high expectations for females in math, science, and technology?
- Do I suggest nontraditional careers for my students?
- Are bulletin boards and posters free of stereotypes?
- Have I taken a leadership role in developing equity in my school and district?
- Am I an effective role model of gender equity for other staff?

Finally, in terms of student-teacher interaction, some issues must be addressed. Females and minorities are shortchanged, according to Myra Sadker, David Sadker, and Sharon Steindam (1989). They found that teachers from elementary school to graduate school ask males more questions and give them more feedback. They also criticize them more often and give them additional time to respond to questions (p. 47).

Myra and David Sadker (1994) proposed four basic teacher reactions to student participation: praise (positive), criticism (explicit statements that an answer is wrong), remediation (helping students to correct a problem), and acceptance (an acknowledgment, such as "okay"). These reactions need to be specific and provide students with an indication of the quality of their work. They found that girls are given more vague, neutral reactions and boys are challenged to think more carefully (Sadker, Sadker, and Stulberg 1993, p. 46).

Along with videotaping for self-assessment, teachers are encouraged to videotape their classrooms in order to assess discipline patterns and how students are reprimanded. They can analyze types of misbehavior that occur, and if boys and girls are treated in the same manner.

Teachers need to encourage female students to participate in productive classroom talk. Sandler and Hoffman (1992) suggest:

- On the first day of class, tell students you expect them to participate equally.
- Call on female students directly, even if they do not have their hands raised.
- Call on both genders in proportion to their ratio in the classroom.
- Use sufficient wait time after asking a question.
- Maintain a teaching diary of student participation in order to identify and encourage silent students (pp. 7-8).

According to Scott and McCollum (1993):

> The research on peer interaction shows that throughout schooling classroom interaction between boys and girls is infrequent. A consequence of this lack of interaction is the reinforcement of stereotypes about sex-segregated activities. Peer contacts count for about 29% of the experiences that children have in a classroom setting. (pp. 181-82)

To enhance peer interaction between the sexes, the teacher should structure group projects, foster cooperative learning, and provide opportunities for females to use equipment typically reserved for males and vice versa.

Teacher Education

Future teachers should receive training in gender equity so that, when they have their own classrooms, they will be able to model appropriate behaviors.

They need to understand gender equity legislation as a foundation to allow them to focus more clearly on the current concerns of equity. The college curriculum for teacher education should include information dealing with the contributions of both sexes, and future teachers should be aware of how males and females are portrayed in their textbooks. Textbooks in methods classes should reflect current research in the field. And the importance of gender equity should be a topic in education methods classes. Information should include selection of appropriate texts and resource materials as well as treatment of students. Human growth and development classes should include studying relationships between men and women along with stereotypes, values, and societal expectations.

The preservice curriculum should prepare future teachers to deal with gender bias in the classroom. They should develop skills through their field experiences in identifying gender issues and using instructional strategies that encourage equity. Future teachers should be able to evaluate students using gender-fair rubrics, authentic assessment instruments or projects, portfolio assessment, and traditional methods of evaluation. They should be familiar with different ways of viewing intelligence, since awareness of multiple intelligences allows teachers to identify the differentiated strengths of males and females in their classrooms.

In addition, future teachers should receive training in career education so that they can teach employability skills and provide information about the world of work. This training should be for all teachers, from preschool through high school. Internships or field experiences in area businesses and industry can give future teachers important firsthand knowledge.

Student teaching is a critical time to check students' awareness of gender equity. College supervisors should help student teachers analyze how many times males are called on in comparison to females and whether critical thinking and analysis skills are expected of females as well as males. Student teachers also should look at their verbal and nonverbal treatment of students.

As teachers enter the workforce, female teachers also need to receive information from the career placement center about options within education. In the United States there is a shortage of female superintendents, which is a powerful position in the school structure. At the college level there are fewer female than male full professors, and fewer female college presidents. "Sixteen percent of academic women are full professors compared to 41% of men. At private universities, the numbers are even worse. Fourteen percent and 48% respectively" (Futter 1991, p. 5).

It would be an interesting project for future teachers to look at the research from other countries to see the roles of and attitudes toward women in schools and the workplace. For example, in Japan an equal opportunity law was passed in April 1986. In November 1992 the Office of the Prime Minister's Secretariat conducted a survey of 5,000 people over the age of 20 concerning opinions about equity. That survey found that only 22% of the respondents felt that equality of the sexes exists in the workplace. The survey reported even lower percentages of equality in other categories, such as politics (13%). The good news is that 61% of the respondents felt that male and female students are treated equally (Fujitake 1993, p. 25).

A second focus on teacher education is inservice training. One way to increase veteran teachers' awareness of gender equity is an awareness workshop. Such a workshop might be designed around three activities: definition, group discussion, and role playing. Following are some suggestions for the workshop coordinator:

Defining terms. Ask workshop participants to write down their definitions of terms to be used in the workshop. Terms will

185

include: gender equity, sexism, harassment, and so on. During the workshop, define the terms and ask the participants to refer to their notes to see the similarities or differences in their definitions. Alternatively, the coordinator may wish to define the terms in advance so that everyone has the same prior knowledge. Either approach can lead to valuable discussions.

Group discussion. Pass around blank index cards and ask workshop participants to write down examples of stereotypical behavior. One example might be asking a woman in a group to be the secretary and a man to chair the group discussion. Another example might be a teacher asking the boys in a classroom to carry books back to the library while the girls straighten up the room. After the examples have been written and turned in, read some of the cards aloud and ask how the situation might be made more equitable. Small-group discussions will focus on the examples.

Role playing. Ask an equal number of males and females (4 or 6) to volunteer as students for a role-playing situation. Then role-play a lesson based on a recent news event. As you proceed, treat males and females differently. This might be in a subtle way, such as eye contact or proximity, or it can be in a more obvious way, such as calling on the males more often than the females. Ask the audience to analyze the situation and write down signs of inequitable treatment.

The workshop coordinator also should provide participants with a packet of background information, such as research summaries and suggestions for making their schools and classrooms more equitable places.

Gender Equity and Parent Involvement

Most children have acquired a gender identity by the age of three, but full development of gender identity takes several more years; thus it is important for children to have role models who exhibit nonstereotypical behaviors (Lewis 1991, p. 3). Just as teachers confront bias in school, parents and guardians need to confront stereotypes at home.

Both boys and girls need to know that family and work roles often are assigned to one sex as a result of custom or tradition. But as they mature, they need to confront these traditions. Males need to realize that, as adults, they probably will be responsible for cooking, cleaning, and managing a household, whether they are married or single. With marriage often comes the additional responsibility of child care. Females need to be aware of how to contribute to the economic health of a family and how to balance a career with family responsibilities.

Parents also should help their children learn about future career opportunities. A wide range of employment choices are available, and new technological occupations are emerging constantly. Adult family members can discuss the pros and cons of their jobs, assist the children in talking to neighbors and friends about their work, and make business and educational contacts related to occupational choice.

Parents who are involved in the school and cooperate with educators have a positive impact on their children's academic achievement (McGee Banks 1993). Families can support the schools in the effort to develop communication skills, math and science skills, global awareness, and other elements in the curriculum that will help their children prepare for careers that might not yet exist. Taking an interest in school activities and checking to see if the schools are stereotyping are part of the parents' role.

Recent statistics indicate that many females will be in the workforce for 30 to 40 years. Therefore, it is imperative that at home and in school, girls be encouraged to plan for the future; to enroll in high-tech courses; to take a full program of science, math, and communication courses; and to investigate a wide variety of career options.

Parents should be able to analyze their own child-rearing practices and to amend them where needed. Parents and educators working together can create gender equity and effectively enhance the self-esteem and academic achievement of all students.

References

Adelman, C. *Women at Thirtysomething: Paradoxes of Attainment.* Washington, D.C.: Office of Educational Research and Improvement, U.S. Department of Education, 1991.

American Association of University Women (AAUW). *Shortchanging Girls, Shortchanging America: A Call to Action.* Washington, D.C.: American Association of University Women Educational Foundation, 1990.

American Association of University Women (AAUW). *How Schools Shortchange Girls: Executive Summary.* Washington, D.C.: American Association of University Women Educational Foundation, 1992.

Biklen, Sari K., and Pollard, Diane. "Sex, Gender, Feminism, and Education." In *Gender and Education: Ninety-Second Yearbook of the National Society for the Study of Education,* edited by Sari K. Biklen and Diane Pollard. Chicago: University of Chicago Press, 1993.

Bitters, B., and Foxwell, S. *Wisconsin Model for Sex Equity in Career and Vocational Education.* Madison: Wisconsin Department of Public Instruction, 1990.

Bitters, B., and Keyes, M. *Classroom Activities in Sex Equity for Developmental Guidance.* Madison: Wisconsin Department of Public Instruction, 1988.

Burstyn, J. "Who Benefits and Who Suffers: Gender and Education at the Dawn of the Age of Information Technology." In *Gender and Education: Ninety-Second Yearbook of the National Society for the Study of Education,* edited by Sari K. Biklen and Diane Pollard. Chicago: University of Chicago Press, 1993.

Campbell, P.B. *Girls and Math: Enough Is Known for Action.* Newton, Mass.: Women's Educational Equity Act Publishing Center, Education Development Center, 1991.

Fujitake, A. "Equality of the Sexes." In *Japan Update.* New York: U.S. Office of Keizai, Koho Center, August 1993.

Futter, Ellen V. "Sex Equity in Education and Society: Appearance Versus Reality." In *Sex Equity in Educational Opportunity, Achievement, and Testing.* Princeton, N.J.: Educational Testing Service, 1991.

Jaffee, L. "Pivotal Years: Health and Self-Esteem Issues for Adolescent Girls, Today's Girls." In *Today's Girls, Tomorrow's Leaders: Symposium Proceedings.* New York: Girl Scouts of the U.S.A., 1991.

Johnston Nicholson, H. "Be Prepared: How Serious Are We About Preparing Today's Girls to Be Tomorrow's Leaders?" In *Today's Girls, Tomorrow's Leaders: Symposium Proceedings.* New York: Girl Scouts of the U.S.A., 1991.

Lewis, M. "Gender Equity: The State of Play in Early Childhood Services." Paper presented at the Early Childhood Convention in New Zealand, September 1991.

Linn, M.C. "Gender Differences in Educational Achievement." In *Sex Equity in Educational Opportunity, Achievement, and Testing.* Princeton, N.J.: Educational Testing Service, 1991.

McGee Banks, C.A. "Restructuring Schools for Equity: What We Have Learned in Two Decades." *Phi Delta Kappan* 75 (September 1993): 42-48.

Measor, L., and Sikes, P.J. *Gender and School.* New York: Cassell, 1992.

Pollard, D.S. "Toward a Pluralistic Perspective on Equity." *Women's Educational Equity Act Publishing Center Digest* (February 1992).

Pollard, D.S. "Gender and Achievement." In *Gender and Education: Ninety-Second Yearbook of the National Society for the Study of Education,* edited by Sari K. Biklen and Diane Pollard. Chicago: University of Chicago Press, 1993.

Rebell, M., and Murdaugh, A. "National Values and Community Values: Gender Equity in the Schools." *Journal of Law and Education* 21 (Spring 1992): 176.

Sadker, Myra. "The Issue of Gender in School." In *Today's Girls, Tomorrow's Leaders: Symposium Proceedings.* New York: Girl Scouts of the U.S.A., 1991.

Sadker, Myra, and Sadker, David. *Failing at Fairness: How America's Schools Cheat Girls.* New York: Charles Scribner's Sons, 1994.

Sadker, M.; Sadker, D.; and Steindam, S. "Gender Equity and Educational Reform." *Educational Leadership* (March 1989): 44-47.

Sadker, M.; Sadker, D.; and Stulberg, L. "Fair and Square? Creating a Nonsexist Classroom." *Instructor* 102 (March 1993): 46.

Sandler, Bernice, and Hoffman, Ellen. "Encouraging Women to Talk in Class." *The Teaching Professor* 6 (August/September 1992): 7-8.

Schuster, Sharon. "Shortchanging Girls, Shortchanging America." In *Today's Girls, Tomorrow's Leaders: Symposium Proceedings.* New York: Girl Scouts of the U.S.A., 1991.

Scott, Elois, and McCollum, Heather. "Gender in Classroom and School Policy." In *Gender and Education: Ninety-Second Yearbook of the National Society for the Study of Education*, edited by Sari K. Biklen and Diane Pollard. Chicago: University of Chicago Press, 1993.

Sheboygan Area School District. *Gender Equity Plan*. Sheboygan, Wis., 1991.

Vandell, K., and Fishbein, L. "Restructuring Education: Getting Girls into America's Goals." *American Association of University Women* (August 1990): 4.

INCLUSION OF STUDENTS WITH DISABILITIES

by Thomas P. Lombardi

As early as the 1960s, I was involved in a federal project to prepare school personnel to meet the needs of students with disabilities in regular classes. Since then, a number of concepts and mandates have emerged under such labels as *normalization*, *mainstreaming*, *least restrictive environment*, and *integrated education*. The latest and perhaps most comprehensive label is *inclusion*.

There is no single, universally accepted definition for *inclusion*. However, it is generally agreed that inclusion involves a commitment to educate each student with a disability in the school and, when appropriate, in the class that child would have attended had the child not had a disability. The guiding principle behind inclusion is to bring the services to the student, rather than the student to the services. All faculty and administrators have as much responsibility in the education and training of students with disabilities as they do with students who do not have formally diagnosed disabilities.

Professional and parent associations, including the Council for Exceptional Children, the Learning Disabilities Association, and the National School Boards Association, have developed position papers on the inclusion movement. Most are cautiously optimistic about the positive potential of inclusion.

Much of the research on inclusion has demonstrated that it has benefits for students with disabilities. These students show significant, consistent educational achievements and increased affective skills when educated in inclusive classrooms.

This essay is condensed from Thomas P. Lombardi, *Responsible Inclusion of Students with Disabilities*, Fastback 373 (Bloomington, Ind.: Phi Delta Kappa Educational Foundation, 1994).

However, critics of inclusion caution that such positive results have been reported from only pilot programs. These critics argue that regular schools may not provide the careful monitoring associated with specially funded inclusion projects and thus might not produce the same benefits for their disabled students. These same critics also warn against total inclusion for all students with disabilities. They caution against abandoning the current continuum of service placements that allows responsible educators to make individualized decisions about the education of disabled students.

With or without funded projects, inclusion is becoming the norm, rather than the exception. As the movement grows, school systems are offering inservice programs to prepare administrators and teachers for their new responsibilities. Collaboration, consultation, cooperative learning, team teaching, peer tutoring, behavior support plans, curriculum adaptations, and environmental accommodations are just a few of the support strategies that need to be instituted in all schools.

Increasing numbers of schools and colleges of education are requiring future teachers and administrators to have both coursework and hands-on experience with students who have disabilities. A 1993 West Virginia Department of Education survey found that 16 of the 18 teacher training programs in that state required all of their teacher trainees to take a course in special education prior to graduation. Some states, such as Maryland, have mandated a course in special education for all teachers.

This essay provides an overview of the philosophical, legal, and research bases of *responsible* inclusion. I believe that inclusion has as much to do with a school's philosophy as it does with specific placement. Educators should not disregard the continuum of service placements, which is legally required, but should recognize that most students with disabilities can be educated in regular classes in their home schools, provided that they have appropriate support systems. This essay includes practical suggestions and strategies for implementing inclusion and describes specific examples of how administrators, regular teachers, special teachers, and parents can work as a team to support an inclusive school and integrated education for students with disabilities. In addition, a series of checklists is included so that administrators, teachers, and parents can see how they are meeting the intent of the inclusion movement.

Responsible inclusion requires careful planning and adequate support before any student with disabilities is placed in a regular class. Both regular and special teachers must be trained properly for their new responsibilities, and that involves more than just changing their titles to "collaborators" or "consultants." It involves learning skills that are not often taught in teacher training programs.

The student's individual education program must be developed before any decision is made on the student's placement. For example, a student who is suddenly blinded may need to be placed in a special class or special school to learn orientation skills before returning to a regular class; but returning to or never leaving the regular class is the basis of inclusion.

Responsible inclusion is hard work. But it may prevent many students with disabilities from becoming handicapped.

The Basis for Inclusion

The basis for inclusion can be found in both legal mandates and moral principles. However, once inclusion is established in a school, it will be up to educators to make appropriate decisions about individual students with disabilities. A disabled student may be assigned to a regular class but not truly accepted or included. Or a student may receive all or part of his instruction in a special class and yet be fully accepted by others and included as a full member of the school community. Ideally, the disabled students should be both physically and socially included in the life of the school and the activities of its students.

Legal Mandates. Educating disabled students with their nondisabled peers was one of the major principles of the Education for Handicapped Children Act (P.L. 94-142), now renamed the Individuals with Disabilities Education Act (P.L. 101-476). (See fastback 360 *Implementing the Disabilities Acts: Implications for*

193

Educators.) How to accomplish inclusion is still being addressed in the courts. Three recent cases are worth noting.

Sacramento City Unified School District v. *Holland* concerned Rachel Holland's school placement. Her parents wanted Rachel, a student with a moderate level of mental retardation, to be placed full time in regular classes. The school administration disagreed. Both parties were in total agreement on the objectives of Rachel's Individual Education Plan (IEP). Although the IEP emphasized socialization skills, the school administration voiced concern that functional skills — doing laundry, counting money, and so on — would be difficult to implement in a regular class even with modifications. However, these functional skills had not been addressed adequately in developing the IEP. Thus the court ruled in favor of the parents, because the objective of socialization could be met in the regular class.

In the case of *Greer* v. *Rome City Schools*, the court ruled that the full range of service configurations was not considered in a placement decision regarding Christy Greer, a 10-year-old with Down syndrome. The school administration believed that Christy's program would best be delivered in a self-contained classroom, and they presented her parents with a proposed IEP prior to the formal IEP meeting. Christy's parents preferred the regular classroom plus specialized speech therapy and so disagreed with the proposed IEP. The court determined that the IEP should have been developed at a meeting by a multidisciplinary team that included the parents and, if feasible, the student.

Unlike Rachel and Christy, Rafael Oberti presented behavior problems. In *Oberti* v. *Clementon School District*, Rafael had experienced a number of different educational placements in the schools. Under a more restricted special class environment with a behavior modification program, his behavior was manageable. When placed in a regular class, his behavior was not manageable. Although the school administration claimed to have considered all placement options for Rafael, the court ruled that they had not. They may have considered all of *their* current placement options, but not all *potential* options. It was felt that the behavior management program offered in the special education class was sufficiently portable to be used in a regular class.

These cases have one key feature in common: The courts gave more consideration to the needs and goals identified in each student's IEP than to actual placement. Placement, by law, follows development of the IEP.

Other legal factors that have been considered in inclusion rulings include the long-term benefits to the student, any detrimental effects a disabled student may have on the education of students without disabilities in the regular classroom, and the costs of establishing or maintaining an inclusive education program for the student. Although the term *inclusion* is not used in any of the current federal acts, the term *least restrictive environment* is used. Thus regular-class placement must be considered seriously before any other placement is made. Removal of disabled students from regular classes should occur only when the special needs cannot be met even with the use of supportive services, teaching adaptations, and curriculum modifications.

Moral Principles. It has been 25 years since Lloyd Dunn wrote his classic article, "Special Education for the Mildly Retarded: Is Much of It Justifiable?" (Dunn 1968). In it he states that "by removing students with disabilities from regular classes we contribute to the delinquency of regular education. We reduce the need for regular teachers to deal with individual differences. It is morally and educationally wrong" (p. 20).

Students with disabilities have a right to be educated with their peers in integrated settings. To deny them this right is a form of discrimination. Students who are educated in separate classes often feel unmotivated, inferior, and helpless.

Recently I heard someone talk about a "tolerance theory" of inclusion. The implications were that some regular teachers have a greater tolerance range than others toward accepting students with disabilities in their classroom. This no doubt is true. However, the education of students with disabilities is too important to be left to teachers' choices of whom they will or will not accept in their classes. Needing assistance, training, materials, and guidance is understandable; arbitrary refusal to accept students with disabilities is not.

One of the criticisms of inclusion is that it could have a detrimental effect on the learning progress of students who are not disabled. Actually, the opposite is more likely. As teachers begin to individualize instruction to accommodate the student with special needs, other students, particularly those considered at risk, also will benefit from the accompanying support systems. Studies of students at risk (Frymier and Gansneder 1989; Lombardi, Odell, and Novotny 1991) indicate that the kinds of support systems needed by such students are similar to those needed by students with disabilities. Having the benefit of both a special teacher and a regular teacher collaborating in a regular class is morally and educationally sound because such collaboration focuses on children's needs, not on their labels.

Segregated settings do not prepare students to live in an integrated society. Responsible inclusion does. Conversely, responsible inclusion does not leave students in regular programs and classes without the necessary support systems to meet their needs.

Research

Although the literature abounds with mission statements, philosophies, theories, principles, opinions, perceptions, and guidelines, there are few studies of the efficacy of inclusion for the broad range of students who are eligible for special education. Most information is in the form of case studies. Since programs for students with special needs should be individualized, perhaps this is as it should be. Following are some noteworthy studies:

Halvorsen and Sailor (1990) reviewed 261 studies that compared special needs students in integrated placements with their peers in segregated placements. They concluded that the students in the integrated programs more often reduced inappropriate behaviors, increased communication skills, exhibited greater independence, and engendered higher parental expectations.

The Learning Together Project (Corbin 1991), conducted in east central Minnesota, targeted students in five elementary schools for full inclusion in general education classrooms. Previously these students had been educated in segregated classrooms. As a result of the new placement, parents reported greater growth in both academic and social learning. Teachers found that the regular education students maintained their academic performance, were understanding and accepting of the disabled students, and became role models for the students with disabilities.

The Ravenswood Project (Lombardi, Nuzzo, Kennedy, and Foshay 1994) assessed the perceptions of 36 teachers, 96 parents, and 232 students regarding an integrated high school inclusion program. All groups were supportive of the program. Positive results included a decrease in dropout rates for students with disabilities, fewer classroom disturbances, and reasonable academic gains. Of the 36 students who had been in resource rooms and special classes, all preferred the regular classroom placement over their previous placement.

A related study of the cost-effectiveness of inclusion was conducted in Madison, Wisconsin. Piuma (1989) found that over a 15-year period, the employment rate for high school graduates with special needs who had been in segregated programs was 53%. But for special needs graduates from integrated programs, the employment rate was 73%. The cost of educating students in segregated programs was double that for educating them in integrated programs. These findings are similar to those of a study by Affleck, Madge, Adams, and Lowenbraun (1988), who demonstrated that the integrated classroom program for students with special needs was more cost-effective than the resource program, even though achievement in reading, math, and language remained basically the same in the two service delivery systems.

Models

A growing number of research reports focus on specific educational approaches and their relationship to the inclusion movement.

The Research Triangle Institute (1993) developed a comprehensive overview of 16 carefully selected and well-documented programs that are effective for students with disabilities. Program models include: the High/Scope Curriculum, Strategy Intervention Model (SIM), Tactics for Thinking, direct instruction, mastery learning, learning styles, SUCCESS, student team learning, classwide student tutoring teams, adaptive learning environments, Vermont Consulting Teacher Model, teacher assistance teams, Project RIDE, North Carolina Lead Team Model, Comprehensive Local School, and Coalition of Essential Schools.

Four of these models are described in this essay, and each description includes a contact person for additional information.

1. *Direct Instruction.* Direct instruction has become a generic term to describe the structured teaching of academic and social behaviors. According to Becker, Englemann, Carnine, and Rhine (1981), direct instruction has eight major components: 1) focus on academic objectives, 2) additional teachers in the classroom, 3) structured use of time, 4) scripted presentation of lessons, 5) efficient teaching methods, 6) careful training and supervision, 7) monitoring of progress, and 8) active parent involvement. It has been used with students of various ages and abilities both in regular and special classes. Its use with students who have severe mental impairments has been limited.

Major cost items involved in using direct instruction are staff training, materials, a supervisor for every 50 to 100 teachers, and a classroom paraprofessional for kindergarten and first-grade classes.

Direct instruction classes look similar to traditional classes. However, direct instruction tends to be more systematic. If you walk into a direct instruction classroom, you might see the teacher working with a small group of seven or eight students, while the rest of the class does independent work. The teacher might tell everyone to "touch" column S in their workbook and say, "First, we are going to read all the words in this column. Then we are going to talk about those words." She then asks the class to repeat what they will be doing. She also calls on individuals to make sure they understand. This individualized attention is particularly helpful for students with special needs. After each correct response, she reinforces the behavior with a smile and verbal praise. Incorrect responses are corrected and the student is then asked the question again.

Some educators believe that direct instruction stifles creativity because it is a step-by-step, fast-paced, structured approach. However, recent research supports its use with large and small groups. White (1988), in a meta-analysis of 25 studies that compared direct instruction to other intervention programs for special needs students, found that 53% of the studies found direct instruction to be statistically the most effective teaching method.

For more information about direct instruction, contact:

> Dr. Douglas Carnine, Co-Director
> Direct Instruction Model Project
> University of Oregon
> 805 Lincoln Street
> Eugene, OR 97401
> (503) 485-1163
>
> or
>
> Karen Sorrentino
> DI Products
> Science Research Associates
> 155 North Wacker Drive
> Chicago, IL 60606
> (800) 722-5351

2. *Strategy Intervention Model (SIM)*. The Strategy Intervention Model was developed by Donald Deshler and his colleagues at the University of Kansas Institute for Research on Learning Disabilities. Using a cognitive orientation, they emphasized developing a learning-strategies curriculum that would allow students to better use their skills in acquiring content. Their original target population of adolescents with learning problems has been expanded to include other age groups and other problem areas.

The heart of the strategy is to teach students how to learn, not what to learn. To date, 16 different learning-strategy instructional programs have been developed. All of the strategies are contained in instructor manuals, many with accompanying student workbooks. At this time, these workbooks are available only to teachers who have participated in training by a certified SIM trainer. Several state education departments have contracted with the institute to prepare SIM trainers for their school systems.

Strategies that are part of the SIM curriculum include: word identification, word imagery, self-questioning, paraphrasing, interpreting visual aids, multipass, listening and taking notes, first-letter mnemonics, pair-associates, sentence writing, paragraph writing, error monitoring, assignment completion, and test taking. There is a recommended sequence for learning and using the strategies. Strategy instruction may be taught in a resource room, special class, or regular class.

A major goal of SIM is learning regular class content. Special and regular teachers work cooperatively to help students learn to use the strategies. If you were to visit a strategies classroom, you might see something like this:

As the teacher hands out a science test, special needs students are prompted to use PIRATES. They immediately write PIRATES and their name on the top of the test. PIRATES is a mnemonic for a SIM test-taking strategy. The acronym stands for: Prepare to succeed; Inspect the instructions; Read, remember, reduce; Answer or abandon; Turn back; Estimate; and Survey.

Next these students individualize the test by deciding the order in which they will answer the questions. They do this by writing a number beside each test section. One student may choose to complete the true-false section first; another may tackle the matching section. As a student proceeds, he may put a star beside an "abandoned" question to remind him to turn back to it later. At the end, the students go back and survey the entire test to make sure they completed it.

For more information about SIM, training requirements, and costs, contact:

Dr. Don Deshler
University of Kansas
Institute for Research on Learning Disabilities
Robert Dole Human Development Center
Lawrence, KS 66045-2342
(913) 854-4780

3. *Teacher Assistance Team (TAT)*. Across the country, teacher assistance teams are being established so that teachers can better serve students with learning and behavior problems in regular classrooms. Typically, a teacher assistance team comprises three or four school faculty members who meet — usually weekly — to help other teachers and staff solve problems. Most of the problems relate to student needs, but they can be as diverse as grading practices or playground schedules.

The TAT model can be used at all school levels; it is not a replacement for special education. Multidisciplinary teams are required by law to determine if a student is eligible for special education; TATs are not required. But the TAT model can support and encourage inclusion by providing assistance to teachers who are trying to individualize instruction. TAT assistance also may include modifying the curriculum, developing a learning strategy, or implementing a behavior-modification program. In an analysis of five studies that included a total of 96 teacher assistance teams, Chalfant and Van Dusen Pysh (1989) found that 59% of the intervention goals addressed managing student behavior and 21% were for academic areas. The remaining 20% included problems in such areas as memory, speech, and motor performance.

TAT is not a typical consulting model, which usually involves giving advice one-on-one. Teacher assistance teams are a collaborative arrangement, where the referring teacher can turn to a team to help solve a problem. One of the first things a team should ask the referring teacher is, "How can we help you?"

An effective TAT requires administrative and faculty commitment, including time to meet and TAT training in analyzing problems, brainstorming, communication, and developing interventions.

Some TAT programs rotate team members so that each teacher eventually gets to serve on a team. Some also invite the parents to serve on the team.

For training information and materials about TAT, contact:

Dr. James Chalfant
College of Education
University of Arizona
Tucson, AZ 85721
(602) 621-3214

4. *Vermont Consulting Teacher Model*. The consulting teacher model (CTM) was used in a number of states even prior to the Education for All Handicapped Children Act (P.L. 94-142). Its basic principle is to help regular education teachers improve their skills in teaching special students. The most noted consulting model is associated with the state of Vermont.

The Vermont model originally was designed to provide direct services to teachers and other service givers and only indirect services to students with disabilities. In addition, all students, regardless of the severity of their disabilities, were to be taught in regular classes. Very few schools use this "total inclusion" design. Rather, most of the school systems using the CTM model give greater emphasis to collaboration and team teaching. This new collaborative emphasis is being supported by the Vermont Department of Education.

Teachers are trained as consulting teachers at St. Michael's College and the University of Vermont. Those who graduate from these programs are prepared to: 1) provide consultation and assistance to teachers with disabled students in regular classes, 2) guide paraprofessionals who provide support to disabled students in regular classes, and 3) team teach in regular classes, resource rooms, or special classes.

The Vermont Consulting Teacher Model lists a wide range of competencies expected from their consulting teachers besides effective consultation skills. These include: providing inservice programs to parents and teachers, developing parent support groups, assessing students for disabilities, suggesting appropriate interventions, evaluating interventions, and overseeing program effectiveness.

In Vermont, many schools include students on Individual Education Plan (IEP) committees. Many of these students are trained by consulting teachers to become advocates for their peers who have disabilities. One process that guides this training is the McGill Action Planning System (Snow and Forest 1987). MAPS teaches how to support peers, family members, and educators in order to integrate the disabled student in the school and community.

For additional information about the Vermont Consulting Teacher Model, contact:

> Susan Hasazi
> Graduate Programs in Special Education
> College of Education and Social Services
> University of Vermont
> Burlington, VT 05405
> (802) 656-2936

Education and Training

Responsible inclusion will require many teachers and administrators to learn new skills and to accept new roles. No longer will the major responsibility for the education of students with disabilities rest solely with the special teacher. More and more states are requiring special education training in general teacher and administrator certification programs.

Teacher Training. In the very near future, all teachers will be expected to know about the special needs of students with learning problems, including students who have disabilities. They also will be expected to modify instruction to better meet these needs. Collaboration and consultation with other personnel, especially the resource teacher, will be an everyday occurrence. Team teaching, peer tutoring, and cooperative learning will become part of their teaching practices.

In anticipation of these requirements, teacher training programs are being reorganized and new inservice requirements are being introduced in schools. Collaboration and cooperative teaching at the college level are becoming the "very essence of learning" (Katz 1987). Many programs that started as pilot projects are being incorporated into quality teacher training. An example is the Benedum Project at the College of Human Resources and Education at West Virginia University. Starting in the 1994-95 academic year, all students seeking teacher certification will take not only coursework associated with students with disabilities but also field and student-teaching experiences before they finish their new five-year degree in education.

Special education teachers also will be trained differently. As our schools become more inclusive, special education teachers will more often function as resource persons and facilitators. Their responsibilities will extend beyond direct instruction to solving problems for the faculty. Categorical teacher certification probably will continue, but only in categories of severe disability or particular special learning needs. Students in these categories, for the most part, will be physically and socially integrated, even when they cannot be academically integrated. The majority of training programs in special education will be noncategorical, with emphasis on special resource teachers providing consultation to and collaboration with general educators and parents. Teacher training programs in Vermont, Massachusetts, and Idaho already have implemented broad-based practices to support successful inclusion.

Administrator Training. Effective inclusion will be impossible to achieve without the support of school administrators. For example, principals must be able to identify teachers who will be successful on inclusion teams, support parent involvement and training, encourage alternative curricula, and develop successful options for graduation. They must allow time for team planning and problem solving. (As a recent consultant to the Ravenswood Project, I found that the main concern of teachers about the inclusion process was time for team planning.)

All administrators need training, particularly at the preservice level, in special education law. This knowledge is needed for two reasons: 1) to ensure that students with special needs receive an appropriate education as required by law and 2) to minimize the potential for inappropriate due-process procedures by parents and other advocates.

A study by Valesky and Hirth (1992) found that no state certification requirement for basic knowledge of special education exists in 45% of administrative endorsements. This oversight needs to be corrected. On a more positive note, these researchers found that 75% of the states annually offer inservice training programs in special education for school administrators.

In all likelihood, the need for special education administrators will continue, though their responsibilities will be somewhat altered. They will be less involved with direct supervision and evaluation and more involved with consultation and collaboration. Their formal training will most likely be a special education endorsement on a general education administrator's certificate.

Training Other Professionals. Speech therapists, physical therapists, occupational therapists, and other service providers will witness a change in how they deliver services in inclusive schools. Rather than take the student with special needs out of the classroom for extended periods of time, they will be required to adapt their therapy to the regular classroom environment. They also will use collaboration and consultation to a greater degree. They will give suggestions to teachers and parents on guiding the therapy process in class and at home.

The role of the school counselor will be especially important if inclusion programs are to be effective. Counselors need to assist disabled students with personal and social concerns, as special and regular education merge into integrated education.

These changing roles will require modifications in training service providers. A model of such modification is adaptive physical education training as a program designed to keep students with disabilities in the mainstream with their nondisabled peers. Interestingly, the organizers of Special Olympics are now re-evaluating their programs in order to promote the integration of persons with and without mental retardation (Block and Moon 1992).

New Roles and Responsibilities

To be effective, responsible inclusion will require consultation and collaboration. A major difference between these two roles is the degree of responsibility for direct service to students with disabilities. Consultants provide information and guidance; they usually have specialized knowledge in such areas as behavior management, physical interventions, and communication development. Collaborators share teaching and training responsibilities. They usually know how to use and, when necessary, how to modify teaching and testing practices to accommodate a broad range of learning levels and styles. Often these two services are combined into a collaborative consultation model.

Consultation. A number of professionals may serve as consultants to regular teachers who have disabled students. These include physical therapists, speech clinicians, and special educators. Consultants observe in the classroom, collect data on the student or teacher performance, suggest intervention strategies, model interventions, and monitor intervention effects. Since consultants are not available on a daily basis, they must train teachers or paraprofessionals to take responsibility for the intervention plan. They do not solve problems directly, but rather help teachers improve skills and become more effective. Consultants must be skilled in interpersonal relations if their assistance is to be accepted.

Examples of how consultation operates both for group and individual problems can be found in Lorna Idol-Maestas' *Special Educator's Consultation Handbook* (1983). Idol-Maestas describes the case of Kenny, a third-grade student with behavior problems that include roaming the classroom, leaving the classroom without permission, arguing with other students, and not completing modified assignments. The special education consultant focused on attention problems in Kenny's disruptive behavior and for eight days observed and recorded his attending/non-attending behaviors using time samples. Positive and negative teacher attention also was observed and recorded.

As a result, the consultant and teacher explained classroom rules to Kenny. Afterward, teacher praise and tokens were awarded when Kenny displayed appropriate behaviors. For the first few days, the consultant modeled the token-economy program; and then the regular teacher took over as the consultant observed. Kenny's attending behavior increased to 67.2% of observed intervals, which was an increase of 39.95% over baseline conditions. Teacher praise increased to an average of 20% of observed intervals, and negative behavior was reduced by one-half.

Collaboration. Whereas consultation is based on a single-expert model, collaboration relies on two or more people sharing their expertise. In most cases a collaborative effort involves a regular teacher and a special education teacher. However, collaboration may involve more than two people and include administrators, counselors, parents, and relevant others. Planning together takes time and the coordination of schedules. Administrators can be supportive by rearranging schedules, providing incentives, and making necessary resources available. These resources often include substitute teachers for collaborative team members. Most teachers, including special education teachers, have not been trained to work collaboratively and thus need inservice training.

Some school systems actually designate someone to serve as an "integration collaborator." The collaborator's duties might include: promoting heterogeneous grouping, broadening the regular curriculum for different learning rates and styles, team teaching, guiding cooperative learning groups, arranging for peer tutoring, and expanding the collaborative effort beyond the classroom.

When two or more people solve problems, the chance for successful integration of students with disabilities is much greater. In addition, students without an identified disability indicate that they also benefit from having more than one teacher in the classroom (Lombardi, Nuzzo, Kennedy, and Foshay 1994). Through collaboration, individualized instruction, once a hallmark of special education, becomes available to all students.

Morgantown High School in Morgantown, West Virginia, provides an example of collaboration in action. As the English teacher, Mr. Hohmann, was lecturing the class on the role of the sender and receiver in following directions in the communication process, Mrs. Lundeen, a special educator, paraphrased some of his comments by writing potentially unfamiliar words on the blackboard. These included such words as *parallel*, *median*, and *exact*. She then reviewed these words with the entire class. Mr. Hohmann took the role of the sender of the communication process by reading specific directions for Mrs. Lundeen to follow. She modeled his message by completing a rectangle drawing. Then students, working in cooperative groups, were given learning packets containing directions for constructing a different figure.

Each cooperative group included three students, one of whom was a special needs student. As the groups constructed their figure, Mr. Hohmann and Mrs. Lundeen circled the room, giving supportive clues when needed. After a specified time, each group turned in their group project, which was compared to a completed model. This exercise stimulated higher-order thinking, peer support, hands-on experience, and social interaction. Most important, it allowed for all class members, including students with special needs, to gain a clear understanding of the importance of following directions.

A number of training programs advocate the use of a combined consultation/collaboration model (Adamson, Cox, and Schuller 1989). In these cases, a special education teacher may serve both roles, depending on the problem.

Modifying Instruction

Recently I heard a keynote address by Larry Lieberman at the West Virginia Council for Administrators of Special Education Conference. Lieberman stressed that a major difference between regular education and special education is that regular education is driven by a system-based curriculum, whereas special education is driven by the needs of the individual. Fortunately for the inclusion movement, this dichotomy gradually is disappearing (Smith 1986). Responsible inclusion requires accepting attitudes by parents, teachers, and administrators; increased interactions between students with disabilities and the nondisabled; and realistic performance expectations for all students. But it also may require modifications in curricula, methods of instruction, and materials.

Curricula. An often-heard criticism is that students with special needs will not be able to benefit from the curriculum. If the curriculum is simply a series of lock-step, sequential bits of information delivered through lectures and textbook readings, then the criticism probably is warranted. But the curriculum can be made much more holistic and personalized by recognizing not only what students need, but also what they already know. Classrooms can become exciting places where group projects and activity centers make the curriculum meaningful for each student. And each student does not have to learn the same things in the same ways.

For example, a third-grade class is doing a science unit dealing with temperature. Most of the students are learning to use Fahrenheit and Celsius scales; a few are learning about molecular movement at different temperatures; and two students are learning to use hot and cold items. There are cooperative group activities and experiments. All students work toward the same basic goal, but individual objectives vary; and all the students benefit from the diversity (Stainback and Stainback 1992).

Methods of Instruction. For the most part, instructional methods used by special educators can be equally effective with general students, and methods used by general teachers can be equally effective with students with disabilities. Good teaching methods have no boundaries. Although an inclusive classroom does focus on the individual, there are some generalized instructional modifications that are especially suited to students with learning problems. These include using advanced organizers, preteaching key vocabulary, providing repetition of instruction, previewing major concepts, making time adjustments, using manipulatives, and providing corrective feedback. Cooperative groups, peer tutoring, whole-language instruction, unit teaching, and behavior modification procedures all have received support in the literature.

Emphasizing how to learn, rather than just what to learn, is important. A learning-strategies approach fits this goal. For example, students who have difficulty remembering what they read may be taught a paraphrasing strategy called RAP, developed by Jean Schumaker, Pegi Denton, and Don Deshler (1984) at the University of Kansas. The mnemonic RAP stands for:

Read the paragraph.
Ask yourself, What is the main idea? Give two details.
Put it into your own words.

Many inclusive schools are teaching such strategies in regular and elective classes. Any student who has difficulty learning is encouraged to take them. In some cases, strategy training is written into a student's IEP. (For a review of learning strategies, see fastback 345 *Learning Strategies for Problem Learners.*)

Another method that has become popular for use with integrated students who have unusual or severe disabilities is called MAPS (McGill Action Planning System), described by Forest and Pearpoint (1992). MAPS is a collaborative process that brings together key people in the student's life to create an action plan to be used in the regular classroom. Vandercook, York, and Forest (1989) provide specific examples of the effective use of MAPS.

Materials. Special teachers and regular teachers may need to locate lower- or higher-level textbooks to meet diverse student learning needs. Although it is time-consuming, many special teachers working as consultant-collaborators redesign materials to retain the original concepts but modify wording and problems in order to better match students' abilities.

Computer-based instruction can allow students with disabilities to be more independent in regular classes. Although a student with a physical disability may not be able to write with a pencil, the student can participate in the regular writing lesson by using the computer as a prosthesis. Students who are unable to read may soon be able to have entire pages read to them using scanners, synthesizers, and special software with a computer. Until such technology is available, teachers may be legally responsible for reading aloud such things as tests. For example, when history teacher Michael Withers refused to give tests orally to a disabled student, the parents sued. The jury ruled in favor of the parents and held Withers liable for compensatory damages, punitive damages, court costs, and attorney's fees (Zirkel 1994).

Lynne Chalmers (1992) provides a variety of suggestions for modifying materials and reformatting worksheets. For example, she suggests using large amounts of visual spacing, breaking worksheets into several sections, limiting the types of questions, providing clear directions and numerous examples, and giving cues for answers.

Inclusion Checklists

The following checklists for administrators, teachers, and parents reflect an inclusion philosophy. Each checklist has 10 questions. The more "yes" answers, the more positive toward responsible inclusion is the respondent.

Administrator Checklist

1. Does your school mission statement embody the belief that all students can learn and respect individual differences?
2. Would the students with disabilities at your school attend this school even if they were not disabled?
3. Do you encourage your regular teachers to accept students with disabilities in their classes? ·
4. Do you allow time and flexible scheduling so that special and regular teachers can consult and collaborate?
5. Do you recommend students with disabilities for placement based on their individual needs, rather than on categorical labels?

6. Do you promote social integration of disabled and nondisabled classmates through school dances, clubs, athletic events, and other activities?
7. Do you promote physical integration of disabled and nondisabled classmates in homeroom assignments, lunch schedules, locker locations, and other placements?
8. Do you expect students with disabilities who have IEPs to be as successful in reaching their goals as nondisabled students are in reaching their goals?
9. Are related services, such as speech and physical therapy, brought to the student in his home school and program, instead of taking the student to the service?
10. Do you encourage parents of students with disabilities to become active members in such school organizations as the PTA?

Teacher Checklist

1. Are you willing to have age-appropriate students with disabilities in your class?
2. Do you modify your curriculum, instructional methods, and materials to meet the diverse needs of students in your class?
3. Are you open to suggestions and modifications in your teaching and classroom management?
4. Are you willing to share your teaching responsibilities with other professionals?
5. Do you expect disabled students to be as successful in meeting their own goals as nondisabled students are in meeting theirs?
6. Do you call on students with disabilities as much as you call on other students in your class?
7. Do you use heterogeneous grouping?
8. Do you use peer tutoring?
9. Do you use adaptive technology and customized software?
10. Have you attended training sessions about responsible inclusion?

Parent Checklist

1. Does your disabled child attend the same school he or she would have attended if not disabled?
2. Do you take your disabled child to the same social functions you would attend if he or she did not have a disability?
3. Are your rules at home the same for your disabled child as for your other children? (If you have only one child, do you set the same rules that you would establish if the child did not have a disability?)
4. Is your disabled child given specific chores and home responsibilities?
5. Do you encourage your disabled child to participate in social and recreational events with nondisabled peers?
6. If your child is capable of doing so, do you encourage him or her to participate in the development of goals and objectives for his or her IEP?
7. Do you discipline your disabled child without special regard to the disability?
8. Will you allow or provide independent living arrangements for your disabled child as he or she matures?
9. Have you attended meetings at which the education of children with your child's type of disability were discussed?
10. Are you willing to serve on a home-school team to encourage appropriate placement of children with disabilities in responsible inclusion programs?

References

Adamson, D.R.; Cox, J.; and Schuller, J. "Collaboration/Consultation: Bridging the Gap from Resource Room to Regular Classroom." *Teacher Education and Special Education* 12 (Winter/Spring 1989): 52-55.

Affleck, J.Q.; Madge, S.; Adams A.; and Lowenbraun S. "Integrated Classrooms Versus Resource Model: Academic Viability and Effectiveness." *Exceptional Children* 54 (January 1988): 339-48.

Becker, W.C.; Englemann, S.; Carnine, D.; and Rhine, W.R. "Direct Instructional Model." In *Encouraging Cheating in America's*

Schools: A Decade of Experimentation, edited by R. Rhine. New York: Academic Press, 1981.

Block, M.E., and Moon, M.S. "Orelove, Wehman, & Wood Revisited: An Evaluative Review of Special Olympics Ten Years Later." *Education and Training in Mental Retardation* 27, no. 4 (1992): 379-86.

Chalfant, J.C., and Van Dusen Pysh, M. "Teacher Assistance Teams: Five Descriptive Studies on 96 Teams." *Remedial and Special Education* 10, no. 6 (1989): 49-58.

Chalmers, L. *Modifying Curriculum for the Special Needs Student in the Regular Classroom*. Moorhead, Minn.: Practical Press, 1992.

Corbin, N. "The Impact of Learning Together." *What's Working*. Minnesota Department of Education. (Spring/Summer 1991).

Dunn, L.M. "Special Education for the Mildly Retarded: Is Much of It Justifiable?" *Exceptional Children* 35 (September 1968): 5-22.

First, P.F., and Curcio, J.L. *Implementing the Disabilities Acts: Implications for Educators*. Fastback 360. Bloomington, Ind.: Phi Delta Kappa Educational Foundation, 1993.

Forest, M., and Pearpoint, J.C. "Putting All Kids on the Map." *Educational Leadership* 50 (October 1992): 26-29.

Frymier, J., and Gansneder, B. "The Phi Delta Kappa Study of Students at Risk." *Phi Delta Kappan* 71 (October 1989): 142-46.

Halvorsen, A.T., and Sailor, W. "Integration of Students with Severe and Profound Disabilities: A Review of the Research." In *Issues and Research in Special Education: Vol. 1*, edited by R. Gaylord-Ross. New York: Teachers College Press, 1990.

Idol-Maestas, L. *Special Educator's Consultation Handbook*. Rockville, Md.: Aspen, 1983.

Katz, J. "Collaborative Learning: How It Works and What It Does." Manuscript. Stony Brook: State University of New York at Stony Brook, 1987.

Lombardi, T.P. *Changing Institutional Structures for Effective Special Education Programs*. Monograph Series No. 4. Tucson: University of Arizona, College of Education, 1971.

Lombardi, T.P. *Learning Strategies for Problem Learners*. Fastback 345. Bloomington, Ind.: Phi Delta Kappa Educational Foundation, 1992.

Lombardi, T.P.; Nuzzo, D.L.; Kennedy, K.D.; and Foshay, J. "Perceptions of Parents, Teachers and Students Regarding an Integrated Education Inclusion Program." *High School Journal* 77 (April/May 1994): 315-21.

Lombardi, T.P.; Odell, K.S.; and Novotny, D.E. "Special Education and Students at Risk: Report from a National Study." *Remedial and Special Education* 12 (January/February 1991): 56-62.

Piuma, M.F. *Benefits and Cost of Integrating Students with Severe Disabilities into Regular School Programs: A Study Summary of Money Well Spent.* San Francisco: San Francisco State University Department of Special Education, 1989.

Research Triangle Institute. *Educational Approaches and Program Options for Integrating Students with Disabilities: A Decision Tool.* Longmont, Colo.: Sopris West, 1993.

Schumaker, J.B.; Denton, P.H.; and Deshler, D.D. *The Paraphrasing Strategy.* Lawrence: University of Kansas, 1984.

Smith, F. *Insult to Intelligence.* New York: Arbor House, 1986.

Snow, J., and Forest, M. "Circles." In *More Education Integration*, edited by M. Forest. Downsview, Ontario: G. Allan Roeher Institute, 1987.

Stainback, S., and Stainback, W. *Curriculum Considerations in Inclusive Classrooms: Facilitating Learning for All Students.* Baltimore: Paul H. Brooke, 1992.

Valesky, T.C., and Hirth, M.A. "Survey of the States: Special Education Knowledge Requirements of School Administrators." *Exceptional Children* 58 (March/April 1992): 399-406.

Vandercook, T.; York, J.; and Forest, M. "The McGill Action Planning System: A Strategy for Building the Vision." *Journal of the Association for Persons with Severe Handicaps* 14, no. 3 (1989): 205-15.

White, W.A.T. "A Meta-Analysis of the Effects of Direct Instruction in Special Education." *Association for Direct Instruction News* 7, no. 4 (1988).

Zirkel, P.A. "Costly Lack of Accommodations." *Phi Delta Kappan* 75 (April 1994): 652-53.

SCHOOL CHOICE

by Susan Uchitelle

School choice is currently the most frequently mentioned method of achieving education reform, a concern that has consumed the education community and the public at large over the past decade. School choice is praised in task force reports and hailed by educators and politicians from coast to coast. Segments from both the public and private school sectors promote school choice as the catalyst for change and reform. In response to the call for restructuring and change, a variety of school choice plans have evolved.

As of February 1992, 42 states have considered, introduced, or enacted some kind of choice legislation. While the legislation in each state varies, clearly school choice has become a priority for many state legislatures in the last several years. Each state has tailored its legislation to meet the specific interests of different constituencies; and each plan has different funding mechanisms and different target audiences.

In some states school choice is restricted to options only within a local school district. In other states the specific choice plans have resulted from school desegregation mandates, including controlled choice, interdistrict or intradistrict transfers, magnet schools, or specialty programs, such those in Kansas City (Mo.), St. Louis, Milwaukee, and Charlotte (N.C.). Other states, such as Minnesota, have enacted legislation to provide interdistrict choice options as well as postsecondary options for high school students. State money follows the student to the receiving school, but transportation is not provided.

This essay is condensed from Susan Uchitelle, *School Choice: Issues and Answers*, Fastback 348 (Bloomington, Ind.: Phi Delta Kappa Educational Foundation, 1993).

This essay provides a brief historical background of the school choice movement, including an analysis of the issues being debated over the marketplace theories and the general philosophy behind school choice. It highlights just a few of the many existing choice plans around the country, both intradistrict and interdistrict, giving the reader a flavor of the kinds of choices that do exist in the public sector. Current state legislation dealing with school choice is reviewed to show the important role of state governments in promoting and facilitating school choice.

This essay also discusses the conditions that must prevail to make choice programs accessible and equitable, including such issues as racial balance, transportation, community participation, financing, and commitment to making choice programs available to those who need them the most. The essay concludes with a discussion of school choice issues still needing to be addressed.

History and Background of the School Choice Movement

The release in 1983 of *A Nation at Risk* by the National Commission on Educational Excellence gave birth to the current reform movement. Designed to be a catalyst for much-needed revitalization and change, the report spawned a flurry of activity — task forces, governors' panels, state legislation, and local reform efforts — all focusing on ways to upgrade our education system, which was viewed as failing to prepare our youth to meet the challenges of the 21st century. A crisis mentality pervaded the nation. Presidents Reagan and Bush saw revitalizing our education system as the key to our nation's future. Both, however, were equally determined that financing these major reforms was to be primarily the responsibility of state and local governments. Funding for education was no longer a federal government priority, as it had been since President Johnson's "Great Society" programs.

The response to *A Nation at Risk* was overwhelming, at least in the policy arena. Educational change became a priority for governors and state departments of education across the country. Restructuring, accountability, and educational excellence were high on the agendas of policy makers — the National Governors' Association, most state commissioners and state boards of education, local school boards, superintendents, and state legislators. State after state responded with reform bills that included such provisions as: increasing graduation requirements, lengthening the school year and day, requiring more science and math for graduation, providing career ladders for teachers, mandating more testing of students, and initiating some kind of school choice within the public sector.

The ultimate goal of these school reforms was to improve the literacy skills of our youth for the work force of the future and to achieve a higher level of productivity and competitiveness for the nation. In the view of many, we were falling further and further behind the rest of the industrialized world in both productivity and academic achievement. Many expressed concern that America's schools were no longer serving their clientele. Student and family needs had changed; yet schools, regardless of various initiatives, remained virtually the same. These concerns became the focus of attention for the National Education Association, the American Federation of Teachers, state education agencies, governors, business communities, school boards, and school districts.

Recommendations from *A Nation at Risk* came on the heels of earlier reforms that had been implemented and were strongly supported by the federal government. During the 1960s and 1970s direct federal dollars, federal matching funds, ESEA funds, and other federally supported programs had become the norm. But in the 1980s these sources dried up. There was virtually no additional federal funding to support these reforms, and state and local resources were at a premium. The fiscal responsibility as well as the decision making were deferred to the state and local districts. Only the rhetoric remained at the federal level.

Among the reform efforts resulting from *A Nation at Risk*, school choice, in particular, somehow was elevated to a policy issue at the national level through the efforts of some prominent scholars who advocated a marketplace theory of schooling. They

219

argued that if parents had a choice of the school their children attended, they would become a powerful force for bringing about school improvement; that is, if you give parents choice, you also give them the leverage for change. And if the school does not improve, it will have no clients and cease to exist. For the first time, the marketplace concept of free choice was to be extended wholesale to education — both public and nonpublic.

School choice became the dominant reform theme for Presidents Reagan and Bush. Both saw choice as a way to bring about education reform and school restructuring with little, if any, federal funds. Reagan wanted to implement a voucher system for both public and nonpublic schooling. Bush initially emphasized choice in the public sector, but later in his term began to include private schools as well. Many politicians saw choice as an inexpensive way to bring about much-needed education reform. On the other hand, most educators who are proponents of choice saw it as a possible catalyst for change but not a panacea for improving public education. Regardless of the different viewpoints, school choice has become a major political and policy issue in the last decade — an issue that is not likely to go away.

During the 1980s "restructuring" became a buzzword. School choice was viewed as one of the means of accomplishing restructuring. School choice would create unique and measurably different kinds of schools. If consumers (parents) could decide on the kind of school they wanted their children to attend, the choice option would change not only the traditional notions about school attendance areas but also would give parents the right to select the educational program they deemed best for their children. Thus schools would have to respond to the desires of their constituents if they were to survive.

Proponents of school choice make many assumptions. Among them are: it gives teachers the opportunity to choose an environment in which they can best teach; it offers parents greater satisfaction; it engages students more effectively and should result in better outcomes because of the match of "shared values"; and student achievement is higher. As yet, however, there are no data sufficient to acknowledge or refute any of these assumptions.

Much has been written about school choice. One of the earliest proponents of school choice was Milton Friedman, the Nobel Prize-winning economist, who proposed a plan for publicly financed education vouchers as early as 1962. In 1978 the federal government experimented with the voucher idea in Alum Rock, California, a project that continued over five years and formed the cornerstone for other choice programs. In 1985 President Reagan proposed a voucher program for the disadvantaged. Following up on Reagan's proposal, the National Governors' Association endorsed parental choice as an educational priority (Elmore 1988). Coons and Sugarman (1978), probably the best-known proponents, advocated that parental preference should take precedence over geographic place of residence.

In fact, this country has long had a form of choice within its several different schooling structures — public, private, and parochial, with many variations within each. However, except for certain federal and state entitlement programs, only public schools are supported by tax dollars.

Perhaps the most controversial issue arising from the school choice movement is: Should public funds be used to educate any children who choose to transfer to a school of their choice, public or private, or should public funds be spent only for public schools?

It took Chubb and Moe in their book, *Politics, Markets, and America's Schools* (1990), to dramatize the controversy over school choice. They argue that the public school system is not working because its structure promotes "characteristics anathema to effective performance" (p. 21). And they go on to assert that a marketplace setting for schooling is the only way to bring about effective reform, contending that school choice is a reform with "its own rationale and justification" (p. 217).

Chubb and Moe postulate that the public school bureaucracy discourages promising practices and inhibits individual initiative, whereas a marketplace approach will force schools to become more flexible and responsive to their clientele. They argue that a free market will promote school autonomy and give parents greater control of school outcomes, since the school will need to satisfy its clientele in order to remain in business.

These authors believe that if schools have a clientele committed to common educational goals, they will be less bureaucratic. They contend that it is the rigid bureaucratic structure that hinders student achievement. Inherent in their argument is the belief that nonpublic schools are more effective than public schools because they are less bureaucratic. Chubb and Moe argue that small, autonomous, nonpublic schools, operating under marketplace principles, produce higher student achievement. They claim that changing a school's bureaucratic structure can raise achievement levels by one full year in a five-year period (p. 180).

There are many unsubstantiated and disputed claims in Chubb and Moe's arguments. It has not yet been shown that the factor of school choice alone results in higher academic achievement. In fact, Henry Levin points out in *Choice and Control in American Education* (1990) that statistically there is only about one-tenth of a standard deviation difference in student performance in private schools compared to public schools and that background factors may account for these differences. Other studies to date show very little convincing evidence that private schools are more effective in improving achievement than are public schools.

Choice in the public sector flourished as part of the reforms of the 1970s in the form of alternative schools, magnet schools, and school-within-a-school structures. The reforms of the 1980s tended to ignore existing school choice alternatives. As will be pointed out in this essay, many different types of school choice plans currently are operating in the public sector. They are programs designed to serve specific student needs and include creative ways to finance alternative school options. Today many schools of choice are working well — in individual districts, in numerous magnet programs, within schools in districts, and across district lines.

Viable choice plans designed to improve education and meet students' needs are complex operations and expensive to implement. If school choice is to be available to all children, we must be willing to pay for high-quality programs, student transportation, and recruitment campaigns targeted at all ethnic and socioeconomic groups.

Spotlight on Public Schools of Choice

This chapter spotlights several public school choice programs. These are programs that offer parents a variety of educational settings and allow them to choose the environment they feel is most appropriate for their children. They are schools that offer parents an alternative to neighborhood schools that they consider inadequate. They strive to overcome educational inequities. They are open to all, not just to those families who know how to take advantage of the system. They do not drain limited resources from the system even though they cost more than the average school in the system. Nor do they siphon off all the most-able students to the detriment of other schools in the system, as is often claimed. Certainly they appeal to the more motivated family. But the solution to improving our schools does not end with implementing school choice; it is but the beginning of a long and ongoing process of change.

When reviewing the choice plans described here, keep in mind the following factors, which undergird the argument for school choice:

1. There are many ways to educate children; there is no one best program.
2. Diversity is desirable, and school choice provides that diversity.
3. The act of choosing empowers parents and makes them more responsible.
4. Schools should not take their clientele for granted.
5. Choice creates new and more involved roles for parents and faculty.
6. Administrators develop new and more dynamic leadership styles.
7. Parents become true participants and partners in the education of their children.
8. Principals feel greater responsibility for the success of their schools.
9. Efforts to find sufficient funds result in some very creative mechanisms for fund raising.

10. When teachers are in a setting that is more congruent with their teaching styles, they take a significant role in developing programs and making decisions.

All the choice plans described here were initiated in different ways. Some of the programs were developed out of a need to remedy historic patterns of racial segregation, with school choice becoming an integral part of that remedy. Others were created by teachers who wanted to engage children and parents. Some were developed by principals who were dissatisfied with the previous program. Still others came from state initiatives.

The school choice plans described here are only a few of the many now operating. They are cited primarily because they have been in existence for a minimum of three to five years and because they represent different kinds of choice programs, thus giving the reader a perspective on the variety of alternatives that exist. For more detailed information about school choice programs, the reader should consult the references at the end of this essay, particularly *Improving Schools and Empowering Parents: Choice in American Education* (Paulu 1989), a report based on the White House workshop on choice in education, and the December 1989 issue of *Phi Delta Kappan*.

The Minnesota Experience. Probably the most extensive options for school choice are found in the state of Minnesota. This state enacted legislation that opened the door to postsecondary enrollment options for high school students, open enrollment across district boundaries, area learning centers, and some public/private transportation opportunities. Minnesota's legislation in effect declares that school choice belongs to families, and the law establishes standard guidelines to encourage choice opportunities. Legislation allows students in the public sector to attend any school they are interested in if they have transportation to the school and there is space. In 1987-1988 the school choice option was implemented giving Minnesota secondary students the opportunity to enroll in alternative schools, special classes in other school districts, college courses at local institutions, and even some specific centers of learning for special students. The only criteria were that the transfer does not disrupt the racial balance of either the sending or the receiving school and that there is space in the receiving school.

Initially, school districts could volunteer to participate in the school choice program. As of 1990, all school districts in the state had to allow students the option of leaving their home district, though individual districts could set criteria governing acceptance of incoming students consistent with space available and district policy. In Minnesota, the state's per-pupil funding follows the student to the receiving district. This is one example of a state initiative available to students throughout the entire state.

Minneapolis and St. Paul are probably the two communities that have taken the greatest advantage of this statewide initiative. St. Paul, with its extensive magnet school program, has about 55 of its schools involved at the elementary, middle school, and high school levels. Students in the St. Paul Public Schools may attend their neighborhood school or apply to attend a magnet school. In some cases, the neighborhood school may be a magnet school. Students who live in a magnet school attendance area are given preference if they choose to attend it. Some magnets are citywide and do not have an attendance area.

Parents who wish to have their children attend a magnet school must complete an application and return it to the magnet school office by early April. Selection of students to the magnet schools is based on racial balance guidelines. Preference is given to students who live in the attendance areas of each magnet school or in preference zones established by the board of education. A sibling priority was implemented for the 1992-93 school year only, as part of a study being conducted by the district. A random selection process is used for accepting students in each of the magnet schools when racial balance is not achieved or when there are more applicants than openings. Students not accepted go on a waiting list and are contacted as openings become available. Transportation is provided according to district eligibility rules.

A joint integration exchange has been established between the St. Paul Public Schools and neighboring Roseville Area Schools. St. Paul students may apply to attend Roseville's Parkview Center Schools, and Roseville students may apply to attend the Open School in St. Paul. Transportation is not provided between districts.

All St. Paul's magnet high schools are specialty programs within comprehensive high schools. Students elect to enroll in the regular program or the specialty program at the high school of their choice. Students may list up to two choices on their application. A counselor from the high school comes to the elementary or junior high school the applicants attend to register them and to make class schedules.

Minneapolis has a smaller school choice program. Its initial choice plan began in 1969-1970 under the leadership of then superintendent John B. Davis. Initially called the South East Alternatives (SEA), the project involved community and school staff in planning a system of alternative elementary schools located in the southeast neighborhood of Minneapolis. The alternatives included a traditional, open, continuous progress, and free school. SEA was implemented as a choice program, not a desegregation program. However, when the district began to desegregate in 1973, the SEA program became the model for the choice program used to facilitate desegregation.

At the elementary level, all families are allowed to choose from among 13 alternative and/or magnet schools. Most families make their choice when their children enter kindergarten. At the secondary level, approximately 10% to 15% of the students are involved in choice programs in some way. At the middle school level, some choices are available. At the high school level, students may choose from among 14 magnets located in comprehensive high schools. The program is primarily intradistrict, though interdistrict transfers are possible. Choice is controlled based on space available and on desegregation guidelines for racial balance. Transportation is provided for all students who participate.

School choice is widely accepted by families in Minneapolis. In fact, many families had been instrumental in promoting the expansion of choice in other parts of the city.

Indianapolis: Key School. The Key School is a K-6 elementary school, one of the choice options in the Indianapolis Public Schools. (Indianapolis also has an interdistrict choice program with nearby suburban districts.) Housed in an older building, the Key School began operation in 1987. Its students come from all parts of the city and are admitted on a lottery basis in accordance with the district's desegregation guidelines. Approximately 40% are African American.

The Key School curriculum is based on Howard Gardner's theory of multiple intelligences (see fastback 342 *Teaching for Multiple Intelligences* by David G. Lazear). This theory postulates that humans possess not one, but seven relatively autonomous intellectual competencies. They are: linguistic, logical-mathematical, musical, spatial, bodily-kinesthetic, intrapersonal, and interpersonal intelligence. Teachers are encouraged to tap into each child's strengths in each of these intelligence areas, not just the linguistic and logical-mathematical areas, which traditionally have dominated the curriculum.

Key School is organized by mixed-age groups (grades 1-3 and grades 4-6). Four days a week students spend time in mixed-age groupings, or "pods," which parents and students select, and work on activities in a particular cognitive area. Students also spend time each week in a special "flow-activity center," which includes games, puzzles, audiotapes, and other materials geared to one of the seven intelligences. By allowing students to pursue areas of interest, teachers hope to capitalize on their intrinsic motivation.

The curriculum is integrated around schoolwide themes, which change every nine weeks. By the end of the nine-week cycle, each student will have carried out a project to illustrate the theme. In addition to the regular academic areas, all students receive daily instruction from specialists in physical education, music (including violin), art, Spanish, and computers.

Student evaluation is done using student portfolios. One component of the portfolio is a videotape that documents children's interests and accomplishments. The portfolio also includes an initial interview and samples of the student's work throughout the

227

year. Students also keep a reflective log with weekly entries about school themes and projects.

The Key School concept is unusual in that it was initiated and designed by the teachers and their principal. The curriculum was developed collaboratively by teachers, parents, and community members. It has been extremely successful in improving attendance, raising achievement, and involving the community. It is visited by educators from around the country.

Controlled School Choice Programs. Other types of school choice programs, found in Seattle, Boston, and Cambridge, Mass., are called "controlled school choice." They were introduced to eliminate segregation, while at the same time allowing students access to all schools and special programs within the school district. Student assignment is determined by space availability and racial balance. Parents may state a school preference, and school officials attempt to match students with the school or program of their choice. In these three communities, parents may choose a particular school or a school-within-a-school plan. The choices range from foreign languages to computer-assisted instruction to open classroom settings.

Boston serves as an example of how controlled choice operates. Its choice plan began in 1989 as a result of complaints from parents that their children were being bused from one segregated school to another. The earlier court-ordered desegregation plan did not take into account demographic changes that caused desegregated schools to become re-segregated.

The Boston controlled choice program has three goals: school desegregation, school improvement, and school choice. All 57,000 students in the Boston school system participate in the program. The city is divided into three attendance zones. Each zone is supposed to be equal in terms of the range and quality of education available. The program is promoted through Parent Information Centers in each zone.

Students may apply to any school in their attendance zone. Parents and students are asked to select five or six schools in order of preference. In early spring the district makes placements based on the applications submitted. No student is guaranteed a placement. However, 85% to 90% of the students get their first- or second-choice school. A lottery is used to place students when there are more applicants than available spaces. All schools within an attendance zone are available to students living in the zone, and 50% of the students in a school's walk zone have preference within school desegregation guidelines. Transportation is provided.

Controlled choice has had a positive impact on parental involvement, especially with the assistance of the Parent Information Centers.

As each school works to make itself attractive to students, school quality has improved. The U.S. District Court has seen fit to withdraw its daily monitoring of desegregation in Boston based on the results of the controlled choice program.

The choice process serves, in a sense, as a referendum on which schools are not measuring up. These schools are targeted for upgrading immediately. Zone School Improvement Councils have been set up to assist in this task. Funding pupil transportation remains a serious problem for Boston's controlled choice program.

Eugene, Oregon. Another good example of school choice is the program in Eugene, Oregon, which has been in existence for about 18 years. In this district with an enrollment of about 17,700, students may attend their neighborhood school or apply to any other school in the district that has room. Students attending a school other than their neighborhood school must provide their own transportation.

The district offers 15 alternative schools and 36 regular schools. The application period for transfers is the first day of school in January through 30 days prior to the beginning of the fall term. If there are more applicants than spaces available, placement is done by lottery in March.

District 4, East Harlem. One of the most widely publicized school choice programs is in Community District 4, East Harlem,

229

in New York City. The program, which began in 1974, is based on the premise that choice is crucial to maintaining the vitality of educational institutions. The open zoning concept in Community District 4 offers a variety of schools for students and parents to select from. Students may choose from among 50 magnet or specialty programs. Options range from environmental studies to performing arts to science and mathematics to the humanities.

Every school allows its teachers and directors to hire the staff and to schedule courses. The schools are organized around particular themes to which administrators, teachers, parents, and students are committed. Students are free to apply to those schools that they feel will best meet their needs.

Each spring, sixth-graders, in consultation with their teacher and parents, go through a decision-making process, beginning with exercises in self-evaluation and making choices. This prepares them to select three junior high schools in order of preference. Some schools address particular interests, such as music or science. Others have a more general liberal arts approach. All schools have their own style and focus, but the focus may change based on parental interest.

Parents are encouraged to attend the School Choice Fair held in December, where each junior high has an exhibit outlining its program. Parents are then urged to visit the three junior high schools that interest them the most. Parents list their preferences on an application, which is returned to the student's current teacher. The teacher forwards the application to the Office of Alternative Schools.

The applications are sent first to the school that students and parents have selected as their first choice. Schools have three weeks to select students using selection criteria that have been included in the descriptions for each school. Schools retain the applications of the students selected and send the applications of children who have not been selected to their second-choice school. The process is continued through a third round for students who have not been selected for their first- or second-choice schools. Students not selected by a school are placed by the Office of Alternative Schools. Acceptance letters for all schools are mailed to parents no later than June 1.

Free or half-priced bus or subway passes are available to all students in the district who live farther than specified distances from the school of their choice. Students from outside the district use public transportation.

The choice program in Community District 4 has resulted in increased reading and math scores, higher teacher morale, a decline in truancy, and a restoration of order. And many more students are placed in specialized high school programs as a result of their increased academic abilities. Because of the unique programs offered, there has been an influx of non-minority students enrolling in a district whose student population is predominantly minority.

Choice Programs for Achieving Desegregation. Some urban school districts have implemented choice programs for purposes of achieving desegregation. For example, the Kansas City, Missouri, school system has developed an extensive system of school choice by converting all schools to magnet schools with specific themes. Students pick the school of their choice according to the magnet theme. Most of the transfers are within the district, though some students attend from the suburbs. The state provides transportation by court order.

Across the state in St. Louis, a significant interdistrict choice program has been developed between the city of St. Louis and 16 suburban school districts. This program resulted from a settlement agreement of a desegregation lawsuit. Students who live in the city may choose to attend any of the 16 suburban districts. Each district submits to the Interdistrict Coordinating Council information about its schools — pupil/teacher ratios, special programs, size of district, number of schools, unique emphasis, college admission rates, school goals, etc. This information is compiled into a booklet and sent to every city family that has children eligible to transfer. Eligibility is based on attendance in a predominantly black, city public school.

Interested parents fill out applications starting in January for the next school year. If there is space, according to the pupil/teacher ratio established by the receiving district's board policy, students are allowed to transfer. Once transferred, the Interdistrict Coordinating Council provides counseling and follow-up services. Transportation is provided, as well as fiscal incentives to both receiving and sending districts. Costs are paid by the state.

The same conditions apply for students from the suburban districts choosing to enroll in St. Louis schools. They may choose to attend one of the 27 magnet schools in the city or any other city school, with transportation provided. Students within the city of St. Louis also may apply to any of 27 magnet schools and programs. The final decision is made by lottery in mid-March. The interdistrict school choice program in St. Louis is currently one of largest in the nation. It has been very successful as an urban-suburban model, but it is expensive to operate because of transportation and incentive payments.

San Diego: Year-Round School Options. The San Diego school system offers still a different kind of choice opportunity. One of its interesting options is its year-round school schedule. Three types of school schedules are available in San Diego:

1. Traditional: September to June
2. Year-round: 45 days on, 15 days off
3. Multi-track year-round: groups of students alternate, with 45 days on, 15 days off

Most secondary schools follow the traditional schedule, while elementary schools may be traditional, year-round, or multi-track year-round. There also are two types of magnet schools: total magnet and school-within-a-school magnet.

Application for magnet schools may be made at any time. However, the ethnic balance of both sending and receiving schools and the enrollment priorities of the magnet program must be considered before applications are approved.

Elementary applications received prior to May 1 receive priority for July (year-round schedule) and September (traditional

232

schedule) openings in magnet programs. Those received after May 1 are processed as additional openings become available. Secondary applications received before March 31 are given priority for September openings. Those received after March 31 are processed as openings become available. Secondary students in certain attendance areas must apply even if the magnet program is at their neighborhood school. No sibling priority is given. The district provides free transportation for students attending magnet programs outside of their geographic school boundary.

Components of a Successful School Choice Program

School choice is being touted by politicians and certain interest groups as a panacea to school reform. Their premise is that if parents can choose the school their children will attend, then they will be more committed to supporting the school, their children will be more eager to go to school, and the school will be more responsive to student needs. What has not been taken into account in many of the school choice proposals are several fundamental factors necessary to make school choice successful. This chapter will discuss some of these factors, using as an example the school choice options in St. Louis.

The St. Louis model is one of the largest urban school choice programs in the country in terms of number of participants. The intradistrict choice component involving magnet schools began in 1976, and the interdistrict program involving suburban districts began in 1981. Although the program was initiated as a result of a court-ordered settlement in a desegregation case, its implementation offers lessons to anyone considering establishing choice options in a school district.

The choice program in St. Louis is very costly. Each student who chooses to transfer to another school is provided free transportation by the state. The state also reimburses to the receiving district the per-pupil cost of educating that student. Although costly, the strength of this program is that choice is truly open to all students, regardless of socioeconomic class or place of residence.

A marketing strategy has been devised to keep families through-out the metropolitan area informed regularly of their choice options. These choices are honored until such time as a receiving district has filled its spaces for the coming year. Currently there are more than 13,000 students transferring from the city of St. Louis public schools to 16 of the 23 suburban school districts in the St. Louis metropolitan area, where the proportion of minority enrollment is 25% or less. Nearly 1,000 students transfer into the city from the suburban districts to attend magnet schools and other specialty programs. Another 8,000 students are transferring within the city to attend magnet schools of their choice.

The first component needed for a choice program is equitable access. Under the St. Louis plan, equitable access is provided to students as long as their transfer does not upset the racial balance in the sending or receiving school. In the case of St. Louis, this makes choice options in the interdistrict component available primarily to black students who live in the city and to white students who live in the suburbs. (City magnet schools are available to all students in St. Louis and to white students living in the cooperating suburban districts.)

To encourage equitable access, families are informed of the choice programs through radio, television, and newspaper advertising. In addition, application forms and brochures with more detailed information are mailed directly to the homes of all eligible families in both the city and suburban districts several times throughout the fall and winter. Also, information about the choice plan is disseminated at community fairs and other public events. Parents are encouraged to investigate their options so that they can make informed decisions. Choice is available to low-, middle-, and high-income families alike.

The second essential component is the provision of complete and free transportation services for participating students. Without free transportation, many families would not be able to participate, thus narrowing the mix of students who could transfer and making equal access impossible. Without free transportation, a choice program is not likely to succeed in urban communities unless the receiving schools are contained in an area that is accessible by walking or by public transportation.

Third, districts accepting transfer students should receive funding for each student equal to the per-pupil cost of educating that student. Since the per-pupil costs vary significantly, depending on the wealth of a district, a fair way to determine an equitable pupil cost would be to average the costs across districts.

Fourth, in any choice plan involving transfers between an urban district and its suburban districts, some resources should be available to help the urban district improve the overall quality of the education it offers. Such resources will help the urban district improve its programs and thus ensure that those students who opt not to exercise choice will have access to quality programs. One of the goals of a choice program should be to maintain overall excellence. If schools lose large numbers of students because they are not doing a good job, then perhaps they should cease to exist. But first they should be given every opportunity to improve within a reasonable period of time.

Fifth, funds should be available to improve school facilities in urban districts where buildings have not been properly maintained. Many parents will not select a dilapidated school if alternatives exist, no matter how sound its educational program may be. Funding for extensive facilities upgrade is an integral component of a choice plan.

A word of caution is in order when analyzing school choice plans. State legislatures are in a quandary over such issues as what kind of choice options to provide, how to fund them, whether it will cost more, how to allocate funds for transferring students, whether to provide transportation, whether to restrict them to public schools or to include private/parochial schools, and whether to offer them to all students or just for students from low-income families. Despite all these unresolved issues, there appears to be a frantic effort to jump on the school choice bandwagon without too much supportive research as yet that a change in schooling will produce better outcomes for children. (Data from Community District 4 in East Harlem do show positive results.)

235

What we can say at this time about school choice is that:

1. It allows different ways for assigning students to schools.
2. It relies on parents' decisions rather than automatic school assignment.
3. It allows for different ways of allocating resources for school choice plans.
4. It tends to increase students' motivation, since they are allowed to go to a school they are interested in.
5. It offers stability for those students who often move from school to school, as often happens in urban areas — especially now with so many homeless children.
6. It tends to result in better morale among school staff, because they are involved in creating and developing a specific program, giving them a sense of ownership and mission.
7. It offers the potential for greater parent and community involvement in school activities.
8. It offers different and sometimes unique curricular opportunities.
9. It facilitates racial integration in settings where this may not have been possible otherwise.

Conclusion

School choice has been hailed by politicians and others as the way to restructure our schools and achieve "quality" in education at very little cost. Despite the rhetoric, school choice, in and of itself, will not restructure schools, or break down the bureaucracy, or make significant improvement in student achievement. What school choice can do is to give families the option to select a school that they think will better meet the needs of their children. Having said that, there are certain things that must be done by those who are responsible for implementing school choice:

1. Provide sufficient options so that parents truly have a choice.
2. Develop an ongoing public information program so that all parents in the community are aware that they have a choice and are apprised of what the choice options are.

3. If the choice plan is to be truly equitable, then transportation must be provided for all students if the school selected is not in the neighborhood or on a public transportation line.
4. Resources must be allocated to help improve schools, particularly those in urban areas from which children are leaving.

School choice cannot be viewed as the sole vehicle for restructuring schools and improving student performance. It can, however, be a component of change and reform when there is input from the school staff as well as from parents and other community members so that everybody feels a sense of ownership. However, choice is but one link in the chain needed to bring about change.

The marketplace approach that views school choice, in and of itself, as the ultimate strategy for reforming our schools needs careful examination. Implicit in the marketplace approach is the assumption that giving parents a choice will improve our schools and increase achievement, since choice would force the schools to be more responsive to their consumers. Yet to date there is very little data to validate this assumption. Parental choice may keep schools from becoming too complacent, may create more curricular diversity, and may give parents a greater sense of ownership and commitment; but it is not a panacea. It can allow access for students who otherwise are assigned to second-class or mediocre environments.

The recent Carnegie report, *School Choice* (Boyer 1992), casts doubt on increased achievement outcomes of students and indicates that most parents do not have an alternate school in mind and that current state plans "widen the gap between the advantaged and disadvantaged."

Yet the report indicates that there are choice programs on a districtwide basis that show many positive results in stimulating parent decision making, reorganizing schools, and putting power in the hands of school people. The report, in essence, supports many of the points mentioned in this essay; namely, that transportation must be provided for students, parents must be involved, public schooling must be reaffirmed, funding must be equitable, and every school should have the opportunity to improve under a fair choice program.

It also is important to mention that recent data indicate that open enrollment programs are becoming more popular. There appears to be growing support for choice in the public sector. Choice can be a catalyst for examining the components of school improvement.

There is no single or simple answer for something as complex as the educational process. We should stop looking for one. In our efforts to improve schools, we must be prepared to serve a diverse constituency with broadly conceived programs that respond to student needs. If school choice can be a catalyst for engaging students and their families, for increasing their motivation, and for reforming the curriculum, then we should support the idea. But if nothing else changes in the delivery of education — no new curricula, no reduction of bureaucratic controls, no staff development for teachers, no coordination of social services, or no community involvement — then choice will remain only a smoke screen.

References

Boyd, W.L., and Kerchner, C.T. *The Politics of Excellence and Choice in Education, 1987 Yearbook of Politics of Education*. New York: Falmer, 1987.

Boyer, Ernest. *School Choice*. Princeton, N.J.: Carnegie Foundation for the Advancement of Teaching, 1992.

Bradley, A., and Snider, W. "Backlash Against Choice Plans Emerges Among Minorities." *Education Week*, 21 June 1989, p. 7.

Capell, F.J. *A Study of Alternatives in American Education, Vol. VI: Student Outcomes at Alum Rock, 1974-1976*. Santa Monica, Calif.: RAND Corporation, 1981.

Chance, W. *The Best of Educators' Reforming America's Public Schools in the 1980's*. Chicago: John D. and Catherine T. MacArthur Foundation, 1986.

Chubb, J.E., and Moe, T.M. *Politics, Markets, and America's Schools*. Washington, D.C.: Brookings Institute, 1990.

Cohen, D., and Farrar, E. "Power to the Parents: The Story of Education Vouchers." *Public Interest* 4, no. 8 (1977): 72-79.

Coons, J.E., and Sugarman, S. *Education by Choice: The Case for Family Control*. Berkeley: University of California Press, 1978.

Elmore, R.F. *Choice in Public Education*. Santa Monica, Calif.: RAND Corporation, 1988.

Kearns, D.J., and Doyle, D.P. *Winning the Brain Race*. San Francisco: ICS Press, 1988.

Levin, Henry M. "The Theory of Choice Applied to Education." In *Choice and Control in American Education, Vol. 1: The Theory of Choice and Control in Education*, edited by William Clune and John Witte. New York: Falmer, 1990.

Nault, R., and Uchitelle, S. "School Choice in the Public Sector: A Case Study of Parental Decision-Making." In *Family Choice in Schooling: Issues and Dilemmas*, edited by M. Manley Casimer. Lexington, Mass.: Lexington Books, 1982.

Olsen, Lynn. "Claims for Choice Exceed Evidence, Carnegie Reports." *Education Week*, 28 October 1992, pp. 1, 12.

Paulu, Nancy. *Improving Schools and Empowering Parents: Choice in American Education: A Report Based on the White House Workshop on Choice in Education*. Washington, D.C.: U.S. Department of Education, OERI, Oct. 1989.

Phi Delta Kappan (December 1989 issue).

Rand Corporation. *A Study of Alternatives in American Education*. R-2170/1-NIE through R 2170/7-NIE. Santa Monica, Calif., 1978.

Raywid, M.S. "Family Choice Arrangements in Public Schools." *Review of Educational Research* 55, no. 4 (1985): 435-67.

Snider, W. "The Call for Choice: Competition in the Educational Marketplace." Special report. *Education Week*, 24 June 1987, pp. 16-17.

Snider, W. "School Choice: New, More Efficient 'Sorting Machine'." *Education Week*, 18 May 1988, pp. 1, 8.

Snider, W. "In Nation's First Open Enrollment State, the Action Begins." *Education Week*, 15 March 1989, p. 18.

SEXUAL HARASSMENT

by Dan H. Wishnietsky

exual harassment in education settings is a serious problem. Although the number of reported incidents varies according to how sexual harassment is defined, both verbal harassment and other crimes of a sexual nature, such as sexual assault, seem to be increasing on school and college campuses. This increase is evident in the number of court cases involving alleged incidents of harassment in education. And the increase in incidents also is a frequent subject of professional articles in education journals and a significant number of newspaper and magazine articles.

A concern consistently expressed in reports on sexual harassment is that the education environment is sexually hostile for many individuals, but especially for females. One repeatedly reported finding is that approximately 25% of female college students report having been sexually harassed by male faculty (Malovich and Stake 1990).

In addition to faculty-student sexual harassment, research has found student-student, faculty-faculty, and student-faculty sexual harassment in secondary and postsecondary institutions. Harassing behaviors included suggestive looks, sexual comments, unwanted touching, sexual assault, and rape. Although most victims were female, male students also reported incidents of sexual harassment. This was particularly true for homosexual males and men enrolled in women's studies classes.

In schools and colleges, where mutual respect is a fundamental condition for a sense of "community," one would expect to find policies that forcefully confront sexual harassment. However, most education institutions fall short of this goal. Some institu-

This essay is condensed from Dan H. Wishnietsky, *Establishing School Policies on Sexual Harassment*, Fastback 370 (Bloomington, Ind.: Phi Delta Kappa Educational Foundation, 1994).

tions find it difficult to develop effective policies because of a lack of consensus on the definition of sexual harassment, the variability of research findings on the extent of the problem, and the overall social complexity of the issue.

The purpose of this essay is to provide information that will help members of the academic community overcome these difficulties and discover ways to eliminate sexual harassment from their schools.

Historical Perspective

Sexual harassment is a complex social problem. Harassment is a behavior by which the harassing individual asserts power over another person. Often, harassment involves a man attempting to manipulate or to control a woman.

To place sexual harassment in context, it is important to understand that women's behaviors nearly always have been more restricted than men's behaviors. The historical distinction between a "good" woman and a "bad" woman was based on a social code of male domination. Until recently, a woman without a man to "protect" her was considered a legitimate target of male sexual desires.

Throughout most of Western history, women have not been regarded as autonomous beings, but rather as male possessions. For example, the rape of a woman throughout much of history was not considered to be a crime against the woman; it was a crime against the property of a husband, a father, a brother, or a son. If a woman went alone in public and was assaulted, the prevailing attitude was that she was asking for trouble and was responsible for the attack. Thus a woman suffered not only the physical trauma of being raped, but also had to endure the public belief that the incident was her own fault.

Many 19th century scientists, such as Edward H. Clarke, believed that women were physically and mentally inferior to males. Clarke (1874) maintained that the development of the sex organs and the development of the brain were at opposite poles of the nervous system. Since the female reproductive system was more complex than that of the male, it required more nervous system energy to develop. This growth took place at the expense of the brain, with the result that the male was more intelligent than the female. Clarke warned that if a female were to educate herself and develop her intellect, the strain on her body would cause her to have a nervous breakdown or to become sterile.

Such views persisted in the United States into this century and helped to produce a culture in which the sexual harassment of women was an accepted practice.

In the 1960s, a major change occurred in the political and legal perspective regarding sexual harassment with the adoption of Title VII of the Civil Rights Act of 1964, which prohibited employers from discriminating against any individual's terms, conditions, or privileges of employment on the basis of sex. Victims of discrimination were entitled to back pay, lost benefits, damages, and job reinstatement. The principles and guidelines of Title VII became applicable to education with the adoption of Title IX of the 1972 Education Amendments. Education institutions that did not take steps to prevent discrimination — sexual harassment being a form of discrimination — faced the possible loss of federal funding.

In 1975 the term *sexual harassment* became a new catch phrase. Publications about the topic rapidly increased as the result of congressional hearings, increased litigation, and the adoption in 1980 of the Equal Employment Opportunity Commission guidelines on harassment. The increased number of articles influenced the editors of the *Education Index* to include "sexual harassment" as a major classification in 1980. (Before that year, articles concerning sexual harassment were listed under "sex discrimination.")

Today, most educators and researchers base their definition of sexual harassment on the 1980 Equal Employment Opportunity Commission guidelines that reflect Title IX of the 1972 Education Amendments:

> Harassment on the basis of sex is a violation of section 703 of Title VII. Unwelcome sexual advances, requests for sexual favors and other verbal or physical conduct of a sexual nature when submission to such conduct is made either

explicitly or implicitly a term or condition of an individual's employment; submission to or rejection of such conduct by an individual is used as the basis for employment decisions affecting the individual; or such conduct has the purpose or effect of unreasonably interfering with an individual's work performance or creating an intimidating, hostile, or offensive working environment.

Sexual harassment consists of verbal or physical conduct of a sexual nature, imposed on the basis of sex, by an employee or agent of a recipient that denies, limits, provides different, or conditions the provision of aid, benefits, services or treatment protected under Title IX. (*Federal Register* 1980)

This definition gives educators considerable freedom in explicitly defining sexual harassment. The text of Title VII states that when determining whether conduct constitutes sexual harassment, the Equal Employment Opportunity Commission will look at the conduct in context on a case-by-case basis.

Sexual Harassment in the School

Research indicates that sexual harassment is a continuing and increasing problem in secondary and postsecondary institutions. In 1982 more than 900 women and men students at the University of Rhode Island responded to a questionnaire regarding their experiences with sexual harassment on campus. Forty percent of the female respondents and 17% of the male respondents reported being the victims of student-student and faculty-student sexual harassment. Both sexes indicated that the harassing individuals usually were men (Lott et al. 1982).

Beyond the physical and mental trauma brought on by sexual harassment, such incidents also have a negative impact on the victim's education. A 1983 article in the *Chronicle of Higher Education* reported that at Harvard University 15% of the graduate students and 12% of the undergraduate students who had been sexually harassed by their professors changed their major or program because of the harassment (McCain 1983). Also in 1983, an article published in the *Journal of College Student Personnel* reported that 13% of the women surveyed stated that they avoided taking a class or working with a professor because of the risk of subjecting themselves to sexual advances (Adams et al. 1983).

Authors of a 1985 study presented at the conference of the American Psychological Association in Los Angeles interviewed 246 women who were enrolled in a graduate psychology program. Of these women, 15.9% reported being directly assaulted, 21% refrained from enrolling in a course to avoid sexual harassment, and 2.6% dropped a course because of harassment (Bailey and Richards 1985).

A 1990 study, published in *Psychology of Women Quarterly*, found that more than 38% of female undergraduate students enrolled in introductory psychology classes at a mid-size Midwestern university had experienced sexual harassment (Malovich and Stake 1990). Approximately 89% of these students were freshmen or sophomores. Another 1990 study, published in *Sex Roles*, studied the sexual harassment of faculty by colleagues and students. Faculty members reported "moderate levels of harassment." Interestingly, female faculty were more likely to report harassment by colleagues, while male faculty were more likely to report harassment by students (McKinney 1990).

Sexual harassment of female students also has been reported in secondary schools. *Education Week* reported that in a 1985 Minnesota study of junior and senior high school students enrolled in a white, middle-class, secondary vocational center, between 33% and 60% of the females had experienced some form of sexual harassment (Stein 1991). A 1991 study of recent North Carolina high school graduates, published in the *Journal of Educational Research*, supported the Minnesota study results. Among the North Carolina females who responded, approximately 50% stated that a high school instructor had sexually harassed them (Wishnietsky 1991).

Although most victims of sexual harassment are women, the number of males alleging sexual harassment also is increasing. In the above study of recent North Carolina high school graduates, approximately 11% of the males who responded stated that they had been sexually harassed. A 1989 study published by Florida State University relates three court cases concerning men who were subjected to sexual harassment (Hazzard 1989). This study predicted that as more women are promoted to supervisory and management positions, the sexual harassment of men will increase dramatically.

A Summary of Judicial Cases

Based on Title IX of the Education Amendments of 1972 and Title VII of the Civil Rights Act of 1964, sexual harassment is a form of sex discrimination and is prohibited under federal law. The federal agency charged with enforcing Title IX is the United States Department of Education Office of Civil Rights (OCR). If any local education agency or postsecondary institution that receives federal assistance does not fully comply with Title IX, the Office of Civil Rights may recommend that the school's federal funding be terminated.

One of the first legal cases involving sexual harassment in education occurred in 1976 when several female students filed suit against Yale University. The students claimed that the university had the responsibility of preventing sexual harassment and mediating any disputes about harassment. Although the court decided in favor of Yale University, the case established a legal precedent for hearing sexual harassment grievances under Title IX of the 1972 Education Amendments (*Alexander* v. *Yale University*, 631 F.2d 178, 2d Cir. 1980).

In 1977 the Supreme Court wrote in *Ingraham* v. *Wright* (430 U.S. 651, 654) that school administrators have "the duty of ensuring that the school environment is a safe one for students." Ten years later, using *Ingraham* as precedent, the federal court serving the Western District of Pennsylvania declared in *Stoneking* v. *Bradford Area School District* (667 F. Supp. 1088, W.D. Pa. 1987) that a safe environment was free of sexual harassment. The case involved a male high school teacher who had sexual relationships with several female students. Testimony indicated that several administrators knew of the teacher's behavior and did not intervene.

Two cases that established the strength of Title VII in protecting employees from sexual harassment are *Kyriazi* v. *Western Electric* (476 F. Supp. 335, D.N.J. 1979) and *Meritor Savings Bank* v. *Vinson* (106 S.Ct. 2399, 1986). In *Kyriazi*, a female engineer sued Western Electric for ignoring her complaints of sexual harassment from three co-workers and two superiors. The court ruled that Western Electric was liable for the harassment and had to pay for lost pay and benefits.

In *Meritor Savings Bank* the Supreme Court held that unwelcome sexual advances that create a hostile or offensive working environment violate Title VII, even if the victim did not suffer economic or tangible injury. Since Title VII is relevant to sexual harassment on campus because of Title IX, these cases also apply to school employees, including student workers.

In October 1991 the Anita Hill-Clarence Thomas inquiry established sexual harassment as a major, nationwide issue as the country watched, read about, and discussed the confirmation hearings of Supreme Court nominee Clarence Thomas. During the confirmation process, Anita Hill, a law professor and Thomas' former aide, testified that Thomas had sexually harassed her in the early 1980s. Thomas emphatically denied the charge, and the Senate confirmed his appointment to the Supreme Court. The fervor unleashed by these hearings persuaded many educators to believe that relationships between men and women have permanently changed. Ellen Futter, president of Barnard College, said that the emotions unleashed by the Anita Hill-Clarence Thomas hearings will not be quieted and will lead to "levels of understanding between men and women not previously achieved or imagined" (Lewis 1991).

Franklin v. *Gwinnett County Public Schools*. The principles of Title IX were designed to prevent federal funds from being allocated to institutions that discriminated on the basis of sex. This changed when the United States Court of Appeals for the Seventh

Circuit ruled in *Cannon* v. *University of Chicago* (710 F.2d 351, 1983) that a student may sue an education institution for discrimination. But until 1992 it was not clear whether a student who prevailed in a sexual harassment case against an education institution could collect monetary damages.

On 26 February 1992, twenty years after its effective date, the Supreme Court confirmed the strength of Title IX when the justices unanimously ruled in *Franklin* v. *Gwinnett County Public Schools* (112 S.Ct. 1028) that victims of sex discrimination in schools and colleges may collect damage payments. Before *Franklin*, the common remedy under the law was a court order to stop the harassment. That recourse is no longer a sufficient remedy for schools to take. According to the Supreme Court, education institutions can be ordered to pay victims compensatory damages.

The *Franklin* case evolved in this way. From September 1985 to August 1989, Christine Franklin was a student at North Gwinnett High School in Gwinnett County, Georgia. North Gwinnett High School is operated by the Gwinnett County School District, which receives federal funds. Franklin alleged that since the fall of 1986 she had been subjected to sexual harassment from Andrew Hill, a teacher and coach at the high school. Franklin claimed that Hill would engage her in sexually oriented conversation that included questions regarding her sexual experiences and whether she would have sexual relations with an older man.

Franklin declared that Hill became increasingly aggressive with his sexual harassment. He telephoned her at home and asked her to meet him socially; forcibly kissed her on the mouth in the school parking lot; and on three occasions during her junior year, raped her while they were on school property. Hill would interrupt a class, request that the teacher excuse Franklin, take her to a private office, and subject her to forced intercourse. Her allegation also claimed that teachers and administrators at North Gwinnett High School became aware that Hill was sexually harassing Franklin and other female students.

Although school personnel investigated Hill's conduct, they took no action to end it; and they discouraged Franklin from press-

248

ing charges against Hill. The school's investigation ended in April 1988, when Hill resigned on the condition that all charges pending against him be dropped (112 S.Ct. 1031).

In August 1988, four months after North Gwinnett High School closed its investigation, Franklin filed a complaint with the Office of Civil Rights. OCR investigated the charges and concluded that the Gwinnett County School District had violated Franklin's rights. This included exposing her to both verbal and physical sexual harassment and then interfering with her right to press charges. The OCR investigation terminated because Hill had resigned and the school district had implemented a grievance procedure that brought it into compliance with Title IX.

Franklin then filed suit in the United States District Court of the Northern District of Georgia under Title IX, seeking damages for gender-based discrimination in connection with sexual harassment and abuse. The district court dismissed the case on the ground that damages are not authorized under Title IX. Franklin appealed to the Court of Appeals for the Eleventh Circuit, which upheld the lower court's decision. Franklin petitioned the Supreme Court to review the lower court's decision. Certiorari was granted. The case was argued 11 December 1991, and decided 26 February 1992.

Relevant Issues. The defendants presented three reasons why the lower courts were correct in dismissing Franklin's complaint. First, they claimed that a monetary award would violate the separation of powers principle by unduly expanding the judicial branch of government into an area rightly reserved for the legislative and executive branches. The Supreme Court rejected this argument, based on the difference between a cause of action and a remedy. The cause of action in this case had already been established by Congress under Title IX, and awarding appropriate relief would not increase judicial power. In fact, the award of damages historically has been within the province of the judicial system and is a crucial protection against unlimited legislative and executive power.

The second argument was that all appropriate remedies should not apply because Title IX was enacted in accordance with the congressional Spending Power Clause. This clause protects state entities from having to pay monetary awards from their treasuries for unintentional violations of federal statutes. Although Spending Clause statutes prohibit monetary damages for unintentional violations, the defendants argued that they should apply equally when the violation was intentional. The Supreme Court rejected this argument, noting that the Court had already ruled in a previous case (*Darrone*, 104 S.Ct. 1251) that the Spending Clause permits monetary damages for intentional violations. The Court also concluded that Congress did not authorize federal funds to support intentional behaviors that are, by congressional mandate, illegal.

The final argument was that the remedies allowed under Title IX should be limited to back pay and prospective relief. However, it was obvious to the Supreme Court that the remedies proposed by the defendants were altogether insufficient. Franklin was a student when the alleged harassment occurred; thus back pay was meaningless. Since Andrew Hill no longer taught at the school and Franklin was not a student in the Gwinnett system, the proposed relief provided no remedy.

In rejecting these arguments, the Supreme Court ruled that a damage remedy is available for an action brought to enforce Title IX. This ruling cleared the way for federal courts to use any available remedy to right a wrong where legal rights have been invaded and federal statute provides the right to sue. With this ruling, the Supreme Court placed Title VII and Title IX on equal footing. The justices asserted that the rules that apply when a supervisor sexually harasses a subordinate also apply when a teacher sexually harasses and abuses a student. Title IX alerts schools not to discriminate on the basis of sex, just as Title VII alerts employers; thus the same remedies should apply in cases of violation.

Implications for Schools. The *Franklin* decision has provided victims of sexual harassment and the many educators who wish to prevent harassment with another avenue of redress. Schools and colleges no longer can afford to ignore reports of sexual harassment on campus or rest content merely to stop the harassment. They now can be ordered to pay victims compensatory damages.

According to Christine Franklin's attorney, Michael Weinstock, the Supreme Court's decision should indicate to every school that it must establish procedures to hear complaints in confidence and must act on complaints promptly, effectively, and in a manner that protects and supports the victim. Policies and procedures should address all types of harassment, whether faculty-student, faculty-faculty, or student-student.

All faculty and students who suffer intentional sex discrimination now may sue for damages under Title IX; and school employees, including student workers, may file a claim under Title VII. In an incident reported in the *New York Times* (11 March 1992, p. B8), a female student received a $15,000 settlement for mental anguish because school officials did not prohibit her male classmates from taunting her and writing vulgarities about her on a bathroom wall.

Considering the financial risks alone, schools and colleges might be expected to move quickly to set in place appropriate policies. However, according to a study published in *Initiatives* in 1994, to date few states have developed and implemented policy changes concerning sexual harassment. Surveys sent to the state boards of education in 50 states and the District of Columbia 15 months after the *Franklin* decision found that only 10% of the reporting states had instituted a change of policy at the state level, while only 22% had changed policies at the local level because of *Franklin* (Wishnietsky and Felder 1994).

Without policies and procedures in place, sex equity specialists predict that many schools will pay monetary damages as future victims of sexual harassment prevail in the courts.

Establishing Written Policies

Educators have a legal and moral responsibility to provide environments that are safe for students and staff. Developing and

251

implementing policies that deter sexual harassment help to provide such security. Ideally, policies are initiated at the state level.

Illinois initiated a statewide sexual harassment policy before the threat of monetary damages became an issue. On 3 October 1986, Illinois Administrative Code, Title 23, Part 200, became law. Section 200.40 states that all policies and practices of the Illinois education system shall comply with Title IX. In addition, each school system is required to have a written policy forbidding discrimination based on sex in all educational programs and activities.

In California the state legislature responded to the Supreme Court ruling in *Franklin* v. *Gwinnett County Public Schools* by drafting and signing into law a bill prohibiting sexual harassment. On 24 September 1992, only seven months after the *Franklin* decision, the governor of California signed into law Assembly Bill No. 2900, which reaffirms an existing law that prohibits sexual harassment and directs each education institution, school district, county office of education, and community college to establish a policy on sexual harassment.

The policy requirements in Illinois and California can serve as models for other states and school entities. Section 200 of the Illinois Administrative Code and Section 212.6 of the California Education Code both address sexual harassment policy and practice at each state's education institutions.

The Illinois code is applicable to all public school districts and mandates that all policies and practices of education systems comply with Title IX of the Education Amendments of 1972. In addition, every education system in Illinois is required to have a written policy on sex equity. This policy must state that schools do not discriminate on the basis of sex in programs, activities, services, or benefits. Students, regardless of their sex, are guaranteed equal access to educational and extracurricular programs and activities.

To enforce the sex equity policy, each school system is required to have a written grievance procedure by which any person in the system may present a complaint alleging discrimination. The grievance procedure includes: 1) the method for initiating and processing a grievance, 2) the parties involved in each step of the grievance procedure, 3) a specific timetable for completing each step and delivering a written decision, and 4) a final appeal process. Each school system is responsible for informing all employees, students, and parents of the sex equity policy and the grievance procedure through such publications as policy manuals, newsletters, and student handbooks. In addition, each school system is required to evaluate their sex equity policy at least every four years.

California Education Code section 212.6 also addresses sex equity issues. According to California law, discrimination of any kind because of sex is prohibited at the state's education institutions. The purpose of Section 212.6 is to define sexual harassment as a form of sex discrimination and therefore prohibited in California schools. By legislative action, this section mandates that each education institution in the state have a written policy on sexual harassment as part of the school's regular policy statement. The institution's written policy is to be in every school publication that details the school's rules and regulations.

Like Illinois, California requires that the education institution's sexual harassment policy include information about where to obtain specific rules and how to make complaints and seek remedies for grievances. The policy must be displayed in a prominent location on the campus or school site. Suggested locations include the main administrative building or other areas where notices regarding the school's regulations, procedures, and standards of conduct are posted. In addition to posting the policy regarding sexual harassment, copies must be provided to all students as part of any orientation process. The education institution also must distribute the sexual harassment policy to all faculty members, administrative staff, and support staff at the beginning of each term or when a new employee is hired.

Human Resources Management Model. Commerce Clearing House publishes *Human Resources Management*, which includes guidelines for establishing a sexual harassment policy and conducting a sexual harassment investigation. The objectives of these policies include preventing sexual harassment and avoiding sexual harassment charges or lawsuits under Title VII. Since Title IX of the Education Amendments is based on Title VII of the Civil Rights Act, the guidelines presented in *Human Resources Management* can be easily modified for education institutions.

The *Human Resources Management* model recommends that any sexual harassment policy include: 1) a definition of sexual harassment, 2) a complaint procedure, 3) a time frame for investigation, 4) a statement of penalties, and 5) an assurance of confidentiality and protection against retaliation. The definition of sexual harassment included in Title VII of the 1980 Equal Employment Opportunity Commission guidelines can be adapted for the education setting by including the academic environment along with the work environment. Any general definition also should describe specific unacceptable behaviors.

The complaint procedure should designate one or more individuals authorized to respond to written complaints. These individuals should not be in the direct line of supervision. It is important that the complaint procedure ensures that the victim will not have to complain to the alleged harasser. In a school setting, the designated individual could be an affirmative action officer, a guidance counselor, or a committee of several educators.

The complaint procedure also should include a timetable for the investigation and specify the penalties that may be levied for policy violations. Such penalties can range from a warning to dismissal. In addition to penalties from the school unit, there may be civil penalties for violating sexual harassment laws.

Sexual harassment often is not reported because victims fear retaliation or social stigma. The *Human Resources Management* model contains a confidentiality provision that stipulates that the identity of all involved individuals will be protected, including the victim, the alleged harasser, and all witnesses. Protection against retaliation for all people involved also is assured.

Sample Sexual Harassment Policy Statement. Many education institutions are developing sexual harassment policy based on the *Human Resources Management* model and the education codes of

Illinois and California. Following is a sample policy statement designed to aid educators in developing appropriate guidelines. This statement on sexual harassment is based on the *Human Resources Model*. It is similar to statements adopted by many schools and school systems, but each individual institution should modify the policy statement to match its specific needs.

Statement of Policy: Sexual harassment by any member of the education community is a violation of both law and school policy. Accordingly, no academic or personnel decisions, such as awarding of grades and jobs, shall be made on the basis of the granting or the denial of sexual favors.

Definition: For purposes of this policy, sexual harassment is defined as unwelcome sexual advances, requests for sexual favors, and other verbal or physical conduct of a sexual nature when submission to such conduct is made either explicitly or implicitly a term or condition of an individual's employment or academic advancement; submission to or rejection of such conduct by an individual is used as the basis for employment decisions or academic decisions affecting the individual; or such conduct has the purpose or effect of unreasonably interfering with an individual's work or academic performance or creating an intimidating, hostile, or offensive working or academic environment.

As defined above, sexual harassment is a specific form of discrimination in which power inherent in a faculty member's or supervisor's relationship to his or her students or subordinates is unfairly exploited. While sexual harassment most often occurs in a situation of power differential between persons involved, this policy recognizes that sexual harassment may take place between persons of the same status, that is, student-student, faculty-faculty, staff-staff.

Purpose of Policy: The sexual harassment policy is designed to encourage students, faculty, and staff to express freely, responsibly, and in an orderly way their opinions and feelings regarding any problem or complaint of sexual harassment. Any act by a school employee or an agent of the school of reprisal, interfer-

255

ence, restraint, penalty, discrimination, coercion, or harassment — overtly or covertly — against a student or employee for using the policy will necessitate appropriate and prompt disciplinary action. This policy shall not be used frivolously, falsely, or maliciously to convey charges against fellow students, faculty members, or employees.

Consensual Relationships: While consenting romantic and sexual relationships between faculty and student, or between supervisor and employee, are not expressly forbidden, such relationships are deemed inappropriate. Where a power differential exists, if a charge of sexual harassment is brought, the defense of mutual consent will be difficult to prove.

Handling Complaints: The complaint officer shall be responsible for receiving and processing any and all complaints of alleged sexual harassment. The initial investigation may lead to one of several steps.

First, an attempt will be made to resolve the question informally through confidential mediation, counseling, or informal discussion. If the complaint cannot be resolved informally, the complainant may file a formal written complaint. The complaint shall set forth in detail the nature of the grievance, against whom the grievance is directed, and the names of any witnesses.

The complaint officer shall contact and forward the complaint to the respondent and request the respondent to reply to the written complaint within 10 days of receipt of the complaint. The filing of such responses shall be mandatory; and the person responding shall be required to indicate denial in whole or in part, or agreement with the assertions in whole or in part. Failure to respond shall be deemed a breach of academic responsibility requiring the complaint officer to notify the appropriate institutional authority. Upon receipt of the response, the complaint officer may further investigate the complaint and may schedule a meeting of the parties. If there is no settlement between the parties, the complaint shall be forwarded to a grievance hearing unless the investigation reveals that the complaint has no merit.

Grievance Hearings: The complaint committee shall conduct grievance hearings for the purpose of advising and fact-finding. A calendar of the hearings in a sexual harassment grievance proceeding shall be fixed by the chair of the complaint committee as promptly as possible. The chair will notify the parties involved of the time and place of the hearing. Any hearing shall be conducted in accordance with basic and traditional principles of fairness and in accordance with procedures that guarantee due process to the complainant and respondent.

The chair of the complaint committee shall preside over the hearing. Both parties may have legal representation. If a complainant or a respondent chooses to hire legal representation, that party shall assume all costs. The charges and the evidence shall be presented by the complainant or complainant's legal representative. Either party may request the privilege of presenting witnesses, subject to the right of cross-examination by the opposing side. The complaint committee chair must be notified in writing five days prior to the hearing date of the names and addresses of all witnesses who will testify. It is each party's responsibility to notify the witnesses of the time, date, and place of the hearing. In addition to the parties named in the complaint, any member of the complaint committee may address questions to any party to the proceedings or to any witness called by the parties or the committee. Inquiry into the complainant's sexual habits or relationships shall be deemed inappropriate.

The hearing shall be confidential and private, unless otherwise agreed upon by both parties. An accurate record of the proceedings shall be made and the record shall be made available to all parties to the hearing. At the end of the hearing, the committee will make its recommendation in a closed executive session. The complaint committee shall make a report to the appropriate person or office and to all parties of the hearing within five working days. It may recommend to dismiss the complaint as being without merit or it may find that the respondent acted in violation of the sexual harassment policy. The committee shall describe the nature of the alleged violation, the evidence that supports its judgment, and the sanction, if any, that it recommends to the appropriate person or office. Final authority for implementing the recommen-

257

dation shall be with the appropriate person or office, who may accept, reject, or modify the decision. The appropriate person or office shall notify all parties of the decision within 10 business days following receipt of the complaint committee report.

Appeals: All appeals shall follow the procedure outlined in the school code, the student handbook, and the State Personnel Act. [These procedures should be already in place to govern grievances other than ones of sexual harassment.] All parties are reminded that sexual harassment is a violation of law and that the decision of the complaint committee does not prevent any party from taking legal action in the courts. By implementing this sexual harassment policy, it is anticipated that resolution will occur during the grievance procedure and the filing of sexual harassment lawsuits will be prevented.

In 1982 a detailed study of the legal implications of sexual contact between teachers and students was published in the *Journal of Law and Education*. The author, Patricia Winks, an attorney who had been a public school teacher and administrator, stated that there was abundant evidence that sexual harassment in academe was widespread. After studying the adverse consequences suffered by victims of sexual harassment in higher and secondary education, Winks alleged that students, teachers, and administrators have all participated in a conspiracy of silence regarding sexual harassment in the schools. Sadly, much of the research published in the years since 1982 supports Winks' allegation.

Instead of silence, educators must forcefully and collectively confront sexual harassment. More important than the legal requirement or a written policy is a faculty and staff that desire a school environment where students and personnel are not sexually harassed. Guidelines may provide the form for policy; but only faculty, staff, and administrators can provide the substance. In fact, a possible deterrent to those who are contemplating inappropriate behaviors is the knowledge that sexual harassment will not be tolerated.

Prevention Programs

Legal mandates and written policies primarily address how to manage situations after harassment has occurred. The *Human Resources Management* model asserts that training is a critical step in the prevention of sexual harassment. The model suggests periodic workshops to explain policy, to identify harassment, and to learn how to interact productively with the harasser.

Sexual harassment workshops attempt to influence behavior by using awareness training as a basis for change. Participants learn what constitutes sexual harassment, its harmful effects, and ways to combat harassment. They also examine and confront individual opinions about sexual harassment. After the training, many schools believe that workshop participants better understand the dynamics of sexual harassment, show more sensitivity toward victims of harassment, and have a lower tolerance for intimidating sexual behavior.

The initial segment of the sexual harassment workshop usually includes a statement by the head of the school or school system or other high-level administrator. The administrator sets the tone for the workshop by emphasizing that sexual harassment cannot be tolerated on campus and that all members of the school community are expected to play an active role in preventing harassment. The administrator also discusses how harassment undermines the mission of education. By involving an influential leader, participants are more likely to recognize that educators at all levels of leadership are united in the institution's war against sexual harassment. Although having this individual appear in person at the workshop is preferred, many schools use a taped introduction because of time constraints on the administrator.

Next, workshop facilitators present and discuss the school's definition of sexual harassment. This may include the explanations found in Title VII of the Civil Rights Act, Title IX of the Education Amendments, or the school's guidelines. After discussing the definition, participants examine different forms of sexually related conduct. This can be accomplished through role playing or by viewing tapes that depict incidents of sexual harassment.

259

A set of 12 tapes, developed at the University of Michigan, demonstrates the complexity and the questions that often surround incidents of harassment. The tapes illustrate basic forms of harassment, such as a male harassing a female, a heterosexual harassing a homosexual, a homosexual harassing a heterosexual, and a female harassing a male. These tapes, the "Tell Someone Training Program," are available from the Affirmative Action Office, University of Michigan, Ann Arbor, MI 48109; (313) 763-0235.

After viewing the tapes, participants discuss whether the incident depicted in each of the scenarios involved sexual harassment and what actions the victim might take. The discussion concerning the tapes or role playing often provides an occasion for discussing personal experiences of harassment at the individual's school. In this way, participants discover firsthand the personal and academic consequences of harassment.

Participants often believe that harassment happens elsewhere, not at their own institution. By viewing sexual harassment as a local problem, workshop members are able to discuss what they can do to help prevent harassment at their school. Participants analyze federal guidelines concerning sexual harassment and review the school's sexual harassment policy statement. The local solutions recommended in the school policy are examined to determine if they conform with federal law. After evaluating the local guidelines, the group suggests how they could be improved. This activity cultivates a sense of shared responsibility for solving the problem.

Finally, each participant receives a reference manual that reviews the aspects of sexual harassment addressed in the workshop.

An Organizational Development Approach. Opposing sexual harassment requires more than establishing policies, instituting grievance procedures, or scheduling workshops. According to an organizational development perspective, intervention must affect the structure and value system of the education setting. Long-term behavioral changes will not occur in individuals unless similar changes occur in the school's social expectations. For example, participants in a sexual harassment workshop might form positive attitudes and behavioral changes; but if the school's culture does not reinforce the new values, the new behaviors soon will be extinguished.

In the fall 1989 edition of *CUPA Journal*, Thomann, Strickland, and Gibbons described how Saint Louis University instituted a sexual harassment policy designed to influence the school's culture. Although the *CUPA Journal* example was developed in a university setting, an organizational development approach can be generalized for all levels of education.

Cultural change at any school requires support from people at the highest levels of the organization. At Saint Louis University, the college president affirmed the institution's commitment to an environment free of sexual harassment. A group of key participants in the organization further strengthened this commitment. They not only provided verbal and written support, but also worked to develop a policy based on their shared value.

As discussion concerning sexual harassment increases, people form shared meanings and definitions, a common understanding of harassment's consequences, and how the individuals and the institution should respond. These new understandings are shared through the school's mission statement, dialogue sessions, workshops, and other methods. As more people participate in the battle against sexual harassment, the orientation of the education community begins to change. Instead of an environment where harassment is ignored or even condoned, the social orientation becomes one where harassment is not tolerated.

Conclusion

Sexual harassment has been illegal since the adoption of Title VII of the Civil Rights Act of 1964 and Title IX of the 1972 Education Amendments. Court cases, such as *Alexander* v. *Yale*, *Ingraham* v. *Wright*, and *Franklin* v. *Gwinnett County Public Schools*, have further defined sexual harassment and have identified appropriate penalties. In spite of these actions, the number of reported sexual harassment cases continues to increase.

A goal of all educators should be to provide an educational environment where sexual harassment is not tolerated. This requires more than legal precedent. All states should require their education institutions to develop policies that will help to create an environment free from all forms of discrimination and conduct that is harassing, coercive, or disruptive. California's Assembly Bill No. 2900 (24 September 1992) and Title 23 of the Illinois Administrative Code, Part 200 (3 October 1986, amended 29 June 1989) provide frameworks for developing sexual harassment policy.

Educators have a legal and ethical responsibility to prevent sexual harassment in the education environment. The ideals of democracy expressed by the academic community indicate an ethical responsibility to provide an environment free of harassment. Although there are no simple solutions, by collaboratively and aggressively confronting sexual harassment, educators can formulate and implement policies that will provide personal security for students and staff and will protect professional integrity.

References

Adams, J.; Kottke, J.; and Padgitt, J. "Sexual Harassment of University Students." *Journal of College Student Personnel* 24 (1983): 484-90.

Bailey, N., and Richards, M. "Tarnishing the Ivory Tower: Sexual Harassment in Graduate Training Programs in Psychology." Paper presented at the conference of the American Psychological Association, Los Angeles, 1985.

Clarke, E.H. *Sex in Education: Or, a Fair Chance for Girls*. Boston: James R. Osgood and Company, 1874.

Federal Register 45, no. 219. Rules and regulations 74676-74677. 10 November 1980.

Hazzard, T. *Sexual Harassment: What's Good for the Goose Is Good for the Gander*. Tallahassee: Florida State University Department of Educational Leadership, 1989.

Lewis, A.C. "Taking Women Seriously." *Phi Delta Kappan* 73 (December 1991): 268-69.

Lott, B.; Reilly, M.; and Howard, D. "Sexual Assault and Harassment: A Campus Community Case Study." *Signs* 8, no. 2 (1982): 296-319.

Malovich, N., and Stake, J. "Sexual Harassment on Campus: Individual Differences in Attitudes and Beliefs." *Psychology of Women Quarterly* 14, no. 1 (1990): 63-81.

McCain, N. "Female Faculty Members and Students at Harvard Report Sexual Harassment." *Chronicle of Higher Education*, 2 November 1983.

McKinney, K. "Sexual Harassment of University Faculty by Colleagues and Students." *Sex Roles* 23, no. 7/8 (1990): 421-38.

Stein, N. "It Happens Here, Too: Sexual Harassment in Schools." *Education Week*, 27 November 1991, p. 32.

Winks, P.L. "Legal Implications of Sexual Contact Between Teacher and Student." *Journal of Law and Education* 11, no. 4 (1982): 437-77.

Wishnietsky, D. "Reported and Unreported Teacher-Student Sexual Harassment." *Journal of Educational Research* 84, no. 3 (1991): 164-69.

Wishnietsky, D., and Felder, D. "The Effect of *Franklin* v. *Gwinnett County* on Sexual Harassment Policy in Secondary Education." *Initiatives* 56, no. 1 (1994): 37-45.

ABOUT THE AUTHORS

Louann A. Bierlein is the Education Policy Advisor to Louisiana Governor Mark Foster and a senior fellow at the Hudson Institute. She formerly was director of the Louisiana Education Policy Research Center at Louisiana State University and assistant director of Education and Social Policy Studies at the Morrison Institute for Public Policy, Arizona State University. Bierlein, a nationally recognized expert on charter schools, began her education career as a middle school science teacher.

Kenneth Burrett is a professor in the School of Education at Duquesne University and an associate of the Center for Character Education, Civic Responsibility, and Teaching. A former elementary and secondary teacher, he also has served as director of student teaching and associate dean at Duquesne University. Burrett was named Teacher Educator of the Year in 1989 by the Pennsylvania Association of Colleges for Teacher Education.

Carol Conway-Gerhardt is director of instruction in the South Milwaukee Schools in Wisconsin. She has served as president of the Sheboygan Wisconsin Chapter of Phi Delta Kappa and is currently PDK Area 5B Coordinator. She previously served as a district department chair and as administrative coordinator of language arts, reading, foreign language, and English-as-a-second-language programs in the Sheboygan Area School District. She also is an adjunct professor at the University of Wisconsin-Oshkosh and Marion College in Fond du Lac, Wisconsin.

Jack Frymier is a Phi Delta Kappa Senior Fellow. He was a professor of education at Ohio State University for many years, where he also was co-director of the Center for the Study of Motivation and Human Abilities. Frymier also served as the national president of the Association for Supervision and Curriculum Develop-

265

ment. The author of 11 books and more than 200 articles, Frymier's recent research includes the PDK study of students at risk and a study of core values education.

Suzanne Gerlach-Downie is a research social scientist at the Center for Education and Human Services, SRI International, in Menlo Park, California. She currently is involved in an evaluation of the Parents as Teachers program. She also provides technical assistance on research and assessment, particularly for projects involving young children.

Geneva D. Haertel is a senior research associate at the Temple University Center for Research in Human Development and Education. She co-edited, with Herbert J. Walberg, *The International Encyclopedia of Educational Evaluation.*

Eileen Veronica Hilke is a professor and chair of the Education Division at Lakeland College in Sheboygan, Wisconsin. She has served as president of the Wisconsin Association of Colleges of Teacher Education and the Sheboygan Wisconsin Chapter of Phi Delta Kappa and vice president of the Kohler, Wisconsin, school board.

Thomas P. Lombardi is professor of special education at West Virginia University. Previously he was an assistant professor at the University of Arizona, director of education and training at the Arizona Children's Colony, and a special educator in Connecticut. Lombardi has published widely in education journals. He is the author of *Career Adaptive Behavior Inventory, Special Students and Our Schools,* and *ITPA: Clinical Interpretation and Remediation.* A certified Strategy Intervention Model trainer, he provides training, workshops, and consultation for schools and industry.

Lori A. Mulholland is a senior research specialist at the Morrison Institute for Public Policy at Arizona State University in Tempe. She has followed the development of charter schools across the nation, conducting legislative analyses on this topic. In addition to tracking this and other school reforms, Mulholland is an evaluation team member for Arizona's Head Start Public School Transition Project and directs the evaluation of a Head Start demonstration project extending services to homeless children and families at a Phoenix shelter.

Timothy Rusnak is the special assistant to the dean and director of the Center for Character Education in the School of Education at Duquesne University. Prior to joining the faculty at Duquesne, he was an elementary and middle school teacher for more than 20 years.

Susan Uchitelle is executive director of the Voluntary Interdistrict Coordinating Council in St. Louis. The council was established to carry out the 1983 settlement agreement by the U.S. Federal District Court for a desegregation plan involving the St. Louis Public Schools and all the suburban school districts — one of the early and most comprehensive school choice plans in an urban area. A former elementary teacher, Uchitelle has been a supervisor for the Missouri Department of Elementary and Secondary Education, assistant to the superintendent of the Parkway School District, a staff member of the Center for the Study of Law in Education at Washington University, a researcher for the Danforth Foundation, and instructor and coordinator of teacher training at Washington University.

Herbert J. Walberg, Research Professor of Education and Psychology at the University of Illinois at Chicago, served as chairman of an advisory committee on education indicators for the Paris-based Organization for Economic Cooperation and Development and served as a founding member and chairman of the Design and Analysis Committee of the National Assessment Governing Board. He has taught educational measurement since 1961 and has served as an advisor on testing and education research in the United States and abroad.

Donovan R. Walling was appointed editor of Special Publications for Phi Delta Kappa International in 1993. Previously, he was director of Instructional Services for the Carmel Clay Schools in Carmel, Indiana, and coordinator of Language Arts and Reading for the Sheboygan Area School District in Wisconsin, where he began his education career in 1970. He has directed programs for gifted education and, from 1981 to 1983, taught in the U.S. Department of Defense schools in Germany.

Dan H. Wishnietsky is an associate professor of mathematics at Winston-Salem State University in North Carolina, where he currently teaches statistics. He also has taught mathematics at high school and community college levels. His research interests include incorporating technology into the curriculum, providing inoffensive learning environments, and helping students develop research projects. Wishnietsky's latest book is *Managing Chronic Illness in the Classroom* (Phi Delta Kappa Educational Foundation, 1996), which he co-authored with his wife, Dorothy Botsch Wishnietsky.

John A. Zahorik is a professor of curriculum and instruction at the University of Wisconsin-Milwaukee, where he teaches graduate courses in instructional research and theory and researches teacher classroom behavior and teacher thinking. Zahorik has published professional articles in a variety of journals, including *Educational Leadership, Elementary School Journal, Journal of Teacher Education, Teaching and Teacher Education, Journal of Curriculum and Supervision*, and other U.S. and European education journals.